PHILOSOPHY *of* RELIGION

PHILOSOPHY
of RELIGION

DAVID ELTON TRUEBLOOD

BAKER BOOK HOUSE
Grand Rapids, Michigan

ISBN: 0-8010-8813-5
Library of Congress Catalog Card Number: 57-7342
Copyright © 1957 by David Elton Trueblood
Reprinted 1973 by Baker Book House Company
by permission of Fleming H. Revell Company

PHOTOLITHOPRINTED BY CUSHING - MALLOY, INC.
ANN ARBOR, MICHIGAN, UNITED STATES OF AMERICA
1973

for VIRGINIA

Contents

Preface

In a way which has not been equally true for years, the philosophy of religion is now both possible and necessary. It is possible because our time has been marked by an astonishing amount of vigorous religious thinking; it is necessary because new challenges to belief are now fully articulate. On the one hand, we can profit by the thinking of Whitehead, Temple, Maritain, Tillich, Niebuhr and many more; on the other hand, we must have an adequate answer to all those who dismiss all theology as meaningless or irrelevant.

The purpose of this book is to develop and to expound the essentials of a philosophy which enables men and women of this century to be both intellectually honest and sincerely devout. Accordingly, I have sought to be continuously aware of both the hope and the danger which have been increasingly evident in our generation. The book arises out of the practical experience of teaching philosophy in several different institutions. In this experience I have learned from students, most of whom are now mature men and women and many of whom, if they read this book, will recognize ideas which have emerged in our common search.

The present decision to do the best I can in a comprehensive effort comes, not only after years of teaching, but also after more than two decades of writing for publication. My first published book, now long out of print, written in the summer of 1935, was called *The Essence of Spiritual Religion*. That work was followed, after four years, by the 1939 Swarthmore Lecture, given and published in England with the title *The Trustworthiness of Religious Experience*. Later the argument was stated more fully in an American book, now also out of print, called *The Knowledge of God*. All of these were direct preparations for a philosophy of religion and led naturally to *The Logic of Belief*, published in 1942. This, the best comprehensive statement of which I was then capable, was written at Stanford University.

After *The Logic of Belief* was published, and the war was on, I became convinced that I ought to try my hand at a different kind of writing, that in which I could deal with the crisis of civilization in short books, made as lean as possible, and directed to the average literate person rather than to specialized scholars. It came to me that we had been attempting the absurdity of a "cut-flower civilization," and that the greatest practical need was a clear understanding of our mistake, along with an intelligent and concerted effort to restore the connection with the roots before it was too late. The result was, first, a slender volume, *The Predicament of Modern Man,* published in 1944, while the war was at its height.

The intervening years have seen the publication of seven other small books, all directed to the same readers, all aiming at clarity, and all concerned with the religious basis of civilization. During the same period I have engaged in one specifically literary work, the editing of *Doctor Johnson's Prayers,* and have written one book on contemporary ethics, *The Life We Prize.* With these behind me, I have felt, with increasing conviction, that the time has come for another new chapter in my life, and that the essence of this chapter is that I must go back to the more strictly academic approach to the philosophy of religion, hoping to produce something that can be used by serious students, both in and out of colleges. The present juncture seems to represent a kind of *Kairos* in my life in the sense in which Professor Tillich has taught us to use this word. In the life of an individual, as in the life of a people, there can come a fullness of time, with its unique opportunity. For better or for worse, this is the time to try to make my major contribution. No person ever feels really prepared for this, but nevertheless the time comes when it must be attempted, even though with a sense of unworthiness. My guess is that every author feels this, so that, if he were to wait for perfection, nothing would be accomplished.

My hope is that, in returning to the kind of writing which I did before the war, I can profit by what I have learned in the intermediate life chapter, in which I tried to discipline myself in such a way that significant things could be said clearly, without confusing verbiage. Very early in my academic life I realized that shallow waters are often muddied to make them look deep, and I vowed to avoid this affectation if I could. Consequently, my hope is that the present volume will profit by the labor of writing the smaller books, while including the substance of *The Logic of Belief* and the other works which preceded it.

Though nearly all which still seems of value in *The Logic of Belief* is included in the present volume, the result is by no means a mere revision of what was published in 1942, because the exciting intellectual developments of the past fifteen years have been such that a completely new structure is required, including new inquiries. These have to do, not only with new problems that have arisen, but also with new answers that have been offered in abundance in a time of undoubted fertility. The consequence is that this volume, while it includes some passages from my earlier books, is not intended as duplication, but rather as completion of former scattered treatments of some of the same topics. I have been encouraged by the words of Aristotle, "It is probably the right way to give first the outline and fill it in afterwards." In any case, it is accurate to say that all through my adult life this book has been in preparation, so that nearly everything that I have done has contributed to the thinking. I am grateful now for the fact that a free period between government service and the return to active teaching has made possible the time and necessary leisure to get the ideas down on paper.

Students who read this book may be interested in my own education, in order to trace influences which have led me to embrace certain conclusions. My undergraduate years were spent at Penn College, in Iowa, which was at that time a place of intellectual and spiritual vigor. Immediately after college I enjoyed a graduate year at Brown University, where for the first time I had to face the challenge of positivism and where I learned to study alone. The following year was spent at Hartford Theological Seminary in an atmosphere that was both liberal and evangelical. My transfer to Harvard Divinity School, where I took a degree in 1926, was occasioned by my desire to study under a number of eminent men, whose help I gratefully acknowledge. The most helpful were Dean Willard L. Sperry, who tried to guide me in the art of expression, both oral and written, Professor George Foot Moore, the most eminent historian of religion whom America has produced, Professor Bliss Perry, who gave me an example of teaching which is still my model, and Professor William Ernest Hocking, whose seminar in Hegel gave me a new understanding of what it is to study.

When the time came later for more strictly philosophical preparation I was fortunate in being able to study for three years at Johns Hopkins University, under the guidance of Professor Arthur O. Lovejoy. He was a hard taskmaster, an exacting critic and an affectionate friend. In my years with Lovejoy he was at the height of his great powers, developing, as something new in America, the history of ideas as an academic discipline and doing his most creative writing. He introduced his students, in seminars, to movements then reasonably new, such as logical positivism and existentialism. I began to read Martin Heidegger, Max Scheler and many more who then seemed alien to the American scene, but today seem so no longer. My doctoral dissertation at Johns Hopkins, which led to the granting of the degree in 1934, was in the field of philosophical anthropology. It has affected much of my later thinking, and I am still convinced that until we are clear on what man is we shall not be clear about much else.

Other people have taught me without being my teachers. Thus, I have profited by serving as a junior colleague of the late Rufus M. Jones, by sharing an ocean voyage with Professor John Baillie of Edinburgh, by personal friendship with Professor Reinhold Niebuhr, when he gave the West Lectures at Stanford University, and by many more. In time spent abroad, particularly at Woodbrooke in England, I came to appreciate the virile mentality of Professor H. G. Wood, both before and after his professorship at the University of Birmingham. In nearly ten years of living and working at Stanford University, I learned most from my colleagues in the natural sciences, including those in chemistry and physics. Some of the issues faced in this book were worked out with such men in long walks over the California hills.

Of those whom I have known only through books I have been most influenced, among contemporary men, by William Temple, and among those of earlier generations, by Blaise Pascal. Though I never saw him, I have been grateful for the thinking of the late Charles A. Bennett of Yale, whose widow graciously made available to me his unpublished manuscripts.

Because everyone who writes writes necessarily from a point of view, it is only fair to state mine. Though I try to be as objective as I can, and though I learned, under George Foot Moore, to appreciate other religions, I am naturally influenced by the fact that I am a Protestant Christian. We are bound to draw more from our own traditions than from others, but I trust that no sectarian bias is revealed by this inevitable practice. It ought to be possible, whatever our particular starting point, to employ the kind of reasoning that can appeal to any honest seeker of any tradition. Whatever the truth may be, it is certainly larger than our particular systems. It is for this reason that no religious thinker dare be limited by the dogmas of his own school. Perhaps the best thing that has been said about Karl Barth is that he has tried strenuously not to be his own follower. Whenever religion is philosophical it is open-ended, in that fundamental inquiry cannot stop at any particular historical point. It is always aware that there is more light to break forth.

My chief ideal in writing is that of coherence, such as is so wonderfully illustrated in Temple's *Nature, Man and God.* In so far as a writer tries to be a philosopher, he does not write disconnected essays and put them together with a cover, but, instead, seeks to make the entire development continuous and consistent in all of its parts. This book, though concerned with religion, is intended as a philosophical book, comparable, in its field, to a philosophy of science or a philosophy of conduct. Accordingly, my purpose is not to clutter shelves with private speculation, but to represent the cooperative effort which philosophy has been since the great days of ancient Greece.

The ideas of this book have come from countless sources and from many books. Some of them are mentioned in footnotes, but it is not practicable to mention them all. Since the ideas are not new, only the organization is new. As I have worked with this theme for thirty years, I have been increasingly conscious of living in a great age. My purpose is to provide students with a guide which will aid them in finding their way through the rich growth which marks our time.

D. E. T.

Earlham College
January, 1957

Part I
THE LOGIC of RELIGION

I

The Necessity of Philosophy

There is nothing in heaven and earth, or beyond them, to which the philosopher must subject himself except the universal logos of being as it gives itself to him in being.
PAUL TILLICH

So great is the religious vitality of the twentieth century that it must be opposed, studied or encouraged; it cannot be neglected. That religion is a prescientific world view and, therefore, bound to fade away with the growth of sophistication or of scientific knowledge is no longer maintained anywhere in the Western world, except perhaps in the Soviet Union. Religious commitment, instead of diminishing with the growth of mature thought as was once predicted, has actually increased. One striking evidence, among others, of the truth of this observation is the phenomenal new burst of religious interest in American colleges and universities.

The new religious vitality, far from answering all of our questions, actually adds to them. That there is a ready response to calls for religious commitment is cause for rejoicing, but at the same time it involves serious dangers, particularly the dangers of easy acceptance of what may prove to be intrinsically unworthy of the commitment. In any case it necessitates careful scrutiny of religious thought. How else can we distinguish between the true and the false, the profound and the superficial? In contrast to that of our immediate predecessors, our time is both more favorable to religion and more ominous.

Times of complete flux produce very little profitable intellectual work, but ours is not really a time of flux. So far as our human judgment is dependable, we are reasonably clear about the main lines of development for an entire generation. The ideological bifurcation of the world will continue, and it will continue along the same major lines that we know now. Though our generation cannot expect real peace, there is reasonable ground for the hope that we shall not have openly declared war. Instead, there will be the constant and unrelenting struggle of *ideas*. We do not have peace, and we do not have war; what we have is a relative stability in the enduring tension.

The present pause in history is not only one in which ideas are of paramount importance; it is also one which is particularly favorable to a careful facing of religious truth. A number of the old problems have been handled so long and so well that, at a certain level of competence, there is a virtual concensus about them, while the new problems have been recognized long enough for the issues to be fairly clear even though adequate answers to them have not yet been developed. Examples of the consensus are numerous and significant. Among these is the problem of the critical study of the Scriptures. Though some fringe groups still resist the fearless application of scientific inquiry to the origin, authorship and composition of the books of the Bible, the agreement among thoughtful people in this area is almost universal. Strikingly, there has resulted not a lessened appreciation of the Bible as a unique revelation, but rather a renewed affirmation among millions of people of its relevance to all times.

In the area of Biblical study the struggle for intellectual integrity has ended in victory, yet we take victory so for granted that we fail to realize how phenomenal it has been. What is amazing is that it has been possible, in spite of years of reverence for the very letter of Scripture, to face the sacred writings with complete scientific honesty, boldly pointing out the mythical and legendary elements in both the Old Testament and the New. Here is an intellectual development which has no parallel in any other religion. Since it has now been virtually completed, it becomes an essential part of any truly current philosophy of religion.

Another problem, no longer in essential flux, is the relation of science to religion. Geology *versus* Genesis is not now a problem for serious groups. How the problem has been solved need not concern us at this point; suffice it to say that a working solution has been reached. In nearly every university in the Western world something of the evidence that a solution has been found is indicated by the obvious religious devotion of a significant number of those engaged in the study of the physical sciences. Modern man no longer needs to choose between faith in science and faith in God.

What has developed in our time that seems so favorable to religion is not so much a new faith as a new openness, a new readiness to listen. This is partly because atheism is now less dogmatic, less sure of itself, and far less comfortable. Many factors have conspired to produce this highly salutary effect. Skepticism about man's ability to produce a good world by his own unaided efforts, a skepticism originally felt by a few intellectuals, is now almost standard. The events which have occurred in the middle of the twentieth century have revealed even to the uncritical the understanding that technology may destroy as easily as it may help. Thus, the demise of the half-gods has enhanced the prospects of a higher religion. Decay of the old dogmatism about natural law leaves the way open for the acceptance of prayer, providing there is any reason to accept it, and the patent insufficiency of mechanism as an explanation of consciousness undermines the force of the strongest argument against immortality. It is precisely because the old self-confidence is gone that man may again open himself humbly to the appeal of religious truth.

Because all who wish to be heard, even on the most important matters, necessarily employ the idiom of their contemporaries, the philosophy of religion must be forever rewritten. We must, accordingly, be sure to deal not merely with the classical problems of the past, but with the challenges felt by the men and women of this day and particularly by the young. It is for this reason that the present volume deals specifically, in Part III, with the current challenge of dialectical materialism, of Freudianism and of Logical Positivism, which do not appear in the older philosophies of religion, but are very real now.

It is important to try to make clear what it is that argumentation about religion can and cannot do. It is sometimes claimed that it cannot really do anything, because, as is said, men do not find God at the conclusion of a syllogism. But such a view misses a point that is crucial to the entire enterprise. It is true that merely by searching men do not find God, but the searching may be extremely valuable if it helps to remove some of the barriers to a vital faith. Most of these barriers are intellectual. Millions would be glad to believe in

God, but are hindered from doing so by what seem to them insuperable intellectual obstacles. Philosophical discussion probably does not ordinarily bring men into the divine encounter, but it can do something of great worth; it can help to remove the barriers which, on the human side, make that encounter virtually impossible. Careful religious argument does not *produce* commitment, but it often, as in the case of T. S. Eliot, *opens the road* to commitment.

Though commitment is intrinsic to religious vitality, the precise object of the commitment is all-important. This is why philosophy is required. Philosophy is necessary when man recognizes competing or mutually incompatible faiths and begins to ask *"Which* faith?" because philosophy is the effort to engage in rational and consistent inquiry concerning the fundamentals of any question. It is the effort to solve problems by disciplined thought. As everybody knows, there are terrible conflicts in the world, with diametrically opposite positions espoused. How are these conflicts to be overcome? The *truth* of an issue cannot be determined by killing one another, for then the outcome merely indicates who is stronger, not who is right. But if violence is no solution, neither is voting, because the majority may be wrong and often has been wrong. The only satisfactory solution is for us to engage in thought, both separately and together, until a viewpoint is reached that is intellectually satisfactory. In so far as we think truly we think together, for dissension is a symptom of our finite ignorance, pride or willful error. We may not, so long as we are in the finite predicament, ever come to full agreement on any important questions, but we can often *approach* agreement, and this, in any case, is our best hope of solving our present problems.

All persons who engage in the philosophy of religion are sincerely trying to be intellectually honest though devout. They recognize that the claims of the great religions are so important that no serious thinker can neglect them, but they recognize also that claims cannot be accepted uncritically. Belief in God, in the sense to be defined later in this book, may be false, and it may be true, but it cannot possibly be trivial. The philosophy of religion is, therefore, a highly important discipline, because it deals with matters which are important, *if true*.

The beginner is often somewhat perplexed about the difference between religion and philosophy, and sometimes tends to equate them. This confusion arises from the fact that both religion and philosophy embrace some of the same subjects. Both are concerned with what is ultimate, in contrast to what is trivial and passing. It is helpful, therefore, to try to clarify the distinction between the two.

The great difference between religion and philosophy is not that of different areas of reference, but of different approaches to all areas. There is a deep sense in which the major human enterprises deal with the same subjects, because each deals with everything. It is well known that philosophy attempts to deal with all reality, yet religion does also, but in a sharply different way. Both philosophy and religion are radically totalitarian in scope, but they are not unique in this regard, other striking examples being science, morality and art.

It is hopeless to try to understand science in terms of the objects which it studies. The child may suppose science to be concerned with chemicals or with botanical specimens or with rocks, but even a slight maturity brings emancipation from these arbitrary limitations. Science is not differentiated by *what* it studies, but by *how* it studies. In short, the heart of science is scientific method or scientific habit or scientific mentality. Science is not a study of special fields, but a study of *any* field in a special way. One can be quite as scientific about the Dead Sea Scrolls as about chemical analysis. Accordingly, it is most unfortunate that academic institutions have come to make a distinction between the sciences, meaning primarily physics, chemistry, biology and geology, and all other subjects of inquiry. This semantic mistake often leads, without definite consciousness or intent, to unnecessary antagonisms.

The late Professor Whitehead, whose well-known book, *Science and the Modern World,* may rightly be considered the most profound and reliable treatment of the theme, has helped all who are willing to listen to understand the universality of science. Having begun by saying that his purpose was to discuss, not the details of scientific discovery, but rather a general scientific state of mind, he elaborated the thesis that the "growth of science has practically recolored our mentality, so that modes of thought, which in former times were exceptional, are now broadly spread throughout the educated world." What is most important, he held, is not the new technology, based on the new sciences, but the "new mentality." In this Professor Whitehead was obviously justified. There are limitations to science, but they are not limitations in the field of valid inquiry. Any claim to truth ought to be submitted to the demand for evidence.

In a similar way morality is concerned with the entire field of human experience. The whole idea of the moral life is defeated if moral considerations are limited to special areas. Morality is as much concerned with what men do in factories as with what they do in homes. Morality is concerned with the way a man pays his taxes, the way he uses his time, the way he spends his money. The good life consists not in performing one special class of actions, but in performing all actions well. There is nothing we can do, say or even think that is totally devoid of ethical significance.

Even art is a totalitarian enterprise in that it recognizes no areas as off limits. The painter finds his scenes in all kinds of situations, not in a conventional few. The poet or dramatist cannot work well unless everything he observes is potential material for his artistic creation. This basic contention Wordsworth made in his justly famous Preface to *Lyrical Ballads,* and it is generally agreed that he made his point persuasively. The artistic enterprise loses some of its validity if beauty is not recognized in every area of common life.

It should be clear, then, that the major human undertakings are not, and must not be, jealous guardians of divided realms. Furthermore, they must not be limited to particular classes of men who enjoy a monopoly. Though we have different emphases, each thoughtful man is to some degree a scientist, each a moralist, and each an artist. In the same way, a man can be both a philosopher and a man of faith. In short, a normal human life is big enough to include and comprehend more than one approach to reality.

Granted, then, that the same person may be both philosophical and religious, it is helpful to try to distinguish between these two approaches. The essential difference may be expressed accurately, not so much by the use of nouns as by the use of verbs. The essence of philosophy is to *think;* the essence of religion is to *dedicate.* Each is more an undertaking than a subject of study. A good course in philosophy does not merely teach students *about* philosophy; far more significantly, it teaches them to *philosophize*. Those who promote religion are never satisfied with imparting information *about* religion; they are concerned, instead, that people *be* religious. Philosophy and religion, both, seek knowledge, but they seek knowledge for different purposes. "Philosophy seeks knowledge for the sake of understanding, while religion seeks knowledge for the sake of worship." [1]

Among modern thinkers who have helped mightily to clarify this *important distinction*, two Gifford Lecturers stand out. The first is William Temple, whose *Nature, Man and God* is one of the shining intellectual achievements of the twentieth century. Archbishop Temple was not only a great practical man of affairs, but also a first-class philosopher and a man of deep personal devotion. As a philosopher he believed in *thought*, as a Christian he believed in *faith*, and as a man he believed in both of them together. He recognized an inevitable yet beneficent tension between philosophy and religion, beneficent because he understood very well that the best music is played upon tight strings. His most quotable aphorism reveals his deepest conclusion concerning the two subjects:

The heart of Religion is not an opinion about God, such as Philosophy might reach as the conclusion of its argument; it is a personal relation with God. [2]

Another famous set of Gifford Lectures, those of Samuel Alexander, called *Space, Time and Deity*, helps in a lesser, but still important way in indicating the essential difference between religion and philosophy. Professor Alexander sharply distinguishes between two kinds of human experience, enjoyment and contemplation, a distinction revealed by C. S. Lewis as a significant factor in his celebrated conversion from atheism. [3] These technical terms in Alexander's philosophy are not identical with their use in popular speech, enjoyment having connection with pleasure. Enjoyment, in Alexander's usage, refers to direct experience. The love of a person is, thus, an act of "enjoyment," while thought about that

---

[1] William Temple, *Nature, Man and God*, London, Macmillan, 1934, p. 30.
[2] *Ibid.*, p. 54.
[3] C. S. Lewis, *Surprised by Joy*, New York, Harcourt, Brace & Co., 1956, 1. 217 ff.

love is "contemplation." Both activities are wholly worthy, but they are radically different and, as Lewis points out, temporally incompatible. "You cannot hope," he says, "and also think about hoping at the same moment; for in hope we look to hope's object and we interrupt this by (so to speak) turning round to look at the hope itself." [4]

While the two activities are widely different, and strictly incompatible at any moment, they can and do alternate with great rapidity. It is important to understand the *difference* and to see the value of both approaches. Things can be different without being better or worse. To say that philosophy and religion are not the same is not to be under the necessity of choosing between them. It is helpful to realize that religion is essentially a matter of "enjoyment," while philosophy is essentially a matter of "contemplation." We need to engage in both, but we need to know which is which. The same point was given its classic though brief formulation three hundred years ago in Pascal's famous ejaculation:

> The difference between the knowledge of God and the love of Him.

Anyone who understands the meaning of Pascal's formulation is ready to engage in the Philosophy of Religion as an intellectual discipline. He will realize that he can engage in the philosophical enterprise without supposing that this is incompatible with the religious enterprise or identical with it. He will know that all such discussion as that involved in this book is far more philosophical than it is religious, though it is *about* religion. Whenever we talk *about,* we are more concerned with contemplation than with enjoyment, but there is no reason to be apologetic about it. It is good to know that we are not trying to produce what is called religious literature. True religious literature is not discursive or critical, but is, characteristically, couched in the language of prayer or of autobiography, in which there is a straightforward attempt to communicate, but not to evaluate the divine-human encounter that has been experienced. This gives us such classics as the *Prayers of Lancelot Andrewes* and *The Imitation of Christ.* Something of this is found in Pascal's *Pensées,* though in these brilliant fragments

[4] *Ibid.,* p. 218.

the mood alternates constantly, with the major emphasis on intellectual justification.

Fundamental to all religion is the experience of commitment or dedication. In its fullest and most mature form this is commitment to the will of God, but, because there are many levels of religious development, it may be commitment to lesser objects. This is why it is worth while to say that dialectical materialism, especially as espoused in Russia, is either a religion or a quasi religion. More precisely, it is *qualitatively* religious, regardless of its poverty of theological content. The dedication is there, though it is not a dedication to the Living God, but to an impersonal dialectical process in which the life of the poor individual seems to be dignified by being a helpless instrument. There is something like a body of scripture; there are ceremonies; there are martyrs; and there is, above all, an evangelical urge to extend the Marxist kingdom. The failure to recognize this religious character is one reason why so many, for so long, underestimated the power of the movement in its ability to influence men's minds. Though this aspect of communism seems to be diminishing in European Russia, it still is an important factor in recently evangelized lands.

The experience of commitment must be appreciated by anyone who wishes to understand religion. Though it may be buttressed by intellectual considerations, it is more than intellectual assent. It is faith, not in the sense of mere belief, but in the sense of courageous involvement. Purely religious insight, as distinguished from philosophical insight, comes from a full and complete self-giving to an object which appears to justify that self-giving. It is intrinsically unconditional. That is why the relation between the divine and the human has so often been illuminated by the metaphor of marriage. Marriage sheds more light on religion than religion sheds on marriage, because marriage is the one voluntary experience which is known almost universally as involving glad and courageous and unlimited commitment to the beloved. Religion is not merely a matter of falling in love; it is joyful dedication to the beloved. It involves unashamedly the whole self, including the emotions.

The contrast between religion, so understood, and all philosophy is very great. While religion thrives and ought to thrive upon "the reasons of the heart," philosophy is possible only when the mood is cool and calm. If religion is the darkening cataract, philosophy is the calm water where we can see to the bottom. It is essential to the paradoxical nature of philosophy that the philosopher, even though he takes a strong position, seeks so hard to be fair to opposing views that he seems to endanger his own. He tries, not merely to prove, but to *disprove* his cherished theory. If he argues merely for victory, he is not a philosopher. The politician seeks to attack the opposition at its weakest point, but the philosopher attacks at the strongest point. However sure he is of the answers, he is honor bound never to minimize the problems or to gloss over the difficulties. Sometimes he states the problems so formidably that it looks as though he cannot escape from his quandary.

The result of this is the further paradox that philosophy, though calm in its effort, is disturbing in its results, the true philosopher being a gadfly who may be forced to drink the hemlock. Santayana's tribute to his teacher and colleague, William James, illustrates this point admirably, the tribute being all the more significant in view of the wide differences between the conclusions of the two men. "His comfortless dissatisfaction with every possible idea," wrote Santayana, "opened vistas and disturbed a too easy dogmatism." [5]

The philosopher is a man who tries to find loopholes in every argument, including his own; whenever a universal proposition is enunciated he seeks deliberately for exceptions; he is incurably critical because he ought to be. Here is one of the greatest known antidotes to self-delusion. Because the philosopher expects difficulties, he does not discard a position merely because it *has* difficulties; he looks first at the alternative positions to see whether they have more. Thus, theism may have problems which are never completely solved, but a wise man, deeply steeped in the mood of philosophical inquiry, does not abandon theism for that reason alone. Instead, he tries to see what the live alternatives are and to examine them with equal sensitivity. He may find that, however great the intellectual difficulties of the theist may be, the intellectual difficulties of the atheist are far greater. One does not escape the problems by becoming an unbeliever, if in doing so one encounters other and harder problems.

This idea, which seems to me to be very important in the philos-

[5] George Santayana, *Persons and Places,* New York, Scribner, 1944, p. 244.

ophy of religion, I owe to two living men, Professor Herbert G. Wood and Professor John Baillie, the one at the University of Birmingham and the other at the University of Edinburgh. Professor Wood's reference to this point is found in his Hulsean Lectures at the University of Cambridge, *Christianity and the Nature of History,* while Professor Baillie's reference is in *Invitation to Pilgrimage.* Baillie's statement has helped me so much in so many situations that I repeat it here:

> I remember well how during my study of philosophy as an undergraduate one of my teachers wrote the following words (or their like) on the margin of an essay in which I had criticized a certain accepted theory: "Every theory has its difficulties, but you have not considered whether any other theory has less difficulties than the one you have criticized." And I remember that the further reflection set up in my mind by that simple remark was, in that particular instance, enough to lead me back to the received doctrine. I am happy to count among my own friends a rather remarkable number of men of high intellectual distinction who have returned to the full Christian outlook after years of defection from it, and I should say that in practically every case the renewed hospitality of their minds to Christian truth came about through their awakening to the essential untenability of the alternative positions, which they had been previously attempting to occupy.[6]

A clear recognition of the importance of this point suggests what the right procedure in religious discussion is. It is a mistake for the believer in religion to accept the role of an apologist in the sense that he continually seeks to defend his faith against attacks from the outside or even against his own doubts. Not only is defense immensely strengthened by offense, but the truth is more likely to be known if the unbeliever is forced to examine the tenability of *his* position or positions. As we shall try to show later, this is the most fruitful way in which to deal with the challenges of Marxian or Freudian thought. Where do they find a solid ground for their basic convictions? What are the difficulties which the atheist must face?

Philosophy is always needed, and needed especially in religion, because philosophy is the only human enterprise in which careful

---

[6] John Baillie, *Invitation to Pilgrimage,* New York, Scribner, 1942, p. 15.

scrutiny not only of intellectual processes, but also of presuppositions is the main business for which there is a professional training. For this there is no substitute whatever. The study of comparative difficulties must continue. We cannot select an official philosopher, whether Hindu or Christian or secular, and stop there, because such selection would end the dialogue and the end of the dialogue would be the end of the enterprise. Unexamined faith is not worth having.

It is because man has, by experience, become highly conscious of the fact of error that he has found it necessary to invent means of avoiding it. Each approach, however, must be relevant to the subject under inquiry. The inquiry about God must be as objective as is the inquiry about uranium, but the appropriate method of investigation is necessarily different. If someone claims that there is uranium in Utah, we have a reasonably simple and direct method of finding out whether the claim is justified. But, in regard to religious assertions, we get no help from a Geiger counter or anything similar to it.

The method most appropriate to the search for religious truth is a method associated with the names of some of the greatest masters of philosophical thought, particularly Plato and Kant. This method we may call either critical or dialectical, since both adjectives refer to the same essential process. Dialectic may be briefly defined as "repeated and thorough criticism of our assumptions." [7]

The essence of this method is that we start with something accepted in the world of facts, as we do in induction, and then reason carefully, as in deduction, but reason *backward* rather than forward. The task is that of starting with results and pressing back to ask what must be true in order that these results may occur. Thus, if we find that there are in the world conscious beings, whom we call persons, we are bound to ask, providing we are critically minded, what kind of world it must be which produces such creatures. What is unreasonable is to accept the known facts while rejecting the other, though not directly known, facts without which the known facts could not be. It is not enough to accept the reality of a measure of freedom or of moral experience; we

[7] A. E. Taylor, *The Faith of a Moralist*, New York, Macmillan, 1930, vol. 1, p. 24.

must go on to ask what else is necessary for the existence of both freedom and morality.

Dialectic is the effort to do justice to competing points of view, not by judging them in terms of some rigid or received system, but by asking in every case what the implications are. A position may be highly plausible, on the surface, as are many of those examined in the Platonic dialogues, but we cannot be satisfied with mere plausibility. Many plausible positions, when examined in the light of their implications, turn out to be based on inherent contradictions, like that of the "thinking Behaviorist," or they are in clear opposition to known facts. In that case they must be rejected, and we try again for something less vulnerable.

In so far as a man is a philosopher, whatever other occupation he may pursue, he is always engaged in asking questions, particularly about presuppositions. He watches for suppressed premises, brings them to the light, and examines them. He is as quick to expose dogmatism in religion as dogmatism in science. The unrelenting demand is that the proposition in question be seen in the light of its implications, implications which may reach into many different fields of human experience. The man who argues for absolute freedom from restraints must be shown that this would involve the freedom to cheat, including the freedom to cheat *him*. If he is unwilling to accept these implications of his position, he has no right to maintain the position.

The best way to expose a position as erroneous is to show, by dialectical development, that it leads to self-contradiction. The point is that *no false premise can be consistently elaborated*. It is because Socrates taught and demonstrated this effectively that he is universally recognized as the father of Western philosophy. The main effort of his inquiry was to keep on asking questions until both he and his companions could see what any position entailed. His conviction was that error is eventually obvious, providing we keep probing, whereas the truth can be consistently elaborated without contradiction. In telling the truth a person could endure endless cross-questioning, but only a person endowed with superhuman genius could succeed forever in maintaining consistency among falsehoods.

The most satisfactory method of reaching the truth "is a process of working round and round the available material until it is found gradually to fit into place and make a coherent scheme." The knowledge of the truth, in important matters, comes not by a simple process along one line, but always by the convergence of many lines. Even then the certainty is never absolute, because we are always dealing with complex materials and our minds are not fully adequate to the situation, but the probability of the truth of a proposition increases with the increase of comprehensiveness and coherence. "The comprehensive mind," said Plato, "is always the dialectical."

2

Faith and Reason

Criticism must be sympathetic, or it will completely miss the mark; but it must also be dispassionate and relentless.

WILLIAM TEMPLE

There are many valid ways in which the immense and interesting subject of religion can be approached. Thus, we may engage in the history of religion, including the history of religious thought; we may, likewise, study religious literature, including the various sacred Scriptures of the world; we may concern ourselves with current practices in regard to worship or social teachings. All of these are important and even necessary if we are to know what it is that we are talking about. Still more important than these, however, is what may be called the sympathetic criticism of religion. The phenomena of religion are rich and varied, but do they have any grounding in reality? In spite of the current vitality of religion in the Western world, the question is an exceedingly live one in many minds. How can we begin to know the truth in regard to such a momentous question? When we try to deal with matters in this area we are concerned with the logic of religion.

A. The Validation of Belief

It is hard to rid our minds completely of the haunting suspicion that the entire religious structure may be nothing more than a grand and beautiful castle in the air. Perhaps there is no Object worthy of our full commitment; perhaps God is just an idea in human minds, an idea as insubstantial as a mirage in the desert. It is easy to construct theories about the world, but we know very well that many of them are purely fanciful. When once we realize that they are fanciful they have very little effect upon either our thought or our conduct, because one can play at that game almost as well as another. The grandeur of the dream provides no certainty that it is more than a dream.

Our natural incredulity in these matters is increased by our study of history. Educated people are well aware of the way in which, in ancient Greece, men continued to talk confidently about the lives and characters of the Olympian gods long after they were reasonably sure that these were fictitious beings. Perhaps we are in a similar situation. Perhaps the millions who flock to church on Sundays in order to pray are only exercising their own imaginations in a world in which there are many to pray, but nowhere One who can listen or care or respond. It is conceivable that the entire evolutionary process, involving millions of years, is purely meaningless, in the sense that it involves no purpose and reflects no mind. It is possible that the only example of consciousness in the entire universe is that which we know in our little lives on one particular planet, and that, beyond the surface of our earth, there is neither life nor consciousness nor understanding anywhere, but only space and planets and stars. To say that we know better by the light of faith is not a convincing answer; the early Greeks had faith, but their faith was centered on nonexistent objects.

Our major concern, therefore, must be the concern for reality. We want to know, if possible, not what would be nice but what *is!* Fiction may be grand, but it can never be as moving as the greatest of biography. The life of one man, like Abraham Lincoln, can tell us more about human nature than can reams of speculation, for a doctrine is of little permanent interest if there is no evidence that it is *true.* What we must do, then, in regard to religious doctrines, is to think as honestly and as carefully as we can. Admittedly, this is not easy, but it is, in any case, a matter of great moment. If it is true that, in addition to our finite minds, there is, in the universe, the Infinite Mind who gives meaning to the world and who has created us for free companionship with Himself, that is obviously tremendous news. We should be foolish not to use all the intelligence we can muster in order to try to know *whether* this is true. To fail to give our minds loyally to this inquiry would not be so much irreverent as stupid.

The wonder is that so many are able to maintain their historic faith while, at the same time, they entertain philosophical and scientific notions which, if taken seriously, make this faith impossible. Beyond the iron curtain a number try to be both Marxians and Christians, while, on this side of the curtain, others actually try to combine positions which are equally incompatible, but this is never possible except by the division of experience into compartments. The laboratory is one thing, men say, and the altar is another. But this will never do. It is quite right to know the difference between the laboratory and the altar, but unless they somehow belong to the same world there is no hope for intellectual integrity at all. If God is the God of the altar only, and not the God of the laboratory also, He is not worthy of our worship, and prayer is idle. Here we can be helped by Christ's own prayer, which began "I thank thee, O Father, Lord of heaven and earth." [1] It is the same as though he had said, "Lord of both factory and church." He was rejecting, with vividness, a compartmentalized faith. A compartmentalized religion is a poor thing and will not endure.

The chief reason why some process of validation is necessary is that most religious propositions are controversial. There is no complete agreement about the existence of God, about life after death, about the basis of religious authority. Such controversial matters are not necessarily something to be deplored. There is, indeed, a sense in which controversial questions are the only questions worth asking. We can welcome religious controversy, provided it is carried on "with gentleness and reverence." [2] Philosophy advances by a system of crosslights. One side says all that it can for its position, and then the other side says what it can for its position, as it seeks to uncover weaknesses or errors in the first. That the hard-hitting dialogue is more fruitful, in serious intellectual inquiry, than is the single monolithic approach is the permanent message of Socrates. We have adopted the system of crosslights in our Western jurisprudence, because experience shows that the truth is more likely to emerge when two sets of lawyers are working, rather than one. Because the truth is complex, we need to entertain claim and counterclaim, each being presented as persuasively as possible.

[1] Matt. 11:25.
[2] "Always be prepared to make a defense to anyone who calls you to account for the hope that is in you, yet do it with gentleness and reverence." I Pet. 3:15.

In one sense the whole history of philosophy has been a continuous dialogue, in which each thinker takes over from where his predecessors leave off. On the whole, this has been both healthy and productive and should be continued in the future. One conclusion is that a student cannot know philosophy except by direct acquaintance with its dynamic movement.[3] We do not understand the answers if we read only the answers. The conduct of controversy in such a way that it becomes truly creative is essential to the philosophical undertaking. In this it is our duty to avoid the temptation to make problems seem easy. The chief way in which we can avoid this pitfall is to feel the problems in ourselves before we try to answer them, so that the ensuing dialogue is really an *inner* dialogue. William Lyon Phelps, of Yale, was bearing witness to this possibility when he wrote, "My religious faith remains in possession of the field only after prolonged civil war with my naturally skeptical mind."

It is unfortunate that people hear about the answers before they have felt the problems in any real sense. This is what makes undergraduate education so nearly impossible—the teacher has to give the answers too soon. A faith that has never been tested is not only not appreciated, it is not even understood. In view of this fact we should never, in pursuing the philosophy of religion, stifle doubt, because doubt, as Galileo taught, is the father of discovery. It is a surprising and beneficent revelation to many young people to learn that their elders have to fight continually within themselves in order to maintain their faith. They then begin to realize that their own experience is neither unique nor necessarily discouraging.

Always in the effort to be reasonable about our faith we must sail between two dangerous reefs. On the left is the danger of dogmatic negativity, in which we make sweeping denials far beyond what is

---

[3] I learned this first from Professor Hocking in the valuable seminar on Hegel, which was held at his house at Harvard. Later I learned it more explicitly from Professor Lovejoy at Johns Hopkins. In the Preface to his highly respected book, *The Revolt Against Dualism*, Lovejoy made it clear that such a method was his own. "The true procedure of philosophy as a science," he wrote, "as distinct from the philosophic idiosyncrasies of individuals, is thus that of a Platonic dialogue on a grand scale, in which the theses, proposed proofs, objections, rejoinders, of numerous interlocutors are focused upon a given question and the argument gradually shapes itself, through its own immanent dialectic, to a conclusion."

reasonable in view of our modest position in the universe. On the right is the danger of easy belief, especially belief in what is comforting or merely traditional and generally accepted. Hope lies in a course in which we are both tender and tough minded, truly critical of every dogmatism, including the dogmatism of the unbeliever. The ideal mood is that which combines a genuine open-mindedness with a constant demand for evidence.

B. THE MEANING OF INVOLVEMENT

While faith alone easily becomes self-deluding, reason alone is sterile, because reason requires something on which to work. It would be idle to develop the reasons of the head if there did not already exist the reasons of the heart. What is required, then, is a beneficent tension in which the conflict between the two is never wholly overcome. As long as we are in the status of finite creatures the tension is never wholly resolved, but it may be an essentially productive tension. While the reasons of the heart give power, the reasons of the head give balance and sanity, and it is always the combination which succeeds, in so far as man ever succeeds.

In the study of religion the ideal of detachment, which is so highly recommended in most fields of inquiry, cannot be adopted, except with important qualifications. It is relatively easy to be both detached and objective on the question whether Pluto is a planet or a satellite of a planet, because this does not affect our personal lives at all, and it is almost as easy to be detached about the nature of the electron. But it is extremely naïve to assume, for that reason, that the detached or indifferent man can reason fruitfully about faith. To be indifferent in the study of religious truth is a contradiction in terms because religion always makes exciting demands, *if true*. Nobody in our generation has seen this more clearly or said it more persuasively than Professor Paul Tillich. His key sentences are as follows:

Unconcerned detachment in matters of religion (if it is more than a methodological self-restriction) implies an *a priori* rejection of the religious demand to be ultimately concerned. It denies the object which it is supposed to study objectively. [4]

[4] Paul Tillich, *The Protestant Era,* University of Chicago Press, 1948, p. xi.

In no field is truth available except to those who have met the conditions. All our primary convictions rest ultimately upon propositions which are self-evident, but propositions can be self-evident without being evident to everybody. Only he who looks in the appropriate way is ever able to see. The Italian astronomers who refused to look through the telescope to see the moons of Jupiter, the existence of which Galileo affirmed, had no scientific significance whatever, because they avoided the one crucial means by which the objective truth might have been revealed to them. We never know what a man's testimony, and especially a negative testimony, is worth until we know whether the reasonable conditions have been met. Truth is revealed in religion not just to anybody, but only to those who seek, and to those who *care*.

There is as little reason to trust the judgment of the irreligious in regard to religion as to trust the unscientific in matters of science. Armchair religion is really no religion at all. Religious understanding comes not primarily in the act of study, but in prayer, in joyous acceptance of God's gifts, and in service to the brethren.

We have a good deal of reason to distrust the judgment of a man in the field of religious knowledge if, as is sometimes the case in universities, his approach is purely abstract or historical. We do not trust the scientist who spurns the laboratory or the musician who never performs. Likewise, there is little reason to respect a scholar in religion who is not in the church, who does not pray, and who does not engage in sacrificial giving or in humble acts of service. A religious scholar is a better scholar if he is also, in some sense, a pastor, not disdaining the practical work of promoting the cause about which it is his business to think.[5]

Though all who think about it agree that religious insight comes only to those who meet the conditions, and though there are several references to this theme in the New Testament,[6] the subject has received relatively little serious consideration in the philosophy of religion. One valuable contribution was made by Frederick W.

[5] For the argument that trust of the insider does not involve any begging of the question, see Samuel M. Thompson, *A Modern Philosophy of Religion*, New York, Henry Regnery, 1955, pp. 133, 134.

[6] We are told, for example, that it is the pure in heart, perhaps the single-minded, who see God, that the way to know the will is to do it, and that only those who are willing to enter as little children enter the Kingdom.

Robertson, in one of his most celebrated sermons, preached at
Brighton on March 2, 1851, the whole point of his discourse being
admirably presented in its title, "Obedience the Organ of Spiritual
Knowledge." It was based on John 7:17 and showed that many
things are revealed only to those who are already obeying what
they already know to be right. Those who wait for all to be shown,
before they are willing to start, never start at all. In a similar vein
it is true to say that love is the organ of knowledge. It is only
those who are rooted and grounded in love who are able to comprehend.[7] We repeat rather stupidly the adage to the effect that
"love is blind," until a man of the intellectual stature of Chesterton
makes us realize the far more important truth that love enables us
to *see*. The lover may, indeed, be blind to some of the defects of the
beloved, but, just because he loves, he can see, in his beloved,
genuine qualities which neither the hostile nor the indifferent can
even suspect.

The major alternative to detachment is *involvement*. Part of the
intellectual vitality of religious thought in our time has come from
a recognition of the importance of involvement, and it has come,
in nearly all instances, from those who have been influenced by
what is generally called existentialism.[8] One does not need to label
himself an existentialist in order to feel the importance of this
approach to all reality and especially to religious reality.

In any case we can be reasonably sure that religious truth will be

[7] Eph. 3:17, 18.

[8] The existential movement takes many forms and includes both theistic and
atheistic thinkers. Among those to whom it is most indebted are Soren Kierkegaard, in the past, and Martin Heidegger, in the present, though Heidegger has
repeatedly disavowed his association with the movement. As a mood, rather than
as a set of doctrines, existentialism has influenced both Christian and Jewish
thinkers in the Western scene, and has now touched Hinduism and Buddhism
in the East. For a Jewish example, see Will Herberg, *Judaism and Modern Man.*
Paul Tillich's affinity for this mood is well known. One of the best introductions
to the subject is *The Existentialist Revolt,* by Kurt Reinhardt. The movement
is not well understood in America, partly because the English word "existence"
is not identical in meaning with its German counterpart. The essence of the
existentialist message is that man is always personally involved in the situations
which he seeks to examine. All man's study of the world must always include
himself, because he is part of the picture. Man, therefore, is marked, not so
much by pure reason as by "concern." All existentialism begins in the recognition that the elimination of the personal equation is impossible and that all
important thinking involves personal decision.

hidden from those who, in the effort to be "wise and prudent," approach it in the mood of tolerance. The notion that religion is a nice thing for those who are interested in it is wholly unproductive and unworthy. It is unproductive because it shows a primary confusion about the nature of the subject studied; it is unworthy because it is basically condescending. Since religious claims involve a man's whole life, it is wholly reasonable for him to *accept* these claims or to *reject* these claims, but it is not reasonable for him to be indifferent to them. How well this is now understood and how deeply existentialism has penetrated our thinking is shown in our new religious vocabulary, which abounds in such words as "care," "concern," "involvement," and "commitment." This is one of the reasons why the present is an auspicious time for religious study. We may not know the answers, but we at least know what some of the problems are, and we feel them at a deep level.

Though there is a popular conviction that all existentialism is atheistic, this is far from accurate. Sartre is, indeed, an atheist, and Heidegger, who was reared as a Jesuit, is one no longer, but Jaspers is a Protestant, and Will Herberg, who is thoroughly existentialist, is a devout Jew. The influence of the existentialist mood is obvious in the published works of Paul Tillich, as when he defines the object of theology as "what concerns us ultimately." It is the truth about man, says Tillich, that he is "ultimately concerned about that which determines his ultimate destiny beyond all preliminary necessities and accidents." [9]

C. The Heritage of Pascal

Closely allied to the spread of the existentialist mood is the renewed admiration for the work of Blaise Pascal, who, three hundred years ago, projected a most ambitious book on the philosophy of religion, left unfinished at the time of his death in 1662. Pascal's cryptic notes included features which have a strong appeal to modern man in so far as he recognizes his serious predicament. Pascal anticipated Kierkegaard in the emphasis on "Either-Or" by his recognition of the existence of forced options. "Yes, but wager you must; there is no option, you have embarked on it," comes as

[9] Paul Tillich, *Systematic Theology*, University of Chicago Press, 1951, vol. 1, p. 14.

a seventeenth-century sophisticated echo of "He that is not for me is against me." There are countless human situations in which tentativeness and indecision are strictly impossible. This has been hidden from us by our intense preoccupation with the characteristic questions of physical science. We can, indeed, postpone the question of whether there is life on Mars; we do not need to decide; it is not a forced option now at all, though we can imagine a situation in which it might become one. Confusion arises when we carry over an intellectual attitude from a situation in which it is appropriate to another in which it has no relevance.

Almost as important as the idea of involvement is the idea of paradox, which has been a common theme in religious thought, but was particularly prominent in the brilliant notes which were left by Pascal when he died. The heart of the idea is that, because the truth is never really simple, it is almost always necessary, when dealing with profound matters, to present at least two propositions rather than one. Often the two propositions are in sharp tension, but this is essential to the effort to represent adequately the complexity of the situation. It is necessary, if we are truthful, to say that man is a wretched creature, a chronic sinner, but it is also necessary to say that he is made in God's image, and that each man is accordingly a being of infinite worth. The mistake of the uncritical is to suppose that the affirmation of the first leads to a denial of the second.

In his exuberance at the discovery of the importance of paradox, Pascal went so far, at one point, as to uphold contradiction, but he did not elaborate this, and, because the notes were never made into a book, we cannot be sure that it represents his matured or critical position. "Contradiction," he wrote in one brief note, "is a poor sign of truth; much that is certain is open to contradiction; much that is false passes without contradiction. Neither is contradiction a mark of untruth, nor absence thereof a mark of truth." The recognition of the importance of paradox does not require such a break with classical logic. That it is possible to emphasize paradox and yet maintain the law of noncontradiction, as absolutely necessary to rational discourse, is made clear by the Aristotelian square of opposition. The closest logical affinity of paradoxical propositions is not with what, in Aristotelian terms, are called contradictions, but rather with those called subcontraries. The fact that one part of a student body is stupid does not keep another part of the student body from being brilliant. The fact that one aspect of human nature is self-centered does not keep another aspect from being akin to the divine. True sophistication is marked by the recognition that both are true and that both are true at once. Striking examples of Pascal's use of paradox, in this sense, are the following:

It is dangerous to show man too clearly how near he stands to the beasts without showing him his greatness. It is equally dangerous to show him his greatness too clearly, and not his lowness. It is yet more dangerous to leave him in ignorance of either. But it is very good for him to show him both.

Man knows that he is miserable; he is miserable because he is miserable, but he is very great because he knows it.

Signs of the greatness and the misery of man are so patent that true religion must necessarily inform us both that there is some great root of greatness in man, and also a great root of misery.

We possess truth and good, but only partially, and mixed with evil and falsehood.

It is not only in regard to the greatness and the wretchedness of man that the conception of paradox applies. It applies equally to the questions of causation and free will, to finitude and infinity, to reason and to revelation. Such an understanding must be kept in mind in connection with nearly every major problem in philosophy, and particularly in the philosophy of religion. When, much impressed with the principle of causation, we proceed to deny the reality of freedom our mistake is that of simple-mindedness. There is no *a priori* reason why both freedom and causation should not exist in our world. Emphasis on faith need not eliminate reason nor emphasis on reason eliminate faith.

It might appear, on first thought, that the concept of paradox is incompatible with the concept of forced option. On one side we say, with Kierkegaard, that we are faced with "either-or," while, on the other side, we say that the truth lies in "both and." The apparent incompatibility of these two positions is avoided when we realize that we are dealing here with two highly different situations. The forced option refers to personal decision, in which what is required is action. The man who refuses to decide whether he will let his weeds go to seed has already decided. It is accurate to say that every living person adopts some attitude toward God, because even neglect is an attitude. Failure to decide is already a decision. Paradox, however, is concerned primarly, not with action, but with the effort to know what is objectively the case. We cannot really follow out contrasting decisions at once, but we *can* see many contrasting aspects of the truth at once. If we do not follow the contrasting aspects, our grasp of the truth is inadequate.

Though it is not limited to religion, the most fundamental of all religious paradoxes is that of faith and reason. Pascal is our highly quotable spokesman here, as he is in so many other areas of serious discussion. Though his major effort was intellectual, as befitted a first-rate mathematician, he is permanently famous for his insistence upon the reasons of the heart. The juxtaposition of faith and reason occurs not merely in religion, but almost equally in science. If we define faith as "conviction apart from or in excess of proof," it is obvious that a vast amount of faith is required even before the scientific effort can begin. The primary faith, wholly unproven and unprovable, includes at least three great convictions:

(1) The conviction that there is a world at all, apart from the consciousness of the individual.
(2) The conviction that the world is conducted along orderly and dependable lines.
(3) The conviction that the future will be like the past.

D. REVELATION AND REASON

While religion shares both faith and reason with other areas of experience, one religious concept, that of revelation, is unique. Revelation differs radically, both from reason and from epistemological faith, in that it claims to refer to an act or to acts of divine self-disclosure. Such a claim is found in so many religions that the philosophy of religion must consider it carefully. What is the use of a painstaking effort to show evidence that God really is if we already know both *that* He is and *what* He is, by virtue of the fact that He has revealed Himself to men? If there is actually revealed religion, why not dispense with natural religion altogether? That we can do so was the conviction or at least the apparent conviction of Karl Barth, when he found himself in the odd position of being a Gifford Lecturer in Scotland. His position was odd, because the Gifford Lectures are specifically and strictly devoted to Natural Theology. Lord Gifford's words are these:

> I wish the Lecturers to treat their subjects as a strictly natural science, the greatest of all possible sciences, indeed, in one sense, the only science, that of Infinite Being, without reference to or reliance upon any supposed special exceptional or so-called miraculous revelation just as astronomy or chemistry is.

One of the most relevant remarks to make about such words is that they are now very largely outdated. The distinction between natural and revealed religion is not nearly so sharp as it formerly seemed to be, and that for several good reasons. One reason is that revelation, if it occurs, is certainly part of the truth about the world and should be included in any study of it. If we depend, in the pursuit of our "science," upon experience, one of the major experiences reported is the experience of receiving revelations. Moreover, the revelation may be far wider than we know. There is nothing intrinsically unreasonable about the hypothesis that, if God really is, He is always reaching out to men in a vast variety of ways. Why should it be assumed that we are seeking Him, but that He is not seeking us? There is nothing implausible about the notion of a double search conducted simultaneously. The figure of speech involved in "Behold, I stand at the door and knock" [10] may, indeed, be accurate.

Once it was widely believed that God, instead of leaving man wholly helpless, even in matters of religion, endowed him at creation with the power of reason. It was supposed that man could, by what was called the "unaided exercise of his reason," come to know God's existence and something of His nature. Later God, so the story went, added something that was different in kind, a direct communication of certain further information which man could never have found out for himself, and this was called revelation. Some said it came to Moses and to the prophets of Israel; some said it came through Christ; some said it came to Mohammed; some

[10] Rev. 3:20.

said it came through the hierarchy of the church. John Baillie speaks for many of his thoughtful contemporaries when he shows how dead this sharp division of knowledge is:

> Our conception of revelation has undergone a profound change, our conception of nature has undergone what is perhaps an even more profound change; and these two changes have been of such a kind as to result in a remarkable approximation or *rapprochement* of the two kinds of knowledge. Our present view of revelation and our present view of nature are such that the distinction between them is no longer the delightfully clear and easily statable thing it used to be.[11]

As we gain a clearer historical understanding of the development of religious experience we are helped to see that the contrast between reason and revelation may be more a matter of object than of method. The main claim of revelation is not that the human recipient is made aware, by a special method, of a set of truths about God, but the far more exciting claim that he is made aware of *God Himself*. This was a point on which Archbishop Temple helped many minds, especially when he dealt with the relationship between what man can learn by observation and what he can learn by revelation. The essence of revelation, he taught, "is intercourse of mind and event, not the communication of doctrine distilled from that intercourse." [12] God may, indeed, break into a man's life as He did into the life of Job, but He does not, for that reason, relieve Job or any other man of the necessity of working out, by careful analysis, his own answer to the problem of evil.

> *From all this it follows that there is no such thing as revealed truth. There are truths of revelation, that is to say, propositions which express the results of correct thinking concerning revelation; but they are not themselves directly revealed.*[13]

This distinction is one of the most helpful that have been made in recent years and, when understood, is one which transcends most of the difficulty that has been felt. The revelation, if it comes, is a religious experience rather than a merely intellectual one, and it requires for its full understanding the addition of thought quite as

---

[11] John Baillie, *Our Knowledge of God*, Oxford University Press, 1939, p. 36.
[12] William Temple, *Nature, Man and God*, p. 316.
[13] *Ibid.*, p. 317. The italics are in the original text.

much as does any other experience. The major reason for this
requirement is that a supposed revelation may be a false one. Since
there are several alleged revelations, many of which are strictly
incompatible with one another, they cannot all be genuine. What
about the supposed revelation to Joseph Smith? Both he and his
immediate followers felt that his revelation was as genuine and as
important as that of the Old or the New Testament. Was he right?
Were the gold plates really there? As soon as we try to answer
this question we are already out of the area of revelation and well
embarked in the area of reason, because we are forced to apply
tests of credibility, and they are highly complex. In short, revelation
is not self-validating! We must always ask the question of *why* it
is reasonable to believe that a revelation has occurred. We have
gained greatly from the widespread application of the historical
method, so that we know something of the steps by which the
alleged revelations have come about. The Bible may, indeed, be
God's direct revelation to finite men, but it is our philosophical
duty to ask how we know that this is true.

The important conclusion here is that the appeal to revelation
is not and cannot be a final appeal, because, if it were, every fanatic
would be justified in his uncritical assertions. If we are told that
the mother of Jesus was perpetually a virgin, we have a right to ask
the nature of the evidence. Was it revealed? Then to whom? Certainly, it does not appear in the Biblical account, where reference is
made to the brothers of Christ. The claim may be a justifiable claim,
but it needs careful substantiation. It is not true just because somebody says so.

The necessary conclusion is that reason and revelation, far from
being incompatible, *need* to go together at all times. If reason is
required to leave out all reference to revelation, it has no religious
material that is worth discussing. When we consider religious
experience, for example, as the heart of the empirical evidence for
the reality of God, the best evidence is the evidence which is in the
Bible, the very book which in the past has been looked upon as
the special preserve of revealed religion. If, on the other hand,
revelation is espoused without the critical examination which reason provides, we have no guarantee against superstition and ecclesiastical pretension. The importance of the philosophy of religion,

in this connection, lies chiefly in the fact that it is the discipline which provides the connection without which both reason and revelation are helpless in the quest for religious reality.

However willing we may be to recognize the value of current theistic existentialism, such existentialism is a source of danger as well as of gain. The danger is that there may be so much emphasis upon the decisiveness of a concerned faith that we do not have any criterion by which to judge *between* faiths. "The decision of faith," says Herberg, "is beyond the abstract reason of science and philosophy." [14] But, in that case, why is one faith better than another? Why espouse the Biblical faith, which Professor Herberg values so highly, rather than some other? If this question is not faced, we have no antidote to superstition; if it is asked, it cannot be answered except by what is called "the abstract reason of science and philosophy." If the choice of faiths is made merely as a matter of personal preference, why is the Biblical theologian any better off than is the logical positivist with his arbitrarily imposed limits upon valid inquiry?

The danger of anti-intellectualism appears among a number of modern interpreters of the highest eminence. We are surprised to find that a man as formidable as Arnold Toynbee writes, "We must recognize the truth that it is a mistake to try to formulate religion in intellectual terms." [15] He does not seem to recognize that, on this basis, there is no valid means of counteracting the very fanaticism which he so fears. In a similar manner, Professor Reinhold Niebuhr says, "This is the final enigma of human existence for which there is no answer except by faith and hope; for all answers transcend the categories of human reason. Yet without these answers human life is threatened with scepticism and nihilism on the one hand, and with fanaticism and pride on the other." [16]

Emil Brunner is more extreme when he says:

Revelation, as the Christian faith understands it, is indeed, by its very nature, something that lies beyond all rational arguments; the argument

[14] *Judaism and Modern Man,* New York, Farrar, Straus, 1951, p. 36.

[15] Arnold Toynbee, "Man Owes His Freedom to God," *Collier's Magazine,* March 30, 1956, p. 82.

[16] Reinhold Niebuhr, *The Nature and Destiny of Man,* New York, Scribner, 1941, vol. 2, p. 149.

which it certainly claims in the support does not lie in the sphere of rational knowledge, but in the sphere of that divine truth which can be attained only through divine self-communication, and not through human research of any kind.[17]

Revelation must be tested by reason for the simple reason that there are false claims to revelation. We know, in advance, that many alleged revelations are false, because there are absolutely contradictory claims. It cannot be true that there is only *one* way by which men may be saved and that there are *many* ways by which men may be saved. Unless the law of noncontradiction is recognized as the necessary condition of all rational discussion, we give up everything. If the law holds, we know that, when contradictory revelations are reported, somebody is wrong. However eager we may be for harmony and tolerance, we cannot be intellectually honest unless we face the fact that there is, for example, a real contradiction between the Roman Catholic and the Protestant version of what it is to be a Christian. The Roman Catholic view is that *theirs* is the only true church; the characteristic Protestant view is that the Christian fellowship is so rich that it can take many valid forms. We do not know, in our finitude, which of these is right, but we do know that somebody is *wrong*.

If there are conflicts and contrasts of revelation between two groups of Christians, there are even greater conflicts when other religions are involved. Assuming that revelation is immune from the tests of rationality, what are we to say about the alleged Moslem revelation? Yet one of the distinguished authors just quoted, Professor Brunner, denies the Moslem revelation and denies it solely by reference to the very "rational arguments" of which revelation is asserted to be independent. Why should not the devout Moslem quote the words given above as a rejoinder to the application of rational tests to *his* revelation? It is precisely because he would be justified in doing so that the arbitrary separation of revelation and reason must never be condoned.

[17] Emil Brunner, *Revelation and Reason,* Philadelphia, Westminster Press, 1946, p. 206.

3

The Possibility of Truth

*Say rather, beloved Agathon, that you cannot refute the truth;
for Socrates is easily refuted.*

SOCRATES

If any religion or any part of religion is not true, we ought to
give it up. To maintain the appearance of a faith merely because it
is socially useful, or comforting, though believed to be false, is to
deny what is asserted. If a religion is not true it is evil! If God
is not, then prayer is a waste of good time and wholly indefensible.
If there is no life after death, the sooner we find that out the better.
In any effort to deal with religion philosophically, we must try to
understand what we mean by truth. If we have differing or ambiguous conceptions of the nature of truth, further fruitful discussion will be impossible, for we may be arguing for different
positions without knowing it.

A. The Danger of Subjectivism

The principle of involvement, which we have seen, in the preceding chapter, to be necessary to religious understanding, may
easily be confused, because of superficial similarity, with the idea
that truth has only subjective reference. The doctrine, as popularly
expressed, is the notion that the truth of any proposition is simply
a matter of what it does to the person who holds it. Thus, it is
common to try to end a theological discussion by saying, "God may
exist *for John,* but He does not exist *for me.*" There is no doubt
that many people suppose such a statement is a final and conclusive one. If they are correct, truth need not involve any trans-
subjective reference at all.

The logical result of the notion of something existing for one
person and not for another would be a theory of the world in which
all knowledge would refer merely to what is in the knower's mind.

In that case not only would God, and the material order, be mere ideas in John's mind, but also Henry would be nothing but an idea in John's mind, and John would be nothing but an idea in Henry's mind. We have not the disposition to argue with anyone who wants to travel that ancient road, but it is not a road that leads to any profitable destination. Certainly when men have worshiped God they have not supposed that they were worshiping ideas in their own minds, for these would not be worthy of worship.

The idea that all religious commitment is based upon personal involvement is a sound idea, but the emphasis on subjectivity need not include any lack of emphasis on the objective truth of religious assertions. The existence of God means little to me unless I personally do something about it, but there is no logical reason why God, when I know Him, should be limited, in His being, to my consciousness. On the contrary, there cannot be any important sense in which God is *for me* unless there is some real and objective sense in which *God is,* irrespective of my belief or my lack of belief.

More than most aspects of experience, religious experience has an enormous stake in philosophical realism. The minimum meaning of all realism is the conviction that objects exist, independent of the experience of the knower. Objects may be physical objects, such as sticks or stones, or they may be universals, such as those for which Plato argued so tirelessly and so cogently. This is why we refer to Platonic realism when we discuss his system. Plato established the great tradition when, following Socrates, he argued that a man who discusses what he ought to do is dealing with something real and objective, rather than merely his own passing ideas, opinions and whims. Though there have frequently been challenges to this tradition, it remains in essential possession of the intellectual field and is stronger today than it has been for a long time.[1]

The temptation to engage in the denial of objectivity arises chiefly from two considerations which occur to almost everyone who thinks at all. First is the consideration that men differ markedly from one another in what they experience. Two men come into a room from two other rooms, one hot and the other cold; to one of them this new room seems cool, and to the other it seems warm.

[1] See, for instance, the carefully argued philosophical work of Paul Weiss, particularly *Man's Freedom,* Yale University Press, 1950.

In a lesser degree the same is true of all human experiences, because each man is affected by his unique background. Thus, we differ about the beauty of buildings. Perhaps we are always talking about ourselves and not, as we suppose, about the external object. The other consideration, and a far more serious one, is that every experience is always an inner and subjective one. Everything that we claim to know about the external world is subjectively known, for we can never succeed in getting outside our own skins. "By the very nature of things," says von Hügel, "we cannot get clean out of our mind, so as to compare things as they are outside it with the same things as we experience them within it."

The argument for the subjectivity of all experience is superficially impressive and, indeed, valid, up to a point. What is important in philosophy is to know where that point is. The color of the red light is, in some sense, my inner experience, since it certainly is not experienced by the color-blind person or by some of the lower animals. Sound is subjective in the same sense. There would not be what we call sound were it not for the sensitive receptors connected with ears. We are aware, always, of the danger of delusion, such as occurs when we interpret the fence post in the foreground as a crag in the distance. We seem to get out of the prison house of subjectivity by walking up to the post and touching it, but we realize that we do not thereby make a real escape, when we note that the experience of touch is just another inner experience. Even if we use instruments, there must always be somebody to read the instruments, and the person's reading is still another inner experience.

To know that every man is in the egocentric predicament is a very great thing, but it need not lead to fundamental skepticism. It is a mark of intellectual sophistication to realize that no man has any privileged way of escaping from the circle of his own subjectivity. Every man inevitably sees the world and all that is in it, including himself, from his own particular point of view. Even the experience of vicarious observation is *his* experience. But it is a *non sequitur* to argue from this to the further proposition that we do not know an objective world. It is especially fallacious to argue, from the necessity of subjective experience, that objects of religious experience are lacking in objective reference when we do not draw the same conclusion in regard to other objects of sensory or scientific experience.

B. THE ARGUMENT FOR REALISM

By realism we mean that theory of the world which holds that there are objects of knowledge which actually enjoy independent existence. Though there are many differences among realists, this is their common faith. All agree that the knower may be deluded and that objects are understood by the knower in the light of his own particular limitations, but they insist that there is something waiting to be known. There are objects which would exist even if they were not known by ourselves or any other mind and which, accordingly, are more than ideas in the mind of the subject who is the alleged knower. The realist insists, in short, that there are existences which are not relative to the cognitive situation, though eventually they may become so. There are, he believes, flowers that bloom unseen.

This faith is to be defended, first, by removing certain intellectual barriers and, second, by positive considerations. The chief intellectual barrier is the notion that an event can be wholly "accounted for" in terms of subjective factors. But this turns out to be nothing but a superstition or a prejudice. How could the existence of subjective factors amount to a denial of the existence of objective factors? I have an idea of a tree, it is true, and this undoubtedly helps me in giving patterned order to the visual sensations which appear, but it is not clear why this eliminates the possibility that there is also something outside my window which gives rise to these curious sensations. I may come to the time of prayer with an idea of God, but this alone is not sufficient to show that the experience of prayer is purely illusory, with no objective revelation of God. In both cases there are, of course, subjective factors, since that is merely another way of saying that we are bound to receive all messages, whatever their origin, by means of our own human faculties. But it does not follow that recognition of subjective causes involves rejection of the presence of objective causes. There is no incompatibility and, indeed, no real difficulty in the hypothesis that what is experienced *inwardly* may exist *outwardly*.

The chief source of confusion on this important point involves the notion of cause. There is the widespread notion, in uncritical thought, that there is a single cause for every event. Thus we ask, "What caused John's illness?" and we are satisfied when we are given the name of a germ. But an illness has *many* causes, most of them exceedingly complex.[2] That the germ alone is insufficient is evident from the fact that germs are often present without the resultant symptoms of illness. The general condition of the human organism, the weather conditions, and many other conditions constitute together the complex "cause" of an illness. *The point is that the discovery of one cause does not entail the elimination of others.* The experience of light may be caused by the fact that I open my eyes, but it may *at the same time* be caused by the fact that there is sunshine. It seems clear that the same principles apply equally to physical knowledge and to religious knowledge. In either case objective status may be lacking, but the existence of subjective conditions is not sufficient to show that this is the case. The fact that we know *with* the mind does not mean that we cannot know what is outside the mind. If we thus rid our minds of the notion of causal simplicity we are prepared to receive the positive arguments for realism. These arguments may be many, but three stand out in sharp relief.

(1) There is a great difference between what we know as perceptual and as nonperceptual experience. Objects which seem to be perceptual have about them a strength, a vividness, a permanence, and a commanding quality which are not involved in the experience which we recognize as imaginative or hallucinatory. This is not explained on the subjectivist hypothesis, but is fully reasonable if there are real objects which help to produce genuine perceptions.

(2) Many of the objects of the external world give evidence of their own continuity even when not observed by our own minds. Thus, a fire which is left burning in a house, where no one is, seems to have been going on during our absence because the fuel is partially burned. There is succession in nature whether we think

---

[2] Professor Joseph calls this the doctrine of the Composition of Causes. Cf. *An Introduction to Logic,* Oxford University Press, 1916, p. 492.

about it or not. How can we account for the filling in of these gaps between subjective experiences other than by an external physical order independent of us?

(3) There is fundamental agreement as between many observers in regard to what is experienced. This does not mean that there is never any difference about the external world, supposing there is an external world, but it does mean that the amount of agreement is so great that it is hard to explain by the miracle of coincidence. There is, thus, good reason to suppose that there is an actual world which makes possible public experience. The pansubjectivist is faced with a tremendous miracle. Though, as we noted above, no two perceptions are identical, it is nevertheless true that they have so much in common that they must be explained by reference to a common source.

The reasonable conclusion is that our ideas, in spite of the fact that they are and must be subjective, have or can have *objective reference*. They have objective reference because they refer to objects, and they partake of the nature of truth when they grasp the character of these objects correctly. Such a statement is epistemological rather than ontological. That is, it says nothing whatever about the constitution of objects. God, according to what most men of recent centuries have believed, is spiritual in nature. To say that God exists really, not merely as a projection of our own minds, is to say that He is an object or that He has objective status, and to say that a stone really exists is to say that it likewise is an object. The notion that only physical things can be objective is, of course, sheer prejudice, with no evidence to support it.

Though we cannot escape from the circle of our subjective ideas, we can find *within these* an order which is indicative of what lies beyond that order. Ideas of imagination and ideas of perception are both ideas, but we can compare them in such a way as to learn much. Thus, experience, in spite of its fallacious tendencies, provides the tests of its own reliability. Otherwise we should have no tests, for we cannot get outside experience. We wish we might have some external standard of veracity, but, since we do not have it, we follow the more humble means of comparing and contrasting the various items in our experience to learn which, among them, are trustworthy and which are untrustworthy. In any case, when we speak of truth in religion we speak of what we discover rather than what we make. "The truth (or falsity) of a proposition *antedates* the process by which it is verified (or refuted)." [3]

C. The Challenge of Pragmatism

The chief challenge to philosophical realism in the modern world does not arise from the subjective idealism which is usually mentioned in the books but which actually has no representatives. Almost anyone can see that subjective idealism, in the sense of the doctrine that the world exists in the knower, rather than the knower existing in the world, would be self-defeating. It would lead inevitably to solipsism, in which the experiencing individual would be the only existent in the world. There would, therefore, be no other persons to hold differing views and, consequently, no philosophical discussion. The subjectivist *philosopher* is, thus, a self-contradiction and ruled out accordingly.

The form of subjectivism which challenges us in the modern world is nearly always some type of pragmatism. Pragmatism gets its strongest popular support from its attack on the representative theory of truth. In common sense a proposition is true if it accurately matches the reality to which it refers. We affirm, let us say, that the moon has no atmosphere, and we normally say that this proposition is true providing it corresponds accurately to the actual state of affairs on the surface of the moon. There is, the ordinary man believes, a real state of affairs in every part of the universe, and the truth appears when our belief or judgment or affirmation *matches* the state of affairs.

The pragmatists of all schools seem to score heavily when they show that we have no way whatever of matching our conviction with what is outside us, since our very effort to verify our belief is one in which we carry ourselves and all our intellectual baggage along. Truth, says the pragmatist, cannot be a copy of reality, because we have no way of observing reality apart from our participation in it. Therefore, says the pragmatist, the only solution is to change our meaning of truth. Since truth, in the fully representative sense, is something of which we are incapable, the path of

[3] W. P. Montague, *The Way of Things,* New York, Prentice-Hall, 1940.

wisdom is to entertain a conception of truth which we can handle. This, it is asserted, is the idea that truth is that which works. We cannot know what the world is apart from human experience of it, but we *can* know what *succeeds*.[4]

Pragmatism as a doctrine of truth has gone far beyond academic philosophy to penetrate common life until it appears among historians and men of letters and in ordinary conversation, including that of religious men and women. It ought to be obvious, however, that the pragmatic approach to truth would undermine nearly all important religious claims. If pragmatism prevails, the future of the great religions is dim.

The way in which pragmatism leads to confusion is shown by considering the religion taught by Adolf Hitler. That Hitlerism was qualitatively religious there is no doubt, for it involved a conception of reality, full commitment to that conception, sacrifice and ceremonial acts. For a while, when Nazi thought was in its ascendancy, this religion certainly worked. It worked, because it made men strong, because it held people together, and because it enabled them to hold off the attacks of a great part of the world for nearly six years. Was the doctrine true *then,* and did it cease to be true after Hitler's suicide in 1945? Does a religion lose its truth when its followers are martyred and dispersed? With how many does it have to work in order to be true, and how long?

Pragmatism has so deeply affected our current mentality that many now espouse the idea that "truth changes," often under the impression that they are holding some advanced or liberating position. But the notion that truth changes involves insuperable difficulties, difficulties which are especially vivid when we deal with history. On many points of fact, of course, we have been forced to change our minds about what occurred long ago, because new evidence has become available. This is true not only of major events, such as wars and revolutions, but of the deeds of particular persons. Thus, modern research has forced us to change our opinion about

---

[4] Even the amateur is quick to realize that pragmatism is highly ambiguous and, therefore, vulnerable in regard to the meaning of "works." Does it mean that which makes me feel good, that which wins military or ideological battles, that which survives, or what? Professor Lovejoy performed a great service to philosophy early in his career by producing his brilliant article, "The Thirteen Pragmatisms." This was first published in the *Journal of Philosophy,* vol. 5, 1908.

the character of Harriet Beecher Stowe's work in the production of *Uncle Tom's Cabin*.[5] If truth changes, we cannot avoid the conclusion that Mrs. Stowe was one kind of writer a hundred years ago and another kind of writer today. But this is too absurd to be believed by anybody. Whatever Mrs. Stowe was she was. Our opinions may change, and they are almost bound to change, because we are fallible and ignorant persons, but the event does not change, and consequently the truth does not change. It is our judgment that is altered. If there is no difference between our judgment and the truth, there is no point in trying to correct our judgments. If our judgments are wrong, they are wrong in terms of *something*, and the only thing in terms of which they can be wrong is the objective truth. But if this reasoning is sound, the pragmatic conception of the meaning of truth cannot stand.[6]

The crucial fallacy of pragmatism is the fallacy of its own inner contradiction. It appears to uphold the idea that all truth is relative, but relative to what? Since it cannot say "relative to objective truth," it is forced to make pragmatism itself its center of reference. A brilliant critic of pragmatism in history has pointed this out in the following passage:

Professor Commager's plea is a plea that we should conform to something, i.e. the pragmatic idea. He refers to what he calls "the first lesson of pragmatism: damn the absolute!" but at the same time he is himself pleading that we should receive the pragmatic ideal as if it were an absolute. The philosophy that damns the absolute is thus strangely revealed as the absolute philosophy.[7]

To make a new absolute out of the doctrine that there is no absolute is obvious confusion. Popularly, it seems to gain credence from the physical principle of relativity and from the remarkable success of technological development, neither of which in fact involves any such conclusion. In technics experimentation seems to be a law unto itself, and always justified by better results. It is right that

[5] Cf. J. C. Furnas, *Goodbye to Uncle Tom*, New York, William Sloane Associates, 1956.

[6] A thorough criticism of the pragmatic conception of truth is that of Brand Blanshard, *The Nature of Thought*, New York, Macmillan, 1940, vol. 1, chapter 10.

[7] J. V. Langmead Casserley, *The Bent World*, Oxford University Press, 1955, p. 122.

men should experiment, not because there is no objective truth but because this is one of the chief ways of knowing what the truth already is. Men should dissent, not for the sake of dissent nor because dissent is absolute but because the truth is hard to know and is more likely to be known if men challenge other men. The truth need not suffer by being challenged.

The confusion which arises from the notion of the absolute relativity of truth comes out especially in connection with the character of God. Radical pragmatists are bound to hold that God's nature has changed as human experience of Him has changed. Thus, we should have to say that God was once bloodthirsty and cruel, whereas later He was forgiving and tender. But a God as changeable as that could not be a worthy object of devotion and dedication. Perhaps He will change again tomorrow. Fortunately, we require no intricate hypothesis to avoid such absurdity. All that is needed is the notion that the truth about God, like the truth about Julius Caesar, has in it a once-for-all quality, though finite men may be slow in understanding it. What we need to recognize is the ancient distinction between truth and opinion.

D. The Error of Inerrancy

Just as it is important, in the philosophy of religion, to see the intellectual danger which lies in pragmatism, so it is likewise important to see, at the same time, the opposite danger of infallibility. It is as much an evil to say that we know the truth perfectly as it is to say that there is no truth to know. It is one thing to argue, against all relativism and subjectivism, that there is an objective truth, but it is quite another to argue that any of us have come in full possession of it.

The doctrine of necessary fallibility is the philosophical equivalent of the religious doctrine of original sin. This latter doctrine asserts, with much factual evidence to support it, that a chronic sinfulness dogs our steps at every point, especially in our claims to virtue, which are tainted with the sin of pride. Every human institution, no matter how noble its aims, is inevitably involved in the struggle for power and prestige, and this, so far as we can see, is not likely to be lessened with the passage of centuries. In short, sin is not a matter of cultural lag but is intrinsic to the situation, part of the price which man pays for his self-consciousness and relative freedom from external constraint. Just as all our efforts to be virtuous are tainted with sin, so all our efforts to achieve the truth are liable to error. We correct some errors only to make others, frequently making one in the very act of correcting another. We are very small; our grasp of reality is very slight; to claim anything else is to be arrogant and presumptuous. Oliver Cromwell's famous advice is permanently valuable because it refers to something basic in human nature. "By the bowels of Christ, I beseech you," he said, "bethink you that you may be mistaken."

Any religious doctrine which claims infallibility, whether it be that of Biblical inerrancy or papal claims or any other, is bound in the end to fail to sustain itself intellectually because it runs head on into the fact of human failure. We are always in the finite predicament, even when we are most religious, and often *especially* when we are most religious. If our human capacity to err needs any demonstration, it is given to us constantly by the fact that we have to reconstruct our theories and reassess our facts. The changes that are necessary, as a result of further insight, include not only the physical world but the spiritual world also

It is conceivable that, by some miracle, God could make an exception to liability to error by creating an infallible Bible or an infallible papacy, but how could we ever know that this is the case? Infallibility necessarily includes not only an infallible revelation but the infallibility of the human mind to *judge* that revelation.[8] It is helpful to realize that the Bible never asserts its own infallibility. Even if there were some institutions which had never made any mistakes, in precisely defined areas of inerrancy, how could we know that must always be the case or is intrinsically the case? In the nature of things the future is not yet, and the evidence is never all in.

It is chiefly by a more realistic appraisal of human nature that we see the error of inerrancy. Man has made great strides in many

[8] "What advantage," wrote Newman, "is an infallible guide, if those who are to be guided have, after all, no more than an opinion?" John Henry Cardinal Newman, *An Essay on the Development of Christian Doctrine,* new ed., Toronto, Longmans, 1949, p. 74.

areas of experience, including the spiritual, the artistic and the scientific, but he always carries his own limitations with him. He is hindered, not only by his own ignorance but even by his own greed and pride. Any group which claims at any point to be free from these limitations is guilty of idolatry, confusing the position of the human with that of the divine. It is against such arrogant pretensions that pragmatism is fighting, though the unfortunate result is that it lands itself in a problem as difficult as that against which it struggles. The great middle ground is that which maintains both the objectivity of truth and man's incapacity, either individually or collectively, to attain it perfectly.

It is because men cannot know the truth simply that we need to devise a multitude of ways of correcting our errors. This is done chiefly by engaging in a series of efforts, in which we subject individual views to the impact of other views which may bring correction or corroboration. Thus, we balance the deliverance of one sense against the deliverance of another. Eye checks ear, and hand checks both. Herein lies the immense advantage of the possession of many senses. We distinguish between mirage and reality chiefly by going to the spot. This, of course, does not bring absolute certainty in any realm of experience, but it, in any case, lessens the probability of delusion. It is still possible to be wrong, but the likelihood is vastly lessened when we use a system of checks and balances.

The ideal of scholarship, which has been consciously cultivated during the past few generations, is one in which a deliberate effort is made, by those who think and experiment and write, to go beyond the individual point of view and to seek to see every problem synoptically. It is still true that we cannot get out of our own skins or live in independence of the particular experiences which have been ours, but much can be done by a conscious effort to transcend the provincial or the partial. This is what the truly judicial mind often achieves to a remarkable degree. Many judges encourage us mightily by the way in which, on attaining the bench, they reject resolutely the temptations to be party men. Scientists are often especially alert to find evidence *against* their pet theories. Lord Acton believed that the ideal stage in the development of historical science would be reached when the life of Martin Luther would be substantially the same whether written by a Protestant or a Roman Catholic. Some scholars now approximate this ideal.

In all this the proper mood is the mood of doubt. It is not, therefore, unreasonable to call Descartes the father of modern philosophy, because, though we may not accept his conclusions, we are forced, as modern men, to accept much of his method. To start by the deliberate practice of doubting what we *can* doubt, and to demand evidence at every point, is the best-known antidote to superstition. All honest doubt has a quasi-religious or at least a moral character about it, because it shows an overriding concern for the truth. Those who do not care tremendously about the truth do not bother to doubt, for doubt entails work. The dangerous man is not the man who doubts, but the man who does not care. *I care, therefore, I doubt* is at least the beginning of a valid method in the philosophy of religion.

It is only just to recognize the significant contribution to this theme made by the distinguished American philosopher Josiah Royce. This excellent scholar, who adorned three universities—California, Johns Hopkins and Harvard—saw, with exceptional clarity, that the place to begin was the fact of error. If we accept the method of doubt and then seek, in the Cartesian spirit, for something that is not doubtful, error provides a solid starting point. It is no idle paradox to point out that we are more sure of error than of anything else, since we imply it even by denying it. Either there is error or there is not. But if there is not, then those specific persons who have believed that there is have, themselves, been in error. It is really easier to be sure of falsehood than of truth, yet if there is falsehood there must be truth, for what can falsehood deviate from, if not the truth? *"The conditions that determine the logical possibility of error must themselves be absolute truth."* [9] A really thoroughgoing skepticism turns out to be that which provides a logical fulcrum.

One thing this skepticism implies—one thing so simple as generally to escape notice among the assumptions of our thought. *It implies that we can be in error about an external world.* Therefore even this extreme skepticism assumes that *there is a difference between true and false state-*

[9] Josiah Royce, *The Religious Aspect of Philosophy*, Boston, Houghton Mifflin, 1885, p. 385.

ments about nature. But now what is involved in saying that a statement is either true or false? To affirm, to deny, to doubt, all imply a real distinction between truth and error; all three then involve in common the assumption that there is such a distinction. That which is involved alike both in the truth and the falsity of a statement must itself be certainly true and cannot be doubted.[10]

The truth *is,* even though it may be beyond us. This is an immense practical help in that, while we are saved from the delusion of supposing that we are more than we are, it is nevertheless worth while to use all the means at our disposal to help one another to get closer and closer to the truth which is. If we hold a philosophy which denies the existence of objective truth we necessarily cut the nerve of moral effort, since there is no use in disciplining our minds for participation in a meaningless endeavor. But the endeavor is neither meaningless nor profitless. Though the truth is something which we cannot grasp with perfection, much of our glory lies in the fact that we can make approximations to it. To see through a glass darkly is better than not to see at all.

[10] *Ibid.,* p. 372.

4
The Mystery of Knowledge

All men by nature desire to know.   ARISTOTLE

We must reject utterly the sometimes popular notion that religion thrives on ignorance, capitalizing on those areas which are unknown. If this were accepted, the area of religious reality would be diminished every time a new scientific discovery was made. This would be both undignified and intolerable. Since valid faith is built not on what is not, but on what *is,* the honest religious thinker welcomes knowledge of every kind. Ignorance is not revealing, but knowledge is.

A. THE CLAIM TO KNOWLEDGE

Though there are many amazing things about the world, as we know it, one of the most amazing is the fact that the capacity to know has been enormously expanded in one creature. We cannot be sure what has emerged in other parts of the universe,[1] but we do know that on one particular planet there are creatures whose capacity for knowledge is truly phenomenal. These creatures can now compute the distance to stars which are millions of light-years away; they know the physical composition of bodies which they have never touched; and they know, with fair accuracy, the story of what occurred on their own planet millions of years ago. Though they are not yet sure whether their atomic discoveries will be ultimately beneficent or disastrous, they know enough of the nature of matter to be able to release almost incredible energy. There are many who claim to know at first hand the Mind which is the source both of themselves and of this same incredible energy.

[1] Henri Bergson believed that there is life and possibly consciousness on many planets. See *The Two Sources of Morality and Religion,* New York, Doubleday Anchor, 1954, p. 255.

Man's claim to knowledge seems very simple until we begin to examine it, and then it is recognized as something highly complex. Our habitual claim is that we are able to have true awareness of natures other than our own, to understand them as they are in themselves, and to grasp something of the relationship both of them and of ourselves to the whole of which all are parts. There is a valid sense in which the universe includes me, but there is an equally valid sense in which the universe is included in my perception and comprehension.

It is a gain in clarity to try to understand the difference between knowledge and truth. Truth is always a quality of propositions and does not refer to minds or to things. If we say "Mars is inhabited," that is a proposition, a statement which is either true or false, even though we may not be able now, or for a long time, to discover *whether* it is true or false. The truth or falsity of such a proposition, as we have argued in the preceding chapter, precedes, both temporally and logically, the operation by which we discover it.

In much the same way in which truth is a quality of propositions, knowledge is a function of minds. The following formula may be helpful in keeping our terms clear:

> *Propositions* may be true or false;
> *Minds* may be knowing or ignorant;
> *Objects* may be real or imaginary.

In spite of our tendency to error, a knowing mind is always in contact, at some point or other, with the actual world. What we know is not merely our ideas, but the real world, our ideas constituting our more or less accurate apprehension of the nature of the real world. One of the purposes of human life is the constant re-examination of these apprehensions in the hope that they will become increasingly more accurate. Knowledge is never simple or easy, delusion is common, and the true apprehension of reality, if it comes, comes at the end of the process rather than at the beginning. Genuine knowledge is always an achievement and never the datum with which we start.

B. THE LEAPS OF KNOWLEDGE

As we study carefully our relationship to the world, parts of which we claim to know, we begin to see that there is a real sense in which we are imprisoned. All that we have is our own sensations, our own impressions, our own thoughts. How do we move from the Beyond that is within to the Beyond that is not within? It is a common practice for those who seek to deny the possibility of the knowledge of God to point out that all reported experiences of God are merely experiences *within* the minds of men. How, then, can religious knowledge be genuine? As we have already seen, however, the same line of reasoning applies to every conceivable item of alleged knowledge. The knowledge of God is, in this regard, in no worse and in no better situation than is the knowledge of "physical objects" or of other persons. If anyone wants to be a complete subjectivist in regard to knowledge, that is his privilege, but we can, at least, ask him to have a decent respect for consistency. He cannot keep our intellectual respect if he plays favorites in his practice of skepticism.

(1) As we analyze the apparently simple relation called knowledge we find that there are three distinct leaps in the process, leaps of which we are not normally conscious because we make them habitually. Of course, we all believe in the existence of the "real world," but it is a wholesome exercise in humility to try to understand *why* we believe in it. We do so by taking a leap, the leap of epistemological faith. This is true whether we are scientists or philosophers or men of common sense, since we are all on the same ground in this important regard. Balfour's account of why we assume the reality of knowledge is hard to improve:

If we do so, it is not, as the candid reader will be prepared to admit, because such a conclusion is justified by such premises, but because we are predisposed to a conclusion of this kind by those instinctive beliefs which, in unreflective moments, the philosopher shares with the savage. In such moments all men conceive themselves (by hypothesis erroneously) as having direct experiences of an independent material universe.[2]

A great part of modern reflective thought has been vitiated by the

[2] Arthur Balfour, *The Foundations of Belief*, 8th ed., New York, Longmans, 1933, p. 128.

original conviction of Descartes, the conviction that the mind deals only with its own ideas. If our own ideas are all that we really know in the beginning, then our own ideas are all we really know in the end, and the bridge by which Descartes crosses the chasm from the self to the objects of knowledge is a purely artificial construction. If we are going to have faith in the end we may as well have it in the beginning, and, as a matter of fact, we do have it in the beginning in an inexpugnable manner. No man really doubts the external world any more than he doubts his own existence.[3] We do not actually go beneath the fundamental subject-object relationship, which is the irreducible unit of all knowledge. "What Descartes indulged in his stove was purely academic doubt," writes Temple; "he was really as sure of the stove as of himself." [4]

Our faith in actual objects of actual knowledge may be sheer animal faith, but it is not a faith which is expelled by any increase in sophistication. What all men actually depend on, in this matter, is the "spontaneous creed of the natural man." Philosophical realism of some sort is an instinctive faith, neither produced by argument nor destroyed by it, because it rests upon assumptions which no man can prove and which no man can really avoid.[5]

(2) The second leap is that by which physical stimuli pass over into conscious experience. There is a vast and fundamental difference between "ether waves" and the experience of sound or the experience of sight, as the case may be. We ordinarily denote this difference by saying that the waves are physical events whereas the experiences are mental events. On the one hand is the realm of things and on the other is the realm of thoughts. Because sound waves have length they can be measured accurately by a number of intricate mechanical devices. Some of these devices are fundamentally similar to those found in the inner ear. Different parts of the intricate apparatus appear to be sensitive to different vibra-

---

[3] It is hard to disagree with Professor Lovejoy when he says, "The occasional lovers of philosophic paradox who have professed such disbelief seem to me merely to display an unconvincing affectation." *Contemporary American Philosophy*, vol. 2, p. 96.

[4] William Temple, *Nature, Man and God,* London, 1934, p. 66.

[5] Cf. A. O. Lovejoy, *The Revolt Against Dualism,* New York, W. W. Norton, 1930, pp. 11-15. Professor Lovejoy presents five items in the epistemological creed of the natural man.

tions and send "messages" accordingly to the brain. But somehow or somewhere the most profound transformation takes place so that there comes to be a reality which has modes of behavior utterly different from the modes of behavior observable in physical objects. It follows a different set of laws. How different the two realms are was stated brilliantly by Blaise Pascal when he said, "All bodies, the firmament, the stars, the earth and its kingdoms, are not equal to the lowest mind; for mind knows all these and itself; and these bodies nothing."

Since the leap in question is better expressed by poetry than by prose, we are wise to be unusually attentive when the late poet laureate of England addresses himself to this theme:

> Tho' measure true
> every wave-length of ether or air that reacheth sense,
> there the hunt checketh, and her keen hounds are at fault;
> for when the waves have passed the gates of ear and eye all
> scent is lost: suddenly escaped the visibles are changed to
> invisible; the fine measured motions to immeasurable emotion;
> the cyphered fractions to a living joy that man feeleth to
> shrive his soul.[6]

The recognition that all knowledge of the external world involves commerce between two kinds of reality is one of the most important lessons that philosophy has to teach. Knowledge ordinarily and continually means that what is physical gives rise to what is not physical, namely, consciousness. The only way in which this interpretation can be avoided is by the adoption of some form of behaviorism, which involves the doctrine that consciousness *is* nothing but physical or electrical motion.

What is important to know is that such behaviorism involves absurdities so great that recognition of them makes the doctrine incredible. All objects have weight and all motions have velocity, but it is nonsense to ask how much the idea of justice weighs or what is the average velocity of a man's conception of social security. The doctrine that thought *is* nothing but a chemical reaction is something for which there is absolutely no known evidence. Certainly a thought does not *act* like a chemical reaction. All that

[6] Robert Bridges, *The Testament of Beauty*, Oxford University Press, 1930, Bk. III, lines 766-773.

anyone can show is that the chemical reaction and the thoughts are *associated*, but association is not identity.

There is a popular confusion, shared by some workers in the life sciences, which identifies mind and brain,[7] but the identification runs counter to all experience. Since we know different realities by what they do and by the laws which they illustrate we are dealing constantly with radically different entities. The relations of physical concomitance and of collision are totally different from the relations of implication and consistency, which can hold only between meanings and never between material objects. No philosopher in our time has made this important distinction more clearly than has Professor Blanshard of Yale University. In his major work he writes:

> That we really do mean something different by consciousness and bodily behavior is made clear again by the different attributes that we assign to them. We speak of an idea as clear or confused, as apposite or inapposite, as witty or dull. Are such terms intelligible when applied to those motions of electrons, atoms, molecules, or muscles, which for the behaviorist are all there is to consciousness? Can a motion be clear, or cogent, or witty? What exactly would a clear motion be like? What sort of thing is a germane or cogent reflex? Or a witty muscular reaction? These adjectives are perfectly in order when applied to ideas; they become at once absurd when applied to movements in muscle or nerve; and how account for this absurdity if we do not mean different things when we speak of ideas and movements?[8]

Every time a person experiences knowledge of the external world he gives a new illustration of the truly remarkable fact that movement gives rise to what is more than movement. We always live in two worlds at once, but in the experience of knowledge the connection is particularly obvious.

(3) A third leap involved in knowledge is that which makes possible public or communicable knowledge. The difficulties inherent in the communication of knowledge seem to be insuperable, and yet we all believe that it is actually communicated. Poets and

---

[7] Many statements of this position are easily available. One of the most plausible is that of Hugh Elliot, *Modern Science and Materialism*, London, Longmans, Green, 1919.

[8] Brand Blanshard, *The Nature of Thought*, New York, Macmillan, 1940, vol. 1, pp. 336, 37. See also Broad, *The Mind and Its Place in Nature*, New York, Harcourt, Brace, 1929, pp. 622, 623.

mystics have long maintained that their experiences are ineffable, but why is not *every* experience ineffable? How do I know that you see what I see? As a matter of fact, we probably do not see exactly the same scene. No matter how close together we are, each has a slightly different perspective and each a different preparation. Even in a single community there are so many different types of training and antecedent experiences that there are vast differences of appreciation. This is well illustrated in any visit to an art gallery. Our social knowledge is based not upon identity of experiences, but on the combinations of similarities and differences in experience.

All of this leads to a radical change in our popular and uncritical understanding of the relationship which exists between knowledge and faith. The ordinary view is that knowledge comes first and that faith comes afterward. We are supposed to know all that can be known and then to press on into the unknown with the eye of faith. The truth, however, lies in the precise opposite of all this. *Faith precedes knowledge* and makes knowledge possible. Apart from faith, defined as "conviction apart from or in excess of proof," we are shut up within the confines of our own minds, separated from any possible knowledge of the world or of other minds with whom we can share our knowledge. Knowledge is produced when the original *sensa* are interpreted and organized by epistemological faith. Upon such faith rest not only the lofty creeds of ethics and religion, but also the maxims of daily life.[9]

The fact that the supreme act of instinctive faith, by which we break out of the prison of our subjective selves, is quite unshaken by any argumentations does not mean that it is a faith wholly independent of reasonable thought. We must, indeed, begin with the faith, since the alternative is to fail to begin at all, but all subsequent developments can be watched to see whether experience based on such primitive faith organizes itself into a coherent whole. In the end all reasoning is circular, in that we may ultimately justify that with which we begin. Circular reasoning is not fallacious, providing the circle is sufficiently large.

[9] Lord Balfour argued this point so well that the argument needs no repetition. See particularly *The Foundations of Belief.*

C. LEVELS OF KNOWLEDGE

We begin to see the necessity of a varied approach to knowledge when we list the kinds of objects which man claims to know.

The first kind of knowledge is knowledge of bodies. Different as these are from our minds, which do the apprehending, we nevertheless know something about them. Probably the first object of the child's knowledge is his mother's body, as he seeks and obtains nourishment. Bodies, of whatever kind, are marked by extension and by weight. They are objects which are susceptible to measurement. Some are so small that their existence is only inferred, but this, assuming their existence, does not change their essential character. The primary way in which bodies are known is by our mental reaction to the sense impressions which bodies make upon our sense organs. How that which has mass and length can give rise to a thought which has neither length nor mass we do not know, but the epistemological event is one which occurs constantly.

The second kind of knowledge is the knowledge of other minds. This knowledge is not as mysterious as is knowledge of bodies, because to know another mind is to have communication with something akin to the knower. A mind is something which has the capacity to *know*. Whenever we discover a being in which there is not only reaction to the environment, but also conscious apprehension of some part of the environment, we are dealing with a mind. Thus, we find knowledge among various animals, even though the knowledge demonstrated is severely limited. The higher animals may know almost nothing of the past or of the world at a distance, but they undoubtedly have adequate knowledge of some of their surroundings and of some immediate events. Though we spend some time in knowing bodies, we spend far more time in knowing other minds, especially other human minds. On the whole, we know minds far better than we know bodies. Millions who have never seen the body of Winston Churchill are reasonably well acquainted with his mind, as a result of his actions and his published thoughts. We can understand a great deal about a number of minds even though we have no idea about the appearance of the corresponding bodies. For instance, we know much of the mind of Christ through the Gospels, but we have no knowledge at all of what the appearance of his body was. The knowledge of a mind, when it is relatively accurate, is the result of a combination of factors, communication arising in a variety of ways. Sometimes it is through art, sometimes through written or spoken words, sometimes through facial expression. So far as finite minds are concerned, we seem to depend upon physical media for the interpretation of the nature of the object studied, even though the object is not itself physical or metrical.

The third object of knowledge is one's own mind. Here knowledge is often accurate and voluminous though it is impossible to have an outside check on accuracy. In this kind of knowledge, independence of the physical is achieved. Thus, we find a series of steps in the direction of independence. In knowledge of bodies the object is physical, in knowledge of other minds the knowledge is mediated by physical acts, but in knowledge of self, where the same being is both knower and known, the knowledge is immediate. Knowledge of one's own thoughts proves the possibility of knowledge apart from the senses. By what sensory experience am I aware of my experience of repentance which I felt so keenly ten minutes ago? Certainly not by hearing, by seeing, by touch, or by any other sense impression at all.[10] That knowledge of one's own thoughts, including those of the immediate past, is real knowledge there is no doubt. This is bound to pose a serious problem for those who claim dogmatically that the only possible knowledge is sensory in origin.

A fourth kind of knowledge is knowledge of values and universals. When we are concerned with what is right or with the beauty of a scene we are dealing with something radically different from either minds or bodies, but we are undoubtedly dealing with *something*. Though the experience of beauty is subjectively conditioned, in that it is only the prepared or the willing who are able to see what is there to be seen, the beauty exists objectively. Both truth and beauty are alike in that they are what is known when the mind discovers, outside itself, that which is akin to itself. Neither truth nor beauty can ever be found by casual sensation, though

[10] For an elaboration of this important point see Alfred North Whitehead, *Adventure of Ideas*, New York, Macmillan, 1933, pp. 233 ff. Whitehead believed this to be a revealing insight.

sensation may be the medium, as it is in knowing other minds. While the physical sensation remains essentially the same as we grow in the appreciation of value, the apprehension does not remain the same.

Value, as an object of knowledge, is not subject to measurement as bodies are, but this is no adequate reason to doubt its objective reality. Why should anyone ever suppose that reality is limited to the measurable? The measurable may be only a tiny fraction of the real world. There are more objects of knowledge which cannot be measured than there are which *can* be measured.

A fifth possible object of knowledge is God. Here we are dealing with mind, but not finite mind. We are not dealing with a body, in the sense of that which has extension, but we are dealing with Mind capable of creating bodies and, to some extent, revealed in those same bodies. The knowledge of God, if it is possible, may be expected to come, not by the mediation of sound or gesture, but by direct contact of consciousness with consciousness. If it occurs it may be as direct as the knowledge of the self, though it is knowledge of Another. It has the same universality as the knowledge of values, but it involves consciousness of a concrete reality rather than an abstract one. Thus, the knowledge of God, if it occurs, is different from each of the other four kinds of knowledge. It is a kind of knowledge to which millions have laid claim. They could be wrong in their claim, but any philosophy is frivolous which does not examine the claim with both open-mindedness and critical vigor. All kinds of knowledge are surprising, and the alleged knowledge of God is no more surprising than any other.

D. Epistemological Humility

It is only when we understand clearly that there are many levels of knowledge that we are emancipated from the notion that there is only one pathway to knowledge. The world of reality is so vast and so complex, and our opportunities to make mistakes are so numerous, that we need to employ a rich variety of means of knowledge. It is clear to all of us, when we think about the matter, that the world is far bigger than we know. The world is bigger physically, but it is also vastly richer in content than we have ever imagined. I do not know that there are any angels, because I have never heard of any convincing evidence on the subject and certainly I have had no direct experience of them, but I should be foolish, indeed, to assert confidently, at this point, that *there are no angels.* There may be creatures of many kinds which I have not even imagined.

This lesson of necessary humility was presented with persuasive simplicity by Charles Kingsley in the well-known passage about the existence of water babies.

> A water-baby? You never heard of a water-baby. Perhaps not. That is the very reason why this story was written. There are a great many things in the world which you have never heard of; and a great many more which nobody ever heard of; and a great many things, too, which nobody will ever hear of, at least until the coming of the Cocqcigrues, when man shall be the measure of all things.
>
> But there are no such things as water-babies. How do you know that? Have you been there to see? And if you had been there to see, and had seen none, that would not prove that there were none. . . . And no one has a right to say that no water-babies exist, till they have seen no water-babies existing; which is quite a different thing, mind, from not seeing water-babies; and a thing which nobody ever did, or perhaps ever will do.

One of the major and potentially beneficent forms of epistemological humility is agnosticism. Agnosticism is often in bad repute because it is identified, in some minds, with the position of those who affirm the impossibility of knowledge, a patently self-contradictory position. To establish complete skepticism a man would have to be omniscient, for we cannot know that nothing can be known unless we already know everything.

The modest and, therefore, defensibe agnosticism is that of the person who admits that he does not know, and is consequently open to learning. No truly devout person can raise any objection to this position. Indeed, the agnostic mood, so defined, is far more fruitful than is the mood of rigid dogmatism, either positive or negative. If an agnostic is one who, in the words of Thomas Huxley, is genuinely willing to sit down before the fact "as a little child," there is a sense in which all of us ought to be agnostics. It is even possible, when this line is followed faithfully, to develop what may be truly called a "reverent agnosticism."

What is very strange is that many who are devoted to the empirical approach arbitrarily limit veridical experience to certain specified objects of knowledge, such as those which are measurable. When we ask why this arbitrary limit should be set we get no intelligible answer. If knowledge comes ultimately from experience, why should we not, with genuine humility, consider *any* type of experience which men report, examining each upon its merits instead of making up our minds in advance?

Because the lesson of humility, in the face of the vastness, complexity and ultimate mystery of the universe, is so much a part of scientific experience, it is not surprising that many practicing scientists are today among the most devout of modern men. Those who know vividly how wrong we have been in the past, when we have dogmatized about what man can and cannot know, have good reason to be careful about setting arbitrary limits. The only justifiable mood is that in which we wait and see and examine, willing to follow the evidence even when it upsets our cherished beliefs.

5
The Nature of Evidence

The truth of our religion, like the truth of common matters, is to be judged by all the evidence taken together. JOSEPH BUTLER

When we think of truth as having an objective status and ourselves as creatures who can approach it by intellectual effort, the search for genuine knowledge takes on an imperious quality. We cannot be true to our vocation as human beings if we believe lightly or if we reject lightly any significant conviction. There is an "ethics of belief" as well as a logic of belief. Since some opinions are undoubtedly nearer to the truth than are other opinions, it is our task to try to discover concrete ways in which opinions can be improved. The improvement of opinion comes by the accumulation and analysis of *evidence*. But before we can weigh evidence profitably we need to know what evidence is. We must learn how to distinguish good evidence from bad evidence and to draw valid conclusions from the evidence that is available. Engagement in this enterprise is one mark of a civilized person.

A. The Limits of Evidence

Few words in the language are used more loosely than the word "proof." We speak of many propositions as being proved, when some analysis of the situation shows that there is abundant room for doubt. Daily we discuss hundreds of supposed "facts," but their factual character rests, for the most part, on flimsy evidence. Often there is a great contrast between our certainty and our ability to defend that certainty. This is clearly illustrated in Dr. Samuel Johnson's celebrated effort to show how hard it was to prove that the English forces had really taken Canada from the French.

I deny that Canada is taken, and I can support my denial by pretty good arguments. The French are a much more numerous people than we; and it is not likely that they would allow us to take it. "But the ministry have assured us, in all the formality of the Gazette, that it is taken."—Very true. But the ministry have put us to an enormous expense by the war in America, and it is their interest to persuade us that we have got something for our money.—"But the fact is confirmed by thousands of men who were at the taking of it." Ay, but these men have still more interest in deceiving us. They don't want that you should think the French have beat them, but that they have beat the French. Now suppose you should go over and find that it really is taken, that would only satisfy yourself; for when you come home, we will not believe you. We will say, you have been bribed.—Yet, Sir, notwithstanding all these plausible objections, we have no doubt that Canada is really ours. Such is the weight of common testimony. How much stronger are the evidences of the Christian religion.[1]

To lampoon our most respected forms of evidence is a beneficent undertaking, inasmuch as we tend to take our "proof" uncritically. The method of fair sampling, though we use it constantly, has led to erroneous conclusions, as it did in the American presidential election of 1948. Failure arises because there is such a wide disparity between the limited observations and the wide scope of the conclusions.

Most of the objects of which we speak familiarly and often have never come within the range of our sensory perception. For example, there is hardly anyone who has seen his own brain, yet each speaks familiarly of this organ and does not doubt its existence. All of our knowledge of historical events and most of our knowledge of contemporary events is at second or third hand. Not many persons have seen their grandparents' grandparents. We usually consider that the best evidence is documentary evidence, but it is not hard to imagine a literary hoax, and more than one has, in fact, been perpetrated. A really successful forgery would not, of course, be detected, and some such there have doubtless been.

Sometimes our belief that propositions are proved rests on little more than a pathetic faith in the printed word.[2] Even direct experience is by no means sufficient to dispel all reasonable doubt, since

[1] *The Life of Samuel Johnson,* by James Boswell, New York, Modern Library, pp. 259-260.
[2] An extreme instance of the unreliability of the printed word occurred in my own experience when I read, in a reputable daily newspaper, of my own death.

our sensory organs frequently lead us into error. Not only are illusions the stock in trade of the conjurer; they also appear in ordinary life. Many court trials have involved contradictory evidence from persons of good faith, reporting on the basis of immediate experience. The difficulty of trustworthy testimony from direct experience can be shown also in psychological experiments. There are many situations in which people "see" what is not there to be seen.

The only proof which is logically coercive is that which depends on strict deduction, as in a mathematical system. We say that it is demonstrably true that, if "a" is the ancestor of "b" and "b" is the ancestor of "c," then "a" is the ancestor of "c." This, indeed, gives certainty, but the certainty is limited to the enclosed system. According to this method, we start with propositions which are supposed to be already assured or fully warranted and work out, with rigorous care, what follows necessarily from these same propositions. This was, in the majority of cases, the primary method of the scholastic philosophers of the Middle Ages and is the major method today, wherever scholasticism has been revived. Whatever else we may think of this we are bound, in honesty, to say that the method necessitates great mental sharpness and has often been followed with astonishing thoroughness. Skill is developed in the ability to detect minute fallacies and to keep in mind, in considering every detail, the comprehensive system of which it is a part.

The weakness of the system is twofold. First, it necessarily depends upon primary premises which, in the nature of the case, cannot be proved by this method. The system is certainly not convincing to anyone who does not accept the starting point. Thus, it is sometimes said, with a measure of justice, that, as induction has no right to its conclusions, deduction has no right to its premises. In any case, there is no initial agreement on which primitive propositions are self-evident.

The second major weakness of this scholastic system is that it leaves no place open for new factual evidence. Its logical rigidity, similar to that of a building which cannot survive an earthquake because it is too stiff, is its downfall. The introduction into a rigid system of any considerable amount of new evidence, such as that provided by the advance of modern science, is bound to break the system to pieces. Any system to be adequate to our need must be an open-ended system, into which new facts are welcomed and one which new facts or new insights cannot destroy.

B. Scientific Method

There is no doubt that the introduction of scientific method into current mentality, about four hundred years ago, represented a great gain in human history. The most obvious feature of this method is the way in which it encourages attention to objective fact. The characteristic haunts of the scientist are the observatory, the museum and the laboratory, as well as the ordinary world of things and men. Charles Darwin's account of *The Voyage of the Beagle* and William James's *Varieties of Religious Experience* are classic illustrations of this direct approach to evidence.

So successful has this method been that the populace has come to accept an erroneous and pathetic conception of the certainty which such a method can provide. Frequently we hear the naïve expression to the effect that all we need to do is to find the facts and pay no attention to theories. Such a position would only be reasonable on the assumption, which is surely false, that facts are easily ascertainable. Which of the alleged facts *are* really facts? In nearly all situations we cannot even begin to answer this question apart from some theories, which are needed to shed light on possible facts and to help us to determine what it is that we are observing. The immense value of Darwinian theory, not primarily in explanation but chiefly as an aid to discovery, is a case in point. Most of the brilliant history of modern science illustrates the valuable point that we cannot begin with facts and then construct theories upon them; it is only by means of much fruitful theorizing that we can apprehend, with any accuracy, what the facts are.

There is a familiar story of how Roentgen, in his discovery of X rays, came one day on a surprising set of events. Later someone asked him what he thought. His famous reply was, "I did not *think;* I investigated." This story has had the unfortunate effect of making it seem that mere laboratory work will suffice. What the famous man was indulging in was a joke, a semipun. And, like many jokes, it is not strictly true. *Of course, he thought.* No amount of investigation apart from rigorous and critical thinking would have been of any value whatever. Moreover, the investigation was profiting from the prodigious amount of thought which he and others had *already* put into the problem.

We lose some of our superstitious reverence for scientific method when we realize that its crucial step, verification, actually involves grave logical difficulties. The essence of verification is the testing of a hypothesis to see whether the effects which ought to appear if the hypothesis is true actually do appear. This conception of verification, which received its classic consideration in the thought of John Stuart Mill, is the heart of what is called the experimental method. Mill emphasized the procedure according to which we observe what happens in circumstances to which the hypothesis applies, deliberately instituting such circumstances if need be. Since this procedure seems to be so reasonable and so harmless, many are surprised when they are made to realize that all verification depends upon a long-recognized logical fallacy.

The fallacy inherent in the process of verification has been known for many years as "the affirmation of the consequent." The logical form is:

> a implies b
> b is true
> Therefore, a is true.

This might be illustrated as follows:

> If John was in the wreck he must have bruises.
> John has bruises on his body
> Therefore, John was in the wreck.

Stated thus baldly, the verification in regard to John's participation is obviously fallacious. The bruised man may have been in the wreck or he may not, for there are many ways of getting bruises. Before the evidence is really convincing one must show that there is no other way in which the bruises could have come in this particular instance, but that is a difficult and circuitous task. Professor Joseph, the celebrated Oxford logician, has pointed out that the fallacy here is the same as the failure to recognize the plurality of causes. Different causes may produce the same effect, and different

theories may have the same implications. "A theory whose consequences conflict with the facts cannot be true," concludes Professor
Joseph, "but so long as there may be more theories than one giving
the same consequences, the agreement of the facts with one of them
furnishes no ground for choosing between it and the others." [3]

When we try to argue back from the consequent to the antecedent
we are acting on the supposition that universal affirmative propositions can be converted simply, and it is common knowledge that
such conversion is not valid. Though all men ar mortal, it does
not follow that all mortals are men. In fact, they are not. Rain
implies wet ground, but wet ground does not imply rain. There
are other reasons for wet ground.

Since verification is based on a logical fallacy, how is it possible
for scientific method, which so stresses verification, to give the
help it clearly gives in the refinement of opinion in such a way
that it approximates the truth? The answer is that *we overcome
the fallacy in great measure by committing it in a refined fashion,
many times instead of once.* This is not a gratuitous paradox, but
a principle of profound importance. We find many and intricate
results which ought to appear if our hypothesis is true, and we
check them one by one. The logical form comes to be not merely

a implies b

with the subsequent verification of b, but rather

a implies b, b1, b2, b3, b4, b5, etc.

Then we check or verify as many of these complicated resultants
as we can, to see whether they are, in fact, found. If all are found,
the process is still the affirmation of the consequent, but by affirming
so many we have a situation in which only a miracle of coincidence
would be the alternative to the validity of our induction. Our
conclusion is based ultimately upon the primitive assumption that
this is the kind of world in which the miracle of coincidence does
not normally occur.

No part of what is called science has caught the public imagination more than has experimentation. There is good reason for this,

---

[3] H. W. B. Joseph, *An Introduction to Logic,* Oxford University Press, 1916,
p. 523.

inasmuch as the major sciences, with the exception of astronomy, use the method with manifest success. That experimentation has been valuable and productive in a number of fields is beyond reasonable doubt. We can be grateful, for example, for what has been discovered experimentally in the production of hybrid seed corn. By trying many combinations an extremely fruitful result has emerged, and one that is bound to have far-reaching effects in the effort to save mankind from the perils of hunger. We are grateful for similar experimentation in the production of new textiles, new building materials and new antibiotics, to name only a few products of the experimental method of extending the borders of knowledge.

Valuable and productive as such experimentation is, it is important to realize that the method has severe limitations. Though it is entirely suitable in working with mere matter or with animal life, it is radically unsuitable in working with persons. It is now universally recognized that human vivisection is indefensible, even when it is performed with the alleged aim of learning more about human diseases. The world-wide revulsion against the experimentation conducted by German doctors on the helpless occupants of Nazi concentration camps represents a healthy reaction. If the experimental method were universally valid, there would be no reason not to *induce* cancer as well as to overcome it. There would be no objection to that kind of brainwashing, which is psychiatry in reverse, in which the sanity of a person is deliberately destroyed. We know how to do these things, because we already do them in our work with animals. If experimentation were universally valid, we could engage deliberately in moral experiments, such as planned infidelity or the breakup of homes. We know something important about human life when we know how nearly universal the rejection of experimentation really is, but we know something still more important when we recognize what the basic reasons for this rejection are.

There is a good philosophical reason for the limitation on the experimental method which is so widely recognized. This is the apprehension of a wide difference in character between two parts of the real world. In one part, that of material things, vegetables and lower animals, experiment is possible and defensible because the class characteristics supersede the individual characteristics in importance. In dealing with corn we are right to be more concerned with the universal than with the individual, because individuality scarcely exists. One grain of seed corn is so much like another that it is not important *which* one is made the subject of the experiment. Indeed, it is far more truly an object than a subject. If one grain is destroyed, nobody cares, because any one will do. The same situation obtains in experiments on animals, though it obtains less fully and, therefore, demands certain moral safeguards. Vivisection on animals, such as guinea pigs, can be defended morally, because of the profit to higher forms of life, but the experimenters are under the moral necessity of seeing to it that needless pain is avoided.[4]

When we come to human life we cross a highly significant line in creation, because once that line is crossed individuality begins to play a dominant role. Men do have characteristics in common, but in our search for the universal we dare never neglect the individual and the particular. Each one is one; each one is precious; and, therefore, none can be wantonly sacrificed.[5]

Fortunately, scientific method is not limited to the method of experimentation or to any laboratory technique. Instead, it is a way of facing the relevant evidence, whatever that may be. This is why the spirit of science can be applied to religious inquiry. It is not a perfect method, and it can never give us the kind of certainty which we find within a mathematical system, but we are satisfied with what we have.

Those who use scientific method most do not ordinarily have for it the superstitious reverence felt by so much of the public but, rather, recognize that it is the best way we have, though admittedly far from perfect. The classic statement on this subject

[4] Dr. Albert Schweitzer, whose philosophy is based on "reverence for life," concurs in this conclusion.

[5] That the observation made above is so widely recognized in the world, the revulsion being great when the rule is transgressed, is one evidence of how deep in the human mind is the fundamental presupposition about man which rests ultimately on religious conviction. It is because man is seen as precious in a religious context that the true nature of his individuality is appreciated. Many uphold a conception of the dignity of man which makes experimentation unthinkable without being aware of what the roots of their conviction are.

is from one of the greatest men in the entire history of science, Sir Isaac Newton:

And although the arguing from experiments and observations by induction be no demonstration of general conclusions yet it is the best way of arguing which the nature of things admits of, and may be looked upon as so much the stronger, by how much the induction is more general.

C. The Reasonableness of Authority

Every proposition is really a judgment. When a man says "King Charles the First was executed" he means "I *believe* King Charles the First was executed." Our dependence appears to be on facts, but it is really a dependence on men. Most *cognoscenda*, "things to be known if possible," are outside our bodies. Most of what we believe about the external world is received at second hand and rests on the prior belief that some men are more trustworthy reporters than others. We believe that the first white man to reach the North Pole was Admiral Peary rather than Dr. Cook, but our chief reasons for this belief depend upon information about the character of these two men.

The area of immediate experience open to any individual is extremely slight—a mere slit in the world's expanse. If, then, we say that we shall believe only what we know directly at first hand we reduce our belief in a fantastic manner. All history would be thereby eliminated, and we should be confined to the *specious present*. A life so ordered would be intellectually poverty-stricken, if, indeed, it were possible at all. Intellectual self-sufficiency, like economic self-sufficiency, is only possible at a level of existence too low to be attractive.

The conclusion to be reached, in view of our individual mental poverty, is that we cannot avoid reliance upon some sort of authority. Because sense experience is so open to error, and because our reflections on our experience may be fragmentary or uncritical, we need to listen to those qualified to know. Characteristically, our reliance is upon the authority of the expert, who may be defined as the man whom there is reason to trust. In all matters in which judgments of great difficulty are demanded it is clearly more reasonable to trust the insight of a few persons than to submit the decision to the many.

In all difficult matters we need something in the nature of a supreme court of learning, and this is what we have in a rough manner. The periodic meetings of the learned societies and of the professional societies point in this direction. The authoritative value of the French Academy and of the Royal Society in Great Britain has been tremendous. Moreover, every university is authoritative in so far as it is a community of learned men, helping and criticizing one another.

Perhaps the experts never fully agree, but they check each other's excesses, corroborate each other's discoveries, and help the laymen to know something about the facts by agreement on some points. The best reason for believing the atomic theory is not that most people have tested it, which they have not, but that the relatively few who have studied it carefully are in substantial agreement.

Herein lies the great importance of those arrangements which help us to know who the few reliable persons are. The Nobel prizes and various lesser prizes are of value in this regard. Since one who gets such a prize has been able to win the high regard of various kinds of fellow experts, we can rest assured concerning his competence. Honorary degrees, when they are not debased by commercial motives on the part of the donor, also help to build up the *complex system of reasonable trust*. The honorary degree is, in fact, the chief method of showing approval that democratic America has developed. And the value of the degree depends upon the esteem in which the granting institution is held. With such intricacy is the authoritative pattern woven.

Not only are we dependent upon authority in affairs of national importance, and in abstruse intellectual matters, but almost equally so in the affairs of everyday life. We submit ourselves and our loved ones to the authority of the physician and, when his opinion differs from ours on some crucial point, we recognize that he is more likely to be correct than we are. Of course, he may not be correct, but the evidence is weighted in his direction. Since we rely on genius in other fields, why should we not do so in religion? "It is impossible to see," writes von Hügel, "why Plato, Aristotle, Leibnitz and Kant, and why again Phidias and Michelangelo, Raphael and Rembrandt, Bach and Beethoven, Homer and Shakespeare, are to be held in deepest gratitude, as revealers respectively of various kinds of reality and truth if Amos and Isaiah, Paul, Augustine and Aquinas, Francis of Assisi and Joan of Arc are to be treated as pure illusionists, in precisely what constitutes their specific greatness." [6]

There are two popular errors concerning authority which such considerations should serve to correct. The first is the notion that authority is chiefly to be found in religion. Authority has a place in religion, not because religion is different from other human pursuits, but because it is like them. The more we deal with intangibles of any kind, that is to say, with really important matters, the more we are forced to rely on authority to a great degree, for there is no simple rule of thumb to which we can appeal. There is a strong tendency to suppose that there is no more reason to listen to one man than to another in spiritual matters, because the subjects considered are notoriously incapable of proof. The proper conclusion to be drawn, however, is the precise opposite of this. It is *because* the subjects are incapable of proof that we need to avail ourselves of superior wisdom wherever we can find it.

The fact that sensitive religious men in all faiths have set great store by religious literary monuments is not hard to understand. We turn to the Hebrew prophets because they were men of undoubted genius in the spiritual life, just as we turn to Bach or Mozart, undoubted geniuses in musical production. We *may* consider our own religious opinions to be better than the opinions of the major prophets, and we *may* consider our own musical opinions to be better than those of the classical composers, but the chance that we are correct in this kind of judgment is not great.

Devout men have turned to the classical expressions of religious experience with reverence and hope, precisely because they have had a salutary humility. We know nothing of an *infallible authority* just as we know nothing of *absolute certainty*, for these seem to be denied to mortals, but we do know that there are some whom it is sensible to trust above ourselves. Any man who has begun to understand the weakness of individualism knows that he needs something to buttress his feeble little life. The long experience of the church is more likely to lead to correct answers than is the

[6] Baron Friedrich von Hügel, *Essays and Addresses on the Philosophy of Religion*, New York, Dutton, 1924, p. 38.

experience of the lone individual. Sometimes the rebel against authority is a prophet, but far more often he is merely a fool. We are not justified in converting the proposition "All prophets have been misunderstood" into "All who have been misunderstood have been prophets."

The dependence upon authority is not confined to religion and is not even found chiefly in religion, but appears wherever men are humble about their own opinions, aware of the complexity of life, and eager to know about difficult matters. The interest which thoughtful men take in literary and artistic criticism is further evidence that this is the case. We do not bow down slavishly to the critics, but we pay attention to the critics; in other words, we regard them as authorities.

The second popular error about authority which calls for correction is the notion that authority and reason are somehow rival ways of coming to know the truth. Even some reputable books on philosophy, like Montague's *Ways of Knowing,* encourage this idea by the arrangement of their chapters. The reader gets the notion that reason is one way of knowing the truth, whereas authority is another. But the analysis of the question, as we have considered it, has already shown that dependence upon authority is itself the path of reason.

When we rely on authority we are, in most cases, doing the most reasonable thing we can do. It is far more reasonable for me to rely on the opinion of the scholars at Oak Ridge than it is to rely on my own unaided and highly amateurish speculations about nuclear studies. The point is that when we rely on authority we are not, *for that reason,* guilty of credulity, because *there is a reason for our reliance.* We trust the men and institutions presenting the most reason for being trusted. We must use reason to determine which authority to follow, just as we use reason to determine which faith to adopt.

D. THE AUTHORITY OF DISCIPLINED INSIGHT

It takes special ability to *observe* intelligently. Any layman who has taken a cross-country walk with a skilled geologist knows how inadequate the layman's observation is, for there are many things obvious to the trained man which the layman actually does not "see." This is even more marked in looking through a microscope or telescope. The instrument may be properly in focus and the conditions of illumination may be right, but often the amateur sees only a blur.

The construction of a fruitful hypothesis depends on human genius to an unusual degree. Hypotheses do not make themselves. They often seem commonplace to later observers, but the original insight is far from commonplace. The invention of a hypothesis which, if sustained, may bring order into an otherwise confused mass of data, is fundamentally similar to the work of a poet or a prophet.[7] We have an abundant autobiographical literature, showing how the happy flash comes in an unpredictable manner and at an unpredictable time, but usually after the problem to be solved has been wrestled with long and patiently, and sometimes temporarily put aside.

The task of seeing what is implied in a hypothesis, and thus to prepare the way for verification, is a matter of intellectual labor which depends for its success, not merely on the nature of external events, but on the quality of the person who performs the labor. Even verification is a matter of individual ability. What is chiefly needed in the physical sciences is persons who can construct novel and "crucial" experiments in order to test the results to see whether what is implied really occurs. But even if it does occur, the original contention is not proved, since there might be more theories than one leading to the same consequences. If we find more and more "predicted consequences" which actually occur we decide that the theory is substantiated, but it is by no means *proved*. When does this point of practical substantiation occur? For this we have no rule, but must depend upon the good sense of men. Professor Joseph has stated this point with admirable clarity as follows:

In such matters we must consider what is called the weight of the evidence for a theory that is not rigorously proved. But no one has shown how weight of evidence can be mechanically estimated; the wisest men, and best acquainted with the matter in hand, are oftenest right.[8]

[7] Poincaré has been particularly convincing on this point. Cf. *Science and Method*, Dover Publications, 1952.

[8] H. W. B. Joseph, *op. cit.*, pp. 523, 524.

As we reach the higher levels of science we find that our dependence on personal trustworthiness becomes more important than in the elementary branches, for the simple reason that the number who can follow their alleged results critically is small. Since dependence on men is so great and so pervasive of our experience, we need to learn all that we can about what it is that makes men trustworthy guides to their fellows.

In the end there is no appeal beyond the actual apprehensions of men. That is our supreme court. It was the great merit of the Cartesian revolution in philosophy that it showed the defects and inapplicability of the scholastic logic and encouraged men to depend on the "natural light" of the mind. But this merit need not make us rest satisfied with the conclusion that one intuition is as good as another. Many things are self-evident to the master which are not self-evident to the pupil. We cannot, in the end, go beyond the intuitions of men, whether in science, ethics or religion, but these intuitions are reliable only when they are the apprehensions of disciplined minds.

This suggests that the function of logic, any kind of logic, is not so much to guide our mental operations *after we have "observed,"* but rather to sharpen our minds in advance so that we shall see what is there to be seen. According to this conception, what we need is a discipline calculated to increase our sensitivity, to sharpen our awareness, to make us recognize the truth when we see it. This makes the biographies and autobiographies of persons of recognized insight extremely important reading. How did men like Pascal and Newton and Darwin achieve the ability to see what others could not see, while looking at the same general scenes? If we could know that, we should be well on our way.

One thing is clear, and that is that the insight comes at the end of a process of experience in a certain field, not at the beginning. When we recognize this we are returning to the doctrine taught by Aristotle at the end of his *Posterior Analytics,* a doctrine which seems to be the final wisdom of his logical inquiries. The *Prior Analytics* give rules for inference from established knowledge, but the *Posterior Analytics* do something better. They deal with the attainment of real and valid knowledge. The last pages not only show the importance of intuition, but show how intuition comes.

So out of sense-perception comes to be what we call memory, and out of frequently repeated memories of the same things develops experience; for a number of memories constitute a single experience. From experience again . . . originate the skill of the craftsman and the knowledge of the man of science, skill in the sphere of coming to be and science in the sphere of being.[9]

Not only is judgment made dependable by anterior discipline; it must be the *appropriate* discipline. The training by experience upon which we rightly depend must be relevant to the problem at hand before it has value. Thus, a good judge of English poetry may not be any judge at all when a nice problem in the age of rock formations is presented. It is a common experience in public life for men who have achieved eminence in one field to begin to dogmatize about some wholly alien field, and thereby make themselves ridiculous. Men in biology are frequently mere tyros in ethics, but quite unaware that this is the case. Natural scientists are more likely to expect attention outside their own fields than are scholars in the humanities, because those outside natural science are well aware that it is a specialized field, made so by the intricacy of the apparatus, if for no other reason.

This point needs to be stressed because it is often overlooked in the field of religious experience. A distinguished physiologist asserts that he does not believe in God; that throughout his life he has never had any sense of the presence of God, and many are impressed by this. Here was a highly intelligent person with a finely trained mind, and the negative evidence provided by his testimony must be given considerable weight. But wait a moment! Are we so sure? Before we give this testimony *any weight at all* we need to know much more. Did the scholar in question submit himself to the kind of situation in which he could expect to be aware of God's presence, if God really is? This scholar would not have expected an opinion concerning physiology to be worthy of attention unless the person announcing the opinion had undertaken a great deal of training in that field. All great things are hard, and there seems no reason to suppose that it would be easier to know God than to know the laws and elements of His creation. Of course, the hypothetical scholar in question may have been a man who engaged

[9] *Analytica Posteriora, 110a.*

in the discipline of his devotional life as assiduously as he engaged in the sharpening of his judgment as a physiologist, for the two are compatible; and, if he did, his words demand respect, but the point is that, if he did not, his opinion is *wholly lacking in value.*

Einstein was a great man in science and a very great man in mathematics, but when he got out of his field of competence, which he often did, the result was pathetic. In an article written expressly for the *New York Times* magazine he said, "It is, therefore, easy to see why the churches have always fought science and persecuted its devotees." The statement is thoroughly false. Indeed, modern science was nourished by the church and by the institutions founded by the church. This includes Princeton University, where Einstein was living when he wrote the article. What this shows is that a man need not be trusted in one field merely because of his competence in another.[10]

The authority we can trust best is that of disciplined insight with experience of an appropriate kind. If we can find, in any field, men who fulfill these conditions, and if there is substantial agreement in their independent judgments, we have as good an indication of what is genuine evidence as men are likely to find in this world.

E. CUMULATIVE EVIDENCE

Since no single line of evidence is ever adequate, our security lies in the phenomenon of convergence. Though every single piece of relevant evidence must be respected, the chance of avoiding error is vastly increased if each item is supported by others. The difference between one line of evidence and two or three pointing in the same direction is tremendous. This is the significance of Butler's famous aphorism, "For probable proofs, by being added, not only *increase* the evidence but *multiply* it." [11]

Consider, for example, a particular crime in which a child is stolen for ransom. Later a man is accused of the crime and stands trial. Usually there is not one *single* line of evidence which is sufficient to constitute proof, even in the vague way in which we use

[10] Cf. *Ideas and Opinions by Albert Einstein,* New York, Crown, 1954, p. 39.
[11] Joseph Butler, *The Analogy of Religion,* Pt. II, chap. 7.

this concept in ordinary speech. The child's nurse may identify the man, but, as was noted above, persons under severe emotional strain are not reliable in regard to their sensory impressions. The man may be caught with the child in his possession, but this is not sufficient, since he may, wittingly or unwittingly, be shielding the kidnaper. Most men, even men of poor reputation, would pick up a lone child found by the roadside. The man may confess that he has committed the crime, but that alone is not enough, since men have confessed crimes which they have not committed, and this they have done for a variety of reasons.

Each *single* bit of evidence is, as we have seen, inconclusive. We cannot *prove* that no two men have the same fingerprints. What is important is to find converging lines of evidence and to find so many that the result is not in practical doubt, even if theoretical doubt is not entirely dispelled. The idea that absolute proof is not part of man's finite lot is a sobering conclusion at which the most thoughtful of men long ago arrived, but it is not particularly disturbing so long as we can find ways of increasing probability. To know that probability is the guide of life is to know something very important, for then, instead of pining over our failure to have complete proof, we are encouraged to go forward in our search for practical tests. The fact that we do not have complete certainty does not involve the denial of the common-sense observation that some things are more certain than others. Evidence does not have to be perfect or complete in order to be good evidence, and some forms of evidence are better than others.

What we must remember is that this difficulty of simple proof, with the attendant necessity of cumulative evidence, applies to everything we know in the realm of matters of fact. It applies not only to evidence for the existence of God, but also to evidence for the existence of atoms and to evidence for the existence of historical characters. This fact needs to be stressed, because it is so often overlooked. One of the most common of popular errors appears at precisely this juncture when we face religious knowledge. There are many who lightly reject belief in God because, they say, the existence of God cannot be "proved," by which they mean that there is no single, obvious, incontrovertible line of evidence for God's existence. The appropriate retort is to ask the critic what

matter of fact there is in the world for which there is some *single,
obvious* and *incontrovertible* line of evidence. So far none is forthcoming. We are saying nothing derogatory about religious knowledge when we say it is a matter of high probability, for this is true
of all matters of fact. There is no valid excuse for the inconsistency
which rejects belief in one field because absolute certainty is lacking,
and is credulous in other fields where it is equally lacking.

The value of our conclusion to the effect that cumulative evidence
is the best evidence applies, with especial relevance, to the primary
question of most living religions, that of whether God is real or
illusory. The sophisticated believer knows very well that he *could*
be wrong, because there is no incontrovertible evidence, but the
path of wisdom is to watch for converging lines. A cable is far
stronger than a single wire. This conception of the nature of evidence is the chief reason for the arrangement of this book.

Part II
THEISTIC REALISM

6

The Theistic Hypothesis

In addition to all finite selves there is a being called God, numerically distinct from them, an independent centre of consciousness, with his own unique life and purposes, with a differential activity of his own.

CHARLES A. BENNETT

God, when carefully defined, either is or is not. Though belief in God appears in many religions, and though Judaism, Islam and Christianity present a common monotheistic front, there are religions, such as classic Buddhism, which involve no such belief. This is all the more reason why the theistic question requires careful treatment; it cannot be assumed. It is the crucial question which the philosopher of religion must face. Most other questions depend upon it and cannot be answered until it is answered.

A. THE CONCEPT OF OBJECTIVE REFERENCE

The belief we are about to examine is the belief that God *is*. The word "is," used in this manner, does not express class inclusion or class membership; it does not refer to equality as it does when it is employed in mathematics; and it does not require a predicate adjective to complete the meaning. To say that God "is" means to give assent to the proposition that the idea of God is not merely an idea in the minds of men, but actually refers to what is objectively the case—something which *was* before we came to be aware of it and which now is, independent of our awareness or lack of awareness. What is exciting is not the subjective entertainment of the idea, but the evidence that the idea has *objective reference*.

The plain man may well be justified if he experiences confusion as a result of some current theological tendencies in regard to existence, especially when the statement "God exists" is rejected as inappropriate. Perhaps the best illustration of such rejection is Tillich's statement in the following words, "God does not exist. He is being-itself beyond essence and existence. Therefore, to argue that God exists, is to deny him." [1] We can see what Professor Tillich means, but it tends to obscure the major issue, which is that between what is and what is not.

The ordinary believer, when he uses the phrase "God exists," is not setting up a contrast between what is in time and what is in eternity. He is, instead, setting up a contrast between what is real and what is illusory. The important question for all who have a deep sense of religious concern is whether the Object of our ultimate concern is nothing but the product of our own hopes and wishes or is something more. Uncle Sam and John Bull are reasonably clear conceptions, but they are not realities. What we want to face is the question whether God is in the same category. The sobering fact is that millions in the modern world actually believe that this is the case. Anything which confuses or obscures this crucial issue is unprofitable and ought to be avoided.

Among propositions that are true, whether we are aware of their truth or not, there is an important difference between those which are "true but trivial" and those which are "true and important." Many of the trivial truths are essentially tautologies which no one doubts and about which no one greatly cares. Important truths are, for the most part, much more difficult to ascertain and far more exciting. Both kinds of propositions may be illustrated among those presented for religious belief. It is one of the merits of Professor Montague's remarkable little volume of Terry Lectures that he presented this difference with uncommon clarity.

Religion as we shall use the term is not a traffic with demons and the dark forces pertaining to them. The belief in such objects is almost certainly false and quite certainly without moral significance. Nor is religion merely a belief in an ultimate reality or in an ultimate ideal. These beliefs are worse than false; they are platitudes, truisms, that nobody will dispute. Religion as we shall conceive it is the acceptance neither of a primitive absurdity nor of a sophisticated truism, but of a momentous possibility— the possibility namely that what is highest in spirit is also deepest in

---

[1] Paul Tillich, *Systematic Theology,* vol. 1, p. 227. See also *The Courage to Be,* Yale University Press, 1952, pp. 172-176.

nature, that the ideal and the real are at least to some extent identified, not merely evanescently in our own lives but enduringly in the universe itself.[2]

Here we have three possibilities, the false, the true but trivial, the true and important. We are most concerned about the propositions which are important *if true*, and what we want to know is whether they are really true. Our only interest in our own ideas is that they should be in conformity with what is objectively the case.

In this connection we may remind ourselves of the distinction so ably made by David Hume between the two fundamental kinds of object of human reason or inquiry, *Relations of Ideas and Matters of Fact*.

Of the first kind are the sciences of Geometry, Algebra and Arithmetic; and in short, every affirmation which is either intuitively or demonstrably certain. *That the square of the hypotenuse is equal to the square of the two sides* is a proposition which expresses a relationship between these figures. *That three times five is equal to the half of thirty* expresses a relation between these numbers. Propositions of this kind are discoverable by the mere operation of thought, without dependence on what is anywhere existent in the universe. Though there never were a circle or triangle in nature, the truths demonstrated by Euclid would forever retain their certainty and evidence.

Matters of fact, which are the second objects of human reason, are not ascertained in the same manner; nor is our evidence of their truth, however great, of a like nature with the foregoing. The contrary of every matter of fact is still possible.[3]

The truth which we seek in the spiritual life is truth in regard to Hume's second class of objects. Actual religion is concerned wholly with *matters of fact*, just as actual science is. The nature of God is not the same as the nature of a tree, inasmuch as God is not known by the physical senses and the tree is, but the question of truth is the same in both cases. In both, the real question is the question of objective existence as a matter of fact. Theistic Realism is a name for the philosophical position which centers on this important point.

It is *because*, in considering the existence of God, we are dealing

[2] William P. Montague, *Belief Unbound*, Yale University Press, 1930, p. 6.
[3] David Hume, *An Enquiry Concerning Human Understanding*, Sec. II, Pt. I.

with the relation of idea to fact rather than the relation of idea to idea that we know we *could be wrong*. We have no right to absolute certainty in this or any other factual situation. The existence of God cannot be demonstrated beyond a shadow of doubt for the simple reason that religious belief refers to something claimed to be objectively real. When Kant pointed out the inability of the classic theistic proofs to give demonstrative evidence he was not doing fundamental harm to religious belief, but rather helping, as others had helped, to set men free from a fantastic ideal of absolute certainty. Kant was, in this regard, supporting the conclusion, at which Bishop Butler arrived earlier in the same century, to the effect that "probability is the very guide of life." Since it is the guide of all actual life, we must expect, both in religion and in ethics, the same conception of the truth and the same dependence upon presumptive evidence that we find in other matters.

B. The Possibility of Atheism

Atheism tends to be a term of disrepute in the Western world, but we ought to do all that we can to change this situation. The honest atheist is simply a person who has looked out upon the world and has come to believe either that there is no adequate evidence that God is or that there is good evidence that God is not. Very seldom does this make a man happy or popular. Indeed, the danger is sufficiently great that men tend to keep their unbelief discreetly to themselves. Many people are in serious doubt of God's real existence, and many more doubt any kind of personal immortality. Their serious conviction is that all consciousness and all personal identity end with the death of the body.

A man who has no practical belief in God may nevertheless be a good man. Sometimes it is the very goodness of a man which makes him an unbeliever; he is so superlatively honest, so eager not to accept anything without adequate evidence, so sensitive to the danger of believing what is comforting, merely *because* it is comforting, that he rejects the very conception which alone could make reasonable his intense effort to be honest. Such a man we can only honor, and trust that he will go on loyally following the evidence wherever it leads, alert to the implications of his own intense concern. It might eventually lead him to the sober conviction that his very concern for the truth cannot be explained if it is an alien development, appearing alone in a world completely insensitive to such experience, but that it makes sense if the love of the good lies at the heart of all things. He may learn the paradox that his brave unbelief, seen in its full implications, may be one of the chief grounds of the very belief which he rejects. In any case, the world is likely to profit more by the testimony of the honest unbeliever than by that of the wishful believer, who believes because his faith is comforting and has never been seriously tested.

The deepest faith is that men and women, in their fierce and faltering struggle to find the right way, are *not alone*. It is conceivable, of course, that the only point in the entire universe which has been marked by loyalty and courage and self-denial, for the sake of the right, is our little earth. It may be that there is no response to our prayers and none to hear them. It may be that all of the remainder of reality, beyond the surface of our planet in the past few thousand years, has been a scene which might be studied by physics, but not one in which ethics has any meaning. It may be that, when our solar system is such that the planet earth is no longer a scene of human habitation, the last concern for goodness will be gone from the universe and the world as a whole will go its way, with no consciousness anywhere of what has thereby been lost.

All this is conceivable, and if we were to learn, by some dependable means, that it is true we should try to go on living out our little day as best we might. We should still try to be honest and to keep promises and to be ashamed when we failed, even if such interests were known to be confined to the race of men and even if there were none else who cared. But, at the same time, we should be wise enough to know that such news would indeed be sad news. A great deal of the lift and joy would necessarily go out of human life. If we were alone in our efforts there would be a constant sense of pathos, because these efforts are truly feeble. We turn frequently against the best that we know, because our characters are often weak. Furthermore, we should be well aware that our efforts were, at best, only temporary, since nothing will survive the inevitable decay. If moral insight is an alien accident in the universe it will not abide.

It is in the light of such possible news that the alternative news is so exciting. Some men believe in God, and some do not, but every intelligent person can see that, if God really is and if we can know it, that is wonderful news indeed! It means that we are not alone; that there is power beyond ourselves waiting to back us up; that the earth's decay is not the end of the story; that the running down of the universe is not final. It means that what is highest in value is deepest in nature, that the things which matter most are not at the mercy of those which matter least. Some men, because the evidence does not convince them, give up such a faith, but in so far as they are intelligent they are saddened by their decision. A world in which men could know that God is *not* might have some good qualities, but it would be strikingly short on *joy*.

Fundamentally, there are only two alternatives in belief concerning the nature of the world. These have been admirably stated by Bishop Gore. One of these, the atheistic alternative, means "that we see in the world of which we form a part no signs of anything corresponding to the mind or spirit or purposes which indisputably exist in man—no signs of a universal spirit or reason with which we can hold communion, nothing but blind and unconscious force." The other alternative, the one to which we now turn, is "the recognition about us, within us and above us, of a universal and eternal reason or purpose, with which we can and ought to correspond." [4] No third possibility is really a live option.

C. The Theistic Alternative

The hypothesis which the immediately succeeding chapters support is not one which some man has worked out in the privacy of his own speculation. It is, rather, one which has come through long years of experience, as men have struggled up through the darkness of spiritism and polytheism to what has appeared to most men to be a more advanced position. The hypothesis most worth examining is not one which has been put together by philosophical glue, but one which has already had severe testing by persons more concerned with doing than with thinking. Many of the faiths which men have held, such as pantheism, are already discarded and, therefore, are not, in the language of William James, "live options." They are not

[4] Charles Gore, *The Reconstruction of Belief*, John Murray, London, 1926, pp. 45, 46.

worth the trouble, but there is at least one conception which *is* worth the trouble, because of the remarkable way in which it has endured the sifting process. Though it is possible that a conception which has been so great a power in human life is altogether illusory, it is not probable.

Nothing is easier than to use the word "God" and mean almost nothing by it. It is easy to be right if we are sufficiently vague or tautologous in what we say. The deepest difficulty with the ontological argument for God is not that the argument is invalid, for it can be so stated that it is not invalid, but rather that the Object to which it points is not worth arguing about. The life of practical religion could not survive by recognizing merely that there is the highest in any series. This no one doubts. What is at stake bears more resemblance to what Blaise Pascal outlined in one of his most famous *Pensées:*

> The God of Christians is not a God who is simply the author of mathematical truths, or of the order of the elements; that is the view of heathens and Epicureans. He is not merely a God who exercises His providence over the lives and fortunes of men, to bestow on those who worship Him a long and happy life. That was the portion of the Jews. But the God of Abraham, the God of Isaac, the God of Jacob, the God of Christians, is a God of love and comfort, a God who fills the soul and heart of those whom He possesses, a God who makes them conscious of their inward wretchedness, and His infinite mercy, who unites Himself with their inmost soul, who fills it with humility and joy, with confidence and love, who renders them incapable of any other end than Himself.

It cannot be too strongly stated that the question of divine being is important or trivial, depending wholly upon the question as to what manner of Being God is. The theistic hypothesis refers, therefore, not to just any "god," but to a particular and concrete conception. Will Herberg has been widely helpful in the contemporary intellectual scene by his teaching that every man has a "god," something which he values most and in deference to which he is willing to sacrifice all else. If this is all that we mean, however, it is obvious that the question of objective reference has no meaning or bearing on our effort to achieve intellectual integrity. If the subjective reference is all that there is, it follows that there are no false gods, but this is a position which satisfies nobody.

The question whether God is derives its interest solely from what kind of Being we are talking about. The Being who now concerns us is One who combines genuine power with perfect love. This is a conception which is perfectly understandable to thoughtful people, even when they do not share it, for it can be described with a minimum of ambiguity or vagueness. It refers to the Living God who is objectively real, who is the Object of worship, and who can, in part, be known as finite persons are known. It is important to insist upon this clarity and objectivity, because there is a widespread opinion in the modern world that men, when they say they believe in God, are uttering propositions which are either meaningless or platitudinous.

The remarkably clear and precise definition of what the being of God means, which appears at the head of this chapter, is strictly in accordance with what the common man undoubtedly means. God, defined by Professor Bennett, is not to be equated with Power or Love or Beauty of Goodness or Truth or Human Aspiration or even the Absolute. In the words of Pascal's most revealing document, we are concerned about the God of Abraham, Isaac and Jacob, not the God of the philosophers. An important insight of a number of philosophers is the recognition that it is the faith of the non-philosophers which is supremely worthy of philosophical consideration.

In making this idea of the Living God clear we must be at great pains to distinguish it sharply from any of the ideas of God which arose in Greek philosophy. Reading the Greek philosophers now, in the light of subsequent intellectual history, and conscious of the Christian adaptation of Greek conceptions, we are inclined to attribute higher notions of divinity to the most influential of the Greek thinkers than their actual teaching warrants. For example, it is almost impossible to read Plato's words about the Good, without equating this with God or supposing that the supreme goodness exists in the mind of God, but Plato did not take this step. It is to the credit of Professor Etienne Gilson that he has insisted on this point until he has made his criticism current philosophical knowledge.[5] It is difficult to point to a single, unifying and fully critical idea of God in the Platonic corpus, and certainly we cannot point

[5] See his *God and Philosophy*, Yale University Press, 1941, chap. 1.

to anything comparable to the advanced notion of God as the all-loving and all-powerful Creator and Sustainer of the universe.

Greek thought, reacting against the primitive mythical conceptions of the gods of Olympus, with their human frailties, adopted a conception which went so far in the opposite direction that divine beings ceased to be contemplated as living realities at all. The satire of Xenophanes was no doubt effective in this radical shift in belief. This is a thoroughly understandable reaction, but essentially an unfortunate one. At best it fails to maintain a sharp distinction between God and the world, and the popular mysticism to which it gives rise is insufficiently ethical in content. Dr. Albert Schweitzer's conclusion on this point is instructive. "In the Graeco-Oriental religion," he says, "there is no living conception of God. To it God is nothing, but pure spirituality. The God of Jesus is an active God, who works in man." [6]

The central Aristotelian conception of God, though not inconsistent with the one which emerged in Palestine, is nevertheless far from identical with it. For Aristotle God was One who gave meaning to the universe, but not One who could be touched by our infirmities or One with whom we could have fellowship in prayer. In fact, Aristotle's God was an "it," not One for whom a fully personal pronoun could reasonably be used. The fully developed theistic view, on the other hand, is that of One for whom we can honestly use not only the third personal pronoun, but the *second.*

The hypothesis which theism thus presents for the consideration of thoughtful minds is a daring one, but it is not preposterous or inherently impossible. The hypothesis is to be distinguished, as sharply as may be, not only from atheism but also from pantheism, on the one hand, and from subjectivism, on the other. It is the conviction that God is, both as transcendent reality and as immanent purpose. It is the belief that God is the Creator of the world, but by no means confined to the world. This conviction is wholly realistic in that God is seen as existing independent of our knowledge of Him. *The idea is that God is, apart from our idea of Him.* His will is expressed in the slow and painful evolution of

[6] Albert Schweitzer, *Christianity and the Religions of the World,* New York, Doran, 1923, p. 28.

the universe; He is witnessed to by conscience; direct experience of acquaintance with Him is reported either explicitly or implicitly by millions. *The hypothesis is that the kind of order we know best, the order of purposive mind, is the ultimate explanation of the universe.*

D. The Process of Verification

Hypothesis is a scientific term, but inasmuch as ours is a scientific age there is nothing strange in our practice of using scientific language, even in our effort to learn the truth about religion. It is obvious that there are no laboratory paraphernalia which are useful and that the concept of experimentation is inappropriate, but these factors are not necessary for a scientific approach. There is no experimentation in astronomy,[7] but astronomy is not rendered thereby less scientific. The scientific approach, in which we seek to draw conclusions on the basis of the evidence, is possible whenever we can have honest observation, clear hypotheses, the facing of difficulties, and some form of verification.

When we use the word "hypothesis" in connection with faith in the Living God we are aware that such faith is not *merely* a hypothesis. It is not entertained in detachment, and in practice it is more akin to courage than it is to belief. It is not normally envisaged as a mere supposition to be tested by scientific method. Nevertheless, the philosopher of religion, knowing this full well, is at liberty to examine theistic faith *as he would examine a scientific hypothesis,* for this is a method which best serves his purpose of rational inquiry. We cannot expect such a method to do justice to the subject, for no method can, but it may shed welcome light upon it.

Here, then, is our method: We present a hypothesis, and we look into various aspects of experience to see whether the hypothesis is supported by the facts. We must consider both those facts which support our thesis and those, if there are any, which make the thesis difficult to maintain. The fact that our thesis appears to be the end product of a long spiritual development in many races and peoples does not prove that our thesis is correct, though it undoubtedly makes any honest thinker approach the subject with unusual respect

---

[7] Unless we include, in astronomy, the launching of artificial satellites.

and actually tips the logical scales somewhat in favor of the hypothesis. It is not enough that our hypothesis appears at the end of a line of manifest progress; we are not satisfied until it is verified by a method harmonious with the method of science. Scientific verification does not, as we have indicated in Chapter V, give absolute proof, but it gives something with which most of us are satisfied.

The fundamental question we face is: "How is the universe to be understood?" We find that there is in the world one bold theory which stands out from its rivals as especially worthy of attention. Is the world more reasonably understood on this basis than on any other? Will this assumption best order all known facts into a reasonable whole?

There are many features of the known world which can be understood on the theistic hypothesis, but which are not understandable on any other that we know. Our procedure is to consider these features ones by one. Singly, they are by no means conclusive, just as a single corroboration is no verification, but together their cumulative effect is very great. And it is in such cumulative effect that the whole strength of verification lies. We have examined the reasons for belief in *anything*; we have presented one particular belief, perhaps the most important in the world; we are now to ask whether the evidence for this belief is good evidence.

7

The Evidence of Scientific Experience

The power of dialectic alone can reveal this, and only to one who is a disciple of the previous sciences.

PLATO

The plain man, when asked to validate his belief in God, normally begins by pointing to nature and particularly to those aspects of nature which seem to him incomprehensible apart from Divine Purpose. Though the evidence provided by the natural order is not adequate, the ordinary believer is undoubtedly right in starting there. It is not the topmost round of the logical ladder, but it is a firm one. In short, Pascal was overstating the case when he wrote disparagingly of those who sought to prove the existence of God from the works of nature. What is important is to try to give each part of the evidence its true weight.

A. THE CLASSIC PROOFS

So far as the Western world is concerned, the philosophy of religion was an invention of the ancient Greeks. The Hebrews and allied peoples, though their belief was strong, and partly because their belief was strong, felt no need of elaborate intellectual vindication, but the Greeks did. Because Book X of Plato's *Laws* represents an important chapter in this intellectual effort, part of it is reproduced, as Appendix A to this book, so that it may be easily available to contemporary students.

The effort, on the part of thinkers, to validate the truth of the hypothesis that God is, has gone on more or less continually during the more than two thousand years which have intervened since Plato's day. By the time that the medieval civilization reached its climax this process achieved a kind of permanence and received

classic expression in the writings of Thomas Aquinas. Though many
subtle distinctions were developed among the "proofs of God's
existence," such as those of the "argument from contingency," "the
argument from motion," and the "henological argument," it was
common by the eighteenth century, when Kant's celebrated attack
occurred, to classify the "proofs" under three heads: the *ontological,*
the *cosmological,* and the *teleological* arguments.[1]

It is not necessary for the modern student to pay a great deal
of attention to these arguments, because all that is of permanent
value in them can be stated better in other ways today. The salvag-
ing process is carried on by means of a new orientation. This is
made necessary not only because of the blows which Kant admin-
istered to these arguments, but even more because of the new pat-
terns of thought which are congenial to our minds today. All that
is required is that the modern student should have some appreciation of what those who formulated the classic proofs were trying
to say.

The *ontological* proof was formulated in its scholastic form by
Anselm (1033-1109) and in a simpler form by Descartes at the
beginning of the modern age. The essence of this approach is that
the existence of God follows necessarily from the idea of God, since
God is a Being than which a greater cannot be conceived, and a
Being which exists in fact and not merely in thought is greater
than one which exists only in thought. In a second formulation
Descartes held that the idea of God, who is infinite and perfect,
could not be produced by any finite object and must, therefore, be
caused by God Himself. Here is the same emphasis on the absolutely
unique nature of one idea, with the principle of sufficient reason
added.

The celebrated Kantian rejoinder that the real contains no more
than the possible and that a hundred real dollars do not contain
a cent more than a hundred possible dollars [2] really misses the point
of the original argument in which reference is made not to any

---

[1] The best contemporary study known to me, in which the various classic
proofs are presented both vigorously and sympathetically, is that of George
H. Joyce, *Principles of Natural Theology,* London, Longmans, 1934. The author
is a Jesuit scholar, especially adept in presenting the Thomistic arguments in
modern form.

[2] In the *Transcendental Dialectic.*

finite object, but only to the infinitely perfect being. We may be sure that Anselm's argument is not so feeble as it appears superficially to be, but nevertheless it does not carry conviction today, largely because it represents a prescientific mentality. It seems irrelevant.

The second of the classic theistic proofs, the *cosmological,* is most often stated in relation to the conception of causality. Plato, in the *Timaeus,* said that every created thing must be created by some cause. In our experienced world all events are preceded by causes. If two trees stand side by side in the forest and one dies while the other lives, all agree that there were different causal factors in the two situations. The dead tree had a disease, but, in turn, there was a cause of the disease, and so on. Thus, among all finite things, the chain of causality runs back, step by step. But an infinite chain of causes is logically impossible. "If no member of the series," writes Joyce, "possesses being otherwise than in virtue of the actual present operation of a higher cause, it follows that in default of a first cause there can be no secondary cause in existence." [3] But there are secondary causes in existence; therefore, beyond all secondary causes and giving rise to the entire series, there must be a first cause, itself uncaused and self-existent. To say that such a first cause exists is to say that God is.

There are many contemporary efforts to state the ancient argument with cogency, but none seems better than the following:

> Let me, then, now try to bring out what I conceive to be the essential truth which the cosmological argument, when rightly stated, establishes. The gist of the argument may be expressed thus: Acknowledging, as we cannot help doing, the existence of a world of nature, we are logically driven to acknowledge that there is a real existence beyond nature, *unless,* indeed, we are prepared to rest in an ultimate inexplicability, and to relinquish the attempt to frame an intelligent conception of nature at all.[4]

The argument is impressive and must always be viewed with respect by thoughtful people. It was not seriously damaged by Kant's criticism. It faces two difficulties, however, in the modern mind. In the first place, we are not sure that the Object arrived at

[3] Joyce, *op. cit.,* p. 65.

[4] G. Dawes Hicks, *The Philosophical Bases of Theism,* New York, Macmillan, 1937, p. 180.

by this intellectual argument is the same as the One mentioned by Pascal, the One whom we can love and worship and partly know. In the second place, modern man has serious doubts about the whole principle of causality. Some contemporary philosophers, taking an extreme position, have attempted to reject the notion of causality completely, and many others have tried to transcend it. Whether they have succeeded in this effort is another question and one which we must face at the appropriate point in our presentation.

The third classic proof is the *teleological*.[5] This argument, always a popular one, argues from the presence of order in the universe to an adequate source of that order. It is, therefore, really a specialized application of the cosmological approach. The order is taken as a token of design and the conclusion is that God must be the source of that design. Though Kant spoke tenderly of this argument, saying "it must be always mentioned with respect," he went on to claim that "all the argument from design can possibly prove is an *architect* of the world, who is very much limited by the adaptability of the material in which he works."

It is obvious that this argument cannot stand alone. Although there is a sense in which it can be validly stated, the argument by itself does not lead necessarily to the belief in an omnipotent creator of the world. Charles Darwin's famous doctrine of natural selection is widely supposed to have destroyed the cogency of the teleological argument, by showing that changes have come by purely natural causes rather than by special design, but this is by no means evident today. Natural selection, we now see, may account for which forms, among several, *survive*, but it cannot account for which *arrive*. The popular notion that modern science has made the conception of cosmic purpose inadmissible is one of the major delusions which careful thought can help to destroy.

Though the classic proofs have strengths as well as weaknesses, they are not needed today. Creative thought has been applied, with unremitting vigor, in our generation to these questions, particularly in the series of lectures in the Scottish universities, supported by the bequest of Lord Gifford. The Gifford Lectures constitute the most honored series of lectures in philosophy in the modern world

---

[5] A splendid contemporary statement of the teleological argument is given by A. E. Taylor in *Does God Exist?* New York, Macmillan, 1947, pp. 57 ff.

and all of them deal, in one way or another, with the validation of theism. The great men who have lectured on this foundation, including James, Royce, Balfour, Sorley and Temple, among many others, have brought the subject we are discussing to a very high point. We are foolish, in the light of their contributions, to go on in the old conventional ways. What is important now is to face the problems anew, especially in the light of our scientific mentality. Since nearly all that is valid in the ancient proofs refers to the external world of nature, it is appropriate to start with nature and to work up, by gradual steps, to that which transcends nature.

If it is really true that, in addition to all finite spirits, there is an infinite Spirit, the divine Mind, who is not only the Companion of our spirits but the Creator and Sustainer of the world order, it is reasonable to expect to find evidences of the divine Mind in the process which goes on relatively independent of the will of men. Specifically, we should expect to find various aspects of the natural order which are not understandable except by reference to the hypothesis in question. If God really is, we should expect the heavens to declare His glory and the firmament to show His handiwork.

B. The Existence of Science

The discipline which we call natural science is the best means at our disposal of knowing the secrets of the external world. Through science we learn more and more about a vast system ranging all the way from distant stars to microscopic phenomena, and all the way from inorganic substance to highly sentient and conscious beings. The process by which we have accomplished so much in the enlargement of the area of scientific knowledge has been slow, laborious and halting. Beginning with an unreflective experience of adjustment between organism and environment, we have finally arrived at the point where we distinguish sharply between subject and object, seeking to consider the world as it is apart from subjective wishes. We are, thus, driven to the conclusion that the world exists independent of our knowing it. Most of the natural order would go on just as it does if there were no scientifically minded creatures on the earth. Perhaps the best evidence of the independence of the natural order is that *it actually did go on a long time before the advent of man.*

Man, when he came to be genuine man, entered into a going world, waiting to be known. The human mind exists in the world, not the world in the human mind. But mind, though a late-comer in the temporal sequence, has been remarkably successful in unlocking the secrets of the world which is older than itself. The world has been able to spawn something which can apprehend that which spawned it.

The most amazing fact about scientific knowledge is the evidence which it provides that there is an actual correlation between the mind and the natural order which it apprehends. This correlation is so great and so fundamental that we seldom reflect upon it. When we do begin to reflect upon it we realize that the most stupendous conclusion to which science leads is the conclusion that ours is the kind of world in which science is possible. There are many ways of adjusting to environment, but the more rational the adjustment the more adequate it becomes, and the test of adequacy is success in manipulation. This tells us something highly significant about our world. It is the kind of world which yields its secrets, in physical and chemical and biological laboratories, to men who conduct precise mathematical calculations. Archbishop Temple has made this point so well that we can do no better than reproduce a few sentences from his Gifford Lectures.

But this fact of knowledge is more remarkable than all the varieties of known objects put together. For the mind which knows is in a perfectly real sense equal to what it knows, and in another real sense transcends it, unless what it knows is another mind which also knows. The mind of the astronomer is equal to so much of the stellar system as he grasps, and transcends it in so far as he knows it while it does not know him. That there should "emerge" in the cosmic process a capacity to apprehend, even in a measure to comprehend, that process is the most remarkable characteristic of the process itself. For though minds emerge as episodes within the process, it is, as will appear, essential to their nature as minds that they are not mere episodes. Thus, the cosmic process gives evidence that it is not only process, and history supplies the proof that reality is more than historical.[6]

When a human mind comes to know an object with any accuracy there is a one-to-one correspondence between the thought and the object. They match! This is what is meant by saying that a mind is equal to what it knows. When an astronomer knows the moon, each feature of the moon's surface is matched by an item of the astronomer's thought. The wonder of such matching becomes most apparent when we engage in actual prediction of physical events, a prediction constantly illustrated in astronomy. Valid mental processes go on for a considerable time, unchecked by reference to events, but when the mental processes *are* checked, they are found to have followed events perfectly. Nature "obeys" the rules of logic; predictions, made on the basis of logical calculations, come true.

Whatever our explanation of this correspondence, and it may be said in passing that the hypothesis of the existence of God, who is at once the Creator of the natural order and the Creator of man's mind, is a fully adequate explanation, there is no avoiding the fact that actual kinship between mind and nature exists. This kinship is the chief basis of whatever success science achieves. It is what we mean when we affirm the existence of an intelligible world. The world, of course, is not now fully intelligible, and it may, for all we know, involve fundamentally irrational elements, but the history of science has been the elimination of many supposed irrationalities, which have finally been understood.

The meaning of these observations becomes more apparent when we consider the significance of *explanation*. Sometimes we say we have explained physical events by reference to prior events of the same order, but reflection shows that this merely pushes the mystery back one step and does not explain at all. To say that it rains today because there was a certain atmospheric disturbance yesterday is to say very little, indeed. All that we do in this case is to enlarge slightly the temporal span of our description of the physical event. The process of explaining must come somewhere to an end, and it comes to an end only when we reach "principles deducible from nothing prior to themselves." [7] In explanation we seek a connection between what is to be explained and what we already understand, at least in some measure. "The business of philosophy is not so much to explain things, as to find the things that explain themselves."

A situation is never understood until we have some intimation

---

6 William Temple, *Nature, Man and God*, p. 129.

of why it has occurred, and we never have an intimation of "why" until we come into contact with purpose. Purpose, in turn, is meaningless apart from a mind which entertains the purpose. "When we find," says Temple, "that the position of a given set of material objects is due to their having been arranged with a view to facilitating the accomplishment of some intelligible purpose, our minds are satisfied. That a plank should lie across a stream may call for much explanation if no human beings have ever placed it there; but if men laid it across to form a bridge, so that they could cross over dry-shod, no further explanation is needed." [8]

Not only is purpose a self-explanatory principle; there is, so far as we are aware, no other. All other types of explanation leave the fundamental questions unanswered. We go on asking "Why?" *in exactly the same way as before.* When we are told that gas pressure is explained by movement of molecules, we ask why the molecules move, and we are asking precisely the same kind of question again. When we trace an occurrence to the purpose of an intelligent being, however, the situation is completely altered. We may, indeed, ask why such a purpose is entertained, but when we do so we are asking a question of a different order. We have come to the end of one road and are starting on another. The causes which *produce* a purpose are entirely different from the set of secondary causes which *result* from a purpose.

If a nail is being driven, we discover a set of secondary causes reaching all the way from the purpose of the carpenter to the completed process. The nail goes in *because* the hammer hits it. The hammer head moves *because* it is moved by the muscles of a man's arm. The arm muscles move *because* they are directed by nerve impulses. But the whole enterprise takes place *because* a man has a reason for driving a nail in a board. Perhaps he wants to build a house for his friend. Our ordinary language obscures the true situation in that we use the same word "because" in each case, but reflection shows that the word in its fourth use means something very different from what it means in the first three uses. The first three do not really explain, but the fourth *does* explain. This remains true even when we ask why the man wants to build the

---

[7] H. W. B. Joseph, *An Introduction to Logic,* p. 503.
[8] William Temple, *op. cit.,* pp. 131, 132.

house. We, then, have solved our first problem and have turned to another.

When we try to explain a purpose we find that our only recourse is to refer to other and more inclusive purposes. Thus, Purpose is really an ultimate principle of explanation, and the only adequate explanation of the world would be the Purpose, which includes the whole process. If the world is understandable, such a Purpose must exist. But the belief in the existence of such a Purpose is theism. Because science shows the world to be intelligible, at least to a considerable degree, science becomes a witness to intelligent Purpose in nature and consequently it bears testimony to the credibility of theism.

Few modern philosophers have grasped this logical conclusion of science better than did the late Baron von Hügel. His words may be used as a summary of and, therefore, a fitting conclusion to this section of our analysis:

Already Mathematics and Mechanics absolutely depend, for the success of their applications to actual Nature, upon a spontaneous correspondence between the human reason and the Rationality of Nature. The immensity of this success is an unanswerable proof that this rationality is not imposed, but found there by man. But Thought without a Thinker is an absurd proposition. Thus faith in Science is faith in God.[9]

C. The Fact of Evolution

Though there are many minor arguments about the precise mode of evolution that has occurred and is occurring in the natural order, there is essential agreement in the modern world about the general principle to the effect that the forms which we see at present have come by innumerable steps, longer or shorter, from other and different forms which have preceded them. The principle of evolution, thus broadly understood, is to be distinguished, both logically and historically, from Darwinism, the special evolutionary theory which seeks to make the notion of natural selection a sufficient means of explanation. The Darwinian is necessarily an evolutionist, but one can be an evolutionist without being a Darwinian.

The conclusion to which most biological scholars have been driven is that all living creatures are the descendants of earlier and,

[9] Baron Friedrich von Hügel, *Essays and Addresses on the Philosophy of Religion,* p. 71.

in many cases, less developed living creatures. Species, we now believe, have not been immutable from the beginning, but have arisen from other species. It is likely that the earliest form of life, and possibly the ancestor of all living things, was a unicellular organism. The evidence we have is by no means adequate to demonstration, and there is truth in the contention of skeptics that evolution is a highly speculative theory, but the evidence is sufficient to satisfy most minds which have considered it fairly.

It is well known that the great intellectual struggle over evolutionary theory which took place almost a century ago was occasioned largely by the inclusion of man in the evolutionary scheme. For a number of reasons it was widely supposed that this inclusion, if sustained, made religious faith difficult or even impossible. Curiously enough, it is this very inclusion which subsequent reflection has fastened upon as one of the chief features of the natural order among those which substantiate and corroborate the theistic hypothesis.

The evidence that man is akin to other living creatures by virtue of descent is abundant. Alfred Russel Wallace's summary of this evidence, though made two generations ago, would hardly be changed by contemporary scholars.

The facts now very briefly summarized amount almost to a demonstration that man, in his bodily structure, has been derived from the lower animals, of which he is the culminating development. In his possession of rudimentary structures which are functional in some of the mammalia; in the numerous variations of his muscles and other organs agreeing with characters which are constant in some apes; in his embryonic development, absolutely identical in character with that of mammalia in general, and closely resembling in its details that of the higher quadrumana; in the diseases which he has in common with other mammalia; and in the wonderful approximation of his skeleton to those of one or other of the anthropoid apes, we have an amount of evidence in this direction which it seems impossible to explain away. And this evidence will appear more forcible if we consider for a moment what the rejection of it implies. For the only alternative supposition is, that man has been specially created—that is to say, has been produced in some quite different way from other animals and altogether independently of them. But in that case the rudimentary structures, the animal-like variations, the identical course of development, and all the other animal characteristics he possesses are deceptive, and inevitably lead us, as thinking beings making use of the reason which is our noblest and most distinctive feature, into gross error.[10]

Wallace, it may be remembered, held back from the conclusion that man's higher life also came out of nature, apparently impelled by the fear that this would involve some disparagement of this higher life. But the higher life of man, found in his mental and spiritual powers, is dependent on the long series of events which Wallace helped so greatly to describe. Unique as man's mind undoubtedly is, man shares much of his mental experience with the humbler creatures. Mind is man's glory, but there are thousands of stages of mental development to be observed in the natural order. Thought and language, now so highly developed, had already been developing for a very long time when they reached the stage illustrated in the most primitive tribes we now know. Many animals have a kind of language, even though it is qualitatively different from human language. "Thinking is grounded in the process of adjustment between oranism and environment and is indeed an extension of that process." [11]

The highest point in creation, so far as we know, is the capacity to comprehend the world, but this capacity has arisen by degrees in the natural order. At one end of the evolutionary series is unconscious life, and at the other is self-conscious life, but *it is all one series*. It is reasonable to suppose, as Aristotle taught, that the conclusion of a process gives a more adequate insight into its character than does the beginning. "Primordial ooze" and scientific accuracy belong to a single comprehensive system of historical and genealogical relations, but the science is more revealing than is the ooze.

The fact that a process is rational does not mean that the ground of that rationality is necessarily revealed in the beginning. In fact the ground of the rationality need not appear until the end of the series of events, but when it appears it illuminates the entire process. This is well illustrated in dramatic poetry and in the lives of good men. Seen in retrospect, such lives are thoroughly rationalized wholes because of what, all along, they were *becoming*.

[10] Alfred Russel Wallace, "Darwinism as Applied to Man" in *Representative Essays in Modern Thought,* New York, Macmillan, 1923, pp. 454, 455.
[11] Temple, *op. cit.,* p. 128.

If the general evolutionary theory is true and if man's life be included in the theory, we cannot escape the conclusion, once more, that mind and nature are akin. We saw earlier that mind and nature are akin because mind truly comprehends nature. We now have an independent line of evidence in that mind arises out of nature. Mind and nature are genealogically, as well as cognitively, akin. The convergence of two lines of evidence on one conclusion is a matter of great importance. The relation "akin to" is a symmetrical relation. If mind is akin to nature, nature likewise is akin to mind.

We are thus led to the conclusion, not that a naturalistic metaphysic is adequate, but that the explanation of nature is to be found in mind. Inasmuch as Archbishop Temple has had the honor of emphasizing this point more than most contemporary thinkers, it is appropriate to quote his conclusion, a conclusion which he rightly prints in italics: *"The more completely we include Mind within Nature, the more inexplicable must Nature become except by reference to Mind."* [12] A boldly accepted naturalism leads directly to supernaturalism! How can nature include mind as an *integral* part unless it is grounded in mind? If mind were seen as something alien or accidental, the case would be different, but the further we go in modern science the clearer it becomes that mental experience is no strange offshoot. Rather it is something which is deeply rooted in the entire structure.

Science knows nothing of the wholly fortuitous. Though there are some events, especially in subatomic physics, to which we cannot assign causes, the general assumption is that this is only a measure of our present ignorance. This assumption has been well justified by former experience in which the apparently fortuitous or haphazard was finally seen as conforming to an intelligible rule. If, as seems likely, there are no truly accidental events, then mind, which comes at the apex of the world process, so far as we know it, is really an integral part of the system and a revelation of the nature of nature.

The most fruitful conclusion of such studies lies in the revelation that "cosmic and biological evolution are one." There seems to be a single orderly development with mind and matter belonging to

[12] *Ibid.*, p. 133.

the same inclusive system. In short, studies regarding the fitness of the environment emphasize in a new way the great lesson of evolution to which we have already pointed. "For undeniably," concludes Professor Henderson, "two things which are related together in a complex manner by reciprocal fitness can make up in a very real sense a unit—something quite different from the two alone or the sum of the two or the relationship between the two. In human affairs such a unit arises only from effective operation of purpose." [13] Thus, the evidence grows that mind is not accidental in nature, and that nature, consequently, is not alien to mind.

D. THE SECOND LAW OF THERMODYNAMICS

Of all the conclusions reached by the past two centuries of careful scientific work, one of the most revealing, as well as disturbing, is that which points to the degradation of energy. The notion of the progressive degradation of energy, which is based on what is called the "Carnot principle" and finds its formal statement in the Second Law of Thermodynamics, has been known for over a century, but we have been surprisingly slow to see its metaphysical implications.

The Second Law of Thermodynamics must be understood in connection with the First Law, that of the conservation of energy. This principle, to be distinguished from the principle of the conservation of matter, was reached independently by several scholars. Mayer, in Germany, announced his conclusions in 1842 and Joule, in England, announced his in 1843. The law holds that the amount of energy in the world is constant though it changes in form. The fact that the amount of energy is constant does not mean that energy is always available. In so far as we can see, the time will come when energy is not available for work. Because there is constant diffusion and because there is no addition to the total energy, we must contemplate a final condition of absolute stagnation. And it is precisely this to which the Second Law points.

In all physical systems we note a leveling process. A stone thrown into a pool raises waves, but these slowly dissipate until they are no longer observable. The hot stove radiates its heat into the closed room until a uniform temperature is reached. Just as nature may be

[13] L. J. Henderson, *The Fitness of the Environment,* New York, Macmillan, 1913, p. 279.

said figuratively to abhor a vacuum, so nature abhors differentiation and concentration of energy. Thus, the stars radiate their energy, and this energy, so far as we know, *never makes a return trip. It is a one-way process.* This increase of leveling is called the "increase of entropy." There are many excellent definitions of this, but the following is one of the clearest: "As the useless energy increases, the useful decreases by the same amount. This ratio of useless to useful energy is called *entropy*. The law of entropy states that the ratio is constantly increasing. This means that the amount of energy available for the energizing process of the world is ever growing less." [14]

The reason why we can get work out of a heat engine is that there is a temperature differential, and the reason we can get work out of a waterfall is that there is a difference in level. The waterfall is useful because there is a low place into which the water can descend. If the leveling process were ever completed, all work would be at an end. "We cannot convert the heat of a cold body into work," says Barnes, "for then, without consumption of fuel, we should get unlimited supplies of motive power. Hence, we may conclude that the efficiency of a perfectly reversible engine is the maximum possible, and further that it depends solely on the temperatures between which the engine works. It is always possible to get work out of the heat of a body which is hotter than surrounding bodies. But, just as you cannot get blood out of a stone, so you cannot get work out of a body which is colder than surrounding bodies. On this simple fact the second law of thermodynamics is based." [15]

Though the law of entropy is partially a matter of speculation, inasmuch as the conclusion is large in comparison with the field of observation, the conclusion reached is far from fanciful. In fact, no less a physicist than Sir Arthur Eddington called this law the most certain and the most grounded of all the laws of physics. "Carnot's principle," wrote Emile Meyerson, "is a fact, and by far the most important fact, of all science." [16] It is always possible for some new force, now unknown, to enter, but, on the basis of present

[14] J. A. McWilliams, *Cosmology*, New York, Macmillan, 1933, p. 42.
[15] E. W. Barnes, *Scientific Theory and Religion*, New York, Macmillan, p. 233.
[16] Emile Meyerson, *Identity and Reality*, New York, Macmillan, 1930, p. 278.

observations, there seems to be no rational escape from the prospect of an ultimate dissipation of all energy. This means not only the "death" of our particular solar system, but of any physical system.

The paradox is that the Second Law, depressing as it seems to be, actually supports the theistic claim in a remarkable way. We are driven, logically, to the conclusion that the physical world is something which not only will have an end, but also something which had a beginning. "If the universe is running down like a clock," says Dr. Inge, "the clock must have been wound up at a date which we could name if we knew it. The world, if it is to have an end in time, must have had a beginning in time." [17] This follows strictly from the fact that the law of entropy is irreversible. A clock which always runs down and is never rewound cannot have been running forever.

At first sight it looks as though there is a possible escape from this conclusion in the concept of the physical world as infinite in extent or in amount of energy. But this, in fact, is no solution of the problem, since the notion of an infinite quantity is really meaningless. The term "infinite sum" has no significance. However much there is of energy or of matter, there is just that much and no more. Energy cannot be infinite in amount, because it is concerned with actuality. Time, however, can be infinite in the sense of the possibility of events.

The chief metaphysical significance of the law of entropy consists not in the evidence of a beginning in time, important as that is, but rather *in the evidence that the natural world is not self-explanatory*. According to natural law, energy loses its efficacy. But without the operation of a totally different principle there would be no energy to lose its efficacy. *Nature points beyond nature for an explanation of nature*. The Second Law of Thermodynamics thus points directly to theism as an explanation of the world, and the reasoning based upon it provides a modern counterpart to the cosmological argument.

Though we have, in this section, referred to development in time, it should be recognized that the reference to time is not strictly necessary to the validity of the argument. All the changes which we know in the world of nature are dependent changes. We refer

[17] W. R. Inge, *God and the Astronomers*, New York, Longmans, 1933, p. 10.

changes in plant growth to changes in soil, we refer the changes in soil to still other changes, and so on. No single step in the process would even occur apart from the other steps upon which it depends. Therefore, the entire chain of causes presupposes the existence of a power which is truly originative, able to account not only for others but also for itself. "The dependence meant in the argument," says Professor A. E. Taylor, "has nothing to do with succession in time. What is really meant is that our knowledge of any event in Nature is not complete until we know the reason for the event. So long as you only know that A is so because B is so, but cannot tell why B is so, your knowledge is incomplete. It only becomes complete when you are in a position to say that ultimately A is so because Z is so, Z being something which is its own *raison d'être*, and, therefore, such that it would be senseless to ask *why* Z is so." [18]

The chief strength of atheistic naturalism has lain in the notion that the material world needs no explanation, *external to itself*, that it is, indeed, a perpetual motion machine, which had no beginning and will have no end. But when we take the Second Law of Thermodynamics seriously we can no longer hold to this doctrine. The universe as we know it, by the aid of modern science, could not have originated without the action of a creative Source of energy outside itself, and it cannot be maintained without it. The more we delve, by the aid of natural science, into the secrets of nature the more it becomes clear that nature cannot account for itself in any of its parts or in its entirety.

The stone which the builders rejected has become the head of the corner. Science, instead of undermining belief in God, today becomes the first witness. Science means knowledge, and what we have to explain about the world is that knowledge has appeared. How, in a nontheistic world, would knowledge of its nontheism be possible? A. E. Taylor is extremely disturbing when he says we must ask of every theory about the world, "Would the truth of the theory be compatible with knowing the theory to be true?" That is a question on which a person may meditate profitably for a long time.

[18] A. E. Taylor, "The Vindication of Religion," in *Essays Catholic and Critical,* ed. by E. G. Selwyn, New York, Macmillan, 1950, p. 50.

8

The Evidence of Moral Experience

The breach between ethical man and pre-human nature consti-
tutes without exception the most important fact which the
universe has to show.

ANDREW SETH

＊

It is not surprising that all the major evidences for the validation
of the theistic hypothesis are connected with human experience,
because it is inevitable that we start where we are. Thus, the evidence of nature, outlined in the previous chapter, is not merely the
evidence provided by the fact that nature exists, but far more by
what scientific knowledge of nature reveals. What kind of world
must it be in which so much knowledge arises and whose secrets
are progressively unlocked by such knowledge? This poses a very
difficult problem for those who deny the theistic hypothesis. But
their problem is made much harder when they consider another
aspect of human experience, that in which men are concerned
with moral values.

A. The Heritage of Kant

It is to the lasting honor of Immanuel Kant that he turned the
thoughts of millions of inquiring minds to what can be learned
from a careful consideration of what he called the practical reason.
One consequence is that, ever since his time, the "moral argument"
has been prominent in discussions of the philosophy of religion.
This does not mean that Kant, himself, produced the finished
argument on this score, for he did not. Kant began by saying that
it is a demand of the moral self that the highest good be realized.

He argued for the necessary union of virtue and happiness, which he called the *summum bonum* and which, he showed, is not possible on naturalistic grounds, since virtue and happiness belong to two different worlds, the former to the intelligible and the latter to the phenomenal world. Therefore, we must postulate the existence of God, since otherwise the required combination cannot be.

This mode of reasoning seems to us artificial and, indeed, awkward, yet the contribution of Kant, in this matter, was really very great. What he did was to give serious thought a new start, after casting doubt upon older ways of thinking. The result is that others have picked up the thread where he left it and have developed it, in the past century and a half, into a really convincing argument.[1] Professor Sorley's Gifford Lectures, *Moral Values and the Idea of God,* represent a kind of climax in this intellectual development. Instead of blaming Kant for not seeing all that was involved in his fresh approach, we ought to be sufficiently gracious to credit him with making a start that was potentially valuable. His major contribution in this regard was twofold. First, he taught men to pay serious attention to the deliverances of the moral consciousness as a really significant part of experience and, second, he indicated the validity of postulational thinking, in which we move from an indubitable experience to those deeper convictions which are required if the indubitable experience is not to be denied or made meaningless.[2] The result of several generations of thought now makes it possible to present the moral argument in a way somewhat different from that in which Kant presented it, yet one which retains his most important insight.

Ours is a world which has men in it. This fact would seem to be so obvious that it could not fail to be observed, since it is usually men who do the observing, but it has, indeed, frequently been overlooked in high places. It is, of course, much easier to exclude the observer from the totality of what is observed, but this can be done only at the price of falsification. Generalization about the nature of reality is greatly simplified if men are left out of consid-

---

[1] Cf. A. E. Taylor, *Does God Exist?* pp. 84, 85. The moral argument is given a brilliant brief statement in C. S. Lewis' *The Case for Christianity,* New York, Macmillan, 1947.

[2] See the excerpt from Kant's reasoning in Appendix B of this book.

eration, for men are highly embarrassing phenomena. The most glaring example of such a radical omission is found in the several varieties of philosophical mechanism. There is a famous story to the effect that Laplace, who sought valiantly to be a consistent mechanist, told Napoleon that in his (Laplace's) system there was no need for the hypothesis of God. He might well have added, as a distinguished Gifford Lecturer has suggested, that there was likewise no place in his system for the creative activity of man.[3] The old-fashioned mechanistic scientist of the nineteenth century, who even yet is not wholly extinct, created "a paradise of intelligibility" by the simple expedient of excluding himself. It is relatively easy to reduce the world to order according to the laws known to physics if one elects to overlook the persons who change the course of events by the discovery and use of the laws of physics. But the truly modern man is so infected with the virus of realism that this simple method is not open to him. Nearly all see the joke when Whitehead writes, "Scientists animated by the purpose of proving that they are purposeless constitute an interesting subject for study." [4]

The augustness of the moral demand is very impressive. This is shown by the witness of men and women of widely different temperaments and vocations, from saints and martyrs to statesmen and scientists. Many scientists could win fame and other rewards for making new discoveries if only they would alter their figures, but in countless cases this temptation is scornfully rejected, even when there is no reasonable probability of detection and exposure. Such action is by no means limited to those who have a positive theistic belief. Few men, for example, have been more uncompromising than W. K. Clifford, who wrote his brilliant and convincing essay on "The Ethics of Belief," with special reference to the religious belief which he did not have. Similarly, the unbelieving Huxley wrote to his friend Kingsley of his refusal to believe in the comforting doctrine of immortality while he was grieving for his dead son, because he could not play fast and loose with truth.

That to which all bear testimony is the fact that a man who

[3] E. W. Barnes, *Scientific Theory and Religion*, p. 583.
[4] Alfred North Whitehead, *The Function of Reason*, Princeton University Press, 1929, p. 12.

genuinely says "I ought" means "I ought, though the heavens fall." The command is not conditional, but categorical. Of course, conditions make a difference, but *once the conditions are recognized* there is a genuine imperative. "Whoever says 'ought' at all, must mean that at least *when* the requisite conditions are fulfilled the obligation is absolute." [5] Though this augustness is not felt in all situations, it seems a misuse of language to call an experience a moral one if this note is wholly absent.

It is beyond dispute that the human animal is concerned very largely *with what he ought to do*. In this enterprise he is, no doubt, frequently confused and baffled, but he goes on asking the question. To describe man without this question would be ridiculous. Man falls to depths such as no mere beast can experience, but he is frequently conscious of his fall and self-condemnatory accordingly. Man is a self-conscious being who not only acts but *judges* his own acts, as well as the acts of others. He not only uses intelligence to gain his ends, but he asks whether certain ends ought to be gained. He not only seeks praise but, at least in fleeting moments, seeks to be worthy of praise. Frequently he does what is customary, but, generation after generation, he asks whether what is customary is really right.

In dealing with the phenomena of conscience we are dealing, therefore, not with something transitory or local, but with something permanent and universal. A great part of the life of man is concerned with ethical judgments. We read history and, as we do so, we distribute praise and blame. All men appear to be concerned that their own actions should be such as to be considered praiseworthy in the eyes of an unprejudiced observer. We are conscious of experiences, and these among the most important in our lives, in which we make difficult moral decisions, sometimes at great cost to our personal comfort or worldly success. When we fail in these decisions we condemn our own actions. We are frequently covered with shame, because of our failures to live up to the highest that we have known. By our remorse we clearly imply that a genuine decision was made, but also that it was made *wrongly*.

In all of this we are conscious of one area of experience which

[5] A. E. Taylor, "The Vindication of Religion," in *Essays Catholic and Critical*, p. 62.

is sharply different from all others. When we condemn our own actions we maintain that there was something which we *ought* to have done and which we did not do. This, by common speech, we put in a class by itself. To say "I ought to do this" is not the same as to say "it is to my advantage" or "it is prudent" or "it is customary" or "it is commanded by the state" or "I desire it." In fact, we habitually decide between all of these and what we think we ought to do. Frequently, there is a clash between them. It may be customary for condemned men to run away if they can, but Socrates stays because he senses a difference between what is moral and what is customary. The martyr distinguishes between what the crowd commands and what seems to him to be right. So pervasive and far-reaching is this experience of moral endeavor or moral failure, as the case may be, that it becomes the deepest source of interest in literature, the most moving scene which the world has to show being that of genuine moral struggle. Thousands of pieces of great literature, with their uncounted millions of readers, bear witness to this fact.

Actually, there would seem more reason to trust the human spirit in its exalted moods than in its more humdrum pursuits. At least, we are conscious of living more adequately in times of courageous moral decision than at other times. No doubt most careful thinkers will have sympathy with the late Paul Elmer More when he asserts that he finds the hypothesis of mass delusion really incredible. "You ask me to believe," he wrote, "that nature has planted in me, and not in me alone, but in all men, desires which I must eradicate as pure deceptions, that I am the victim of a cosmic jest only the more cruel if unintended, that the ultimate fact of existence is a malignant mockery." [6]

Now the point to make clear is that an experience so lofty and so indubitable must be given great weight in our effort to know the nature of reality. All that we know we know by experience, and it would be absurd to pay attention to lesser experiences while we neglect the obviously greater ones. The enduring contribution of Kant is that he, more than any other modern philosopher, has made men ask, "What conception of the universe is required if we are to

[6] Paul Elmer More, *The Sceptical Approach to Religion,* Princeton University Press, 1934, p. 24.

make sense out of the most august experiences which men enjoy?" Our debt to Kant is not so much that he gave the right answers. but that he made us ask the right questions.

B. THE OBJECTIVE FACTOR IN MORAL EXPERIENCE

If the first step in the moral argument for theism is the recognition that moral experience may be truly revealing of reality, the second step is the necessary postulation of objective reference. Every person who engages in moral judgment implies by his judgment the existence of an objective moral order. This is because the relationship called judging involves at least three terms: the person who judges, the action that is judged, and the standard of judgment by which the judged action is measured. This last, if moral experience is to make sense at all, must be something independent of both of the other terms.

There is hardly any field in which sensitive men have been so concerned with the distinction between appearance and reality as that of moral experience. This has led, in all generations, to the rejection of mores in favor of what is held to be really right. Good men in all ages have interpreted their moral decisions not in terms of something they have *made,* but in terms of something to which they have become sensitive. The record of experience is that the moral law is discovered rather than invented.

That ethical propositions are genuine propositions, i.e., statements capable of being true or false, is something to which we bear witness whenever we criticize either ourselves or others for doing wrong or for making wrong decisions. Our criticism implies the fact of error, but if there is the possibility of moral error there is also the possibility of moral truth. If there is a possibility of moral truth, which is what we miss when we go wrong, then ethical propositions refer to a realm which is as independent of the individual observer as are natural laws.

It helps greatly, in the effort to avoid confusion in these matters, to omit the word "absolute" and concentrate, instead, on "objective." Absolute is, unfortunately, a word with emotional overtones, which hinder understanding, especially by the suggestion of changelessness. We are not wise enough to know much about the changeless, but we do have, as human beings, a peculiar flair for trying to ascertain the objectively real. The objective reference which is inherent in all ethical judgment is fully consistent with a species of relativity, in that the precise relationship to the objective order is different in each particular situation. The duty of the married man is not the same, in certain emergencies, as is the duty of the single person. This kind of relativity is not only consistent with the notion of objectivity, but is necessitated by it. Two men starting from opposite shores to swim to an island in a stream must swim in different directions in order to reach their common goal, not because there is no objective order *but because there is.* Though the fundamental truths about what is really right no doubt remain the same, as do the fundamental truths about physics and chemistry, new and different acts are demanded when situations change if moral consistency is to be maintained.

Because modern literate people are well acquainted with what is known as sociological relativism,[7] according to which it is widely believed that the study of different cultures undermines any belief in any moral law at all, it is necessary to try to state what the major arguments for ethical realism are. By ethical realism is meant the conception according to which ethical propositions are genuine propositions, capable of being true or false. The case is strictly parallel to that for physical realism. There are the same reasons for believing in a moral order, to which our judgments may or may not conform, as there are for believing in a physical order to which our scientific judgments may or may not conform. The moon had a definite size even when men differed about it.

The first argument is dialectical. If no ethical judgment involves anything more than subjective reference, if, that is, each man who says "This is right" is merely talking about a feeling which he happens to have, we cannot escape the startling conclusion that no two people have ever differed on any ethical question. If we are referring to something confined to ourselves, as the thoroughgoing subjectivist holds, we are referring to *our* whims, and the other

---

[7] This particular relativism has been associated especially with the name and books of Professor Westermarck. In fairness to this famous scholar, it should be noted that his researches do not show the utter confusion in moral ideas, even among backward peoples, which they are popularly believed to show.

fellow is referring to *his* whims. It is as though Paul, when he says "This murder was unjustified," should say "I don't like spinach," and Peter, when he says "This murder was justified," should say "I do like spinach." *Unless there is objective reference, the one is not even denying what the other says, for they are not talking about the same thing.*

Now, it is well known that men *do* differ on ethical questions, that they differ on these more than on anything else, and that they constantly refuse to let each man be an ethical solipsist. When, to "I like murder," Peter replies, "But *you ought not to* like murder," he doesn't mean "I don't like it." Apart from some belief in ethical realism, no moral judgment was ever in error, but this is a manifest absurdity. Apart from the ascription of objective reference, ethical questions could not even be discussed, but they *are* discussed, even by confirmed subjectivists, and they have received the most careful discussion from the men, such as Plato and Kant, whom we have had most reason to honor. Ethical realism holds the field, because its denial leads to self-contradiction.[8]

The best evidence for ethical objectivity, however, is not this dialectical argument, but the fact that there is really a significant agreement in moral convictions, an agreement too great to be accounted for by coincidence. The convergence of ethical testimony is parallel to the convergence of opinion regarding physical factors. Just as people on the savage level exhibit the widest difference of judgment in reference to astronomical or geographical objects, so people on the same level exhibit considerable difference of opinion on moral questions, but, with the growth of sensitiveness and the development of the human mind, the difference of judgment concerning both the moral and the material order is greatly diminished. That there is never full agreement is easily accounted for by the fact that there are even more reasons for moral blindness than there are for physical blindness.

In our reaction against the provincialism of our earlier moral ideas we have tended to exaggerate the differences in moral judgment which appear in different cultures. What exists is neither full agreement nor absolute confusion, but *authentic development,*

[8] For a fuller statement of this interesting argument, see G. E. Moore, *Ethics,* New York, Henry Holt, 1912.

roughly parallel to what we observe in scientific development from magic to modern science. At a high level of competence the agreement among moralists is very striking. As one example of this, Dr. Bell points out that "not a single outstanding teacher of moral wisdom has failed to warn that riches tend to isolate their owners, make them petty, vulnerable, a little ridiculous."[9]

C. The Theistic Implication

The first and second steps of the moral argument are impressive, but they are manifestly incomplete. A third step is required as the conclusion of the logical structure. The entire pattern, then, is as follows:

1. Moral experience is a true revelation of the nature of reality.
2. Moral experience is meaningless unless there is an objective moral order.
3. The objective moral order is meaningless unless there is a Divine Being.

This third step is so important and so easily misunderstood that it must be considered with great care. Why not end with a moral order? Perhaps the ascription of this to God is unnecessary. That the third step is unnecessary has, indeed, been the conviction of some eminent thinkers of whom Nikolai Hartmann is representative. Why is not the moral law, in and of itself, a sufficient object of reverence?

A good way to face this question is to ask how and where a moral law could exist. We can think of natural law, like that of gravitation, existing in the material structure, but it would be absurd to think of the moral law as so existing. There is nothing moral about gravitational pull. Moreover, the moral law cannot exist in *me*. I know this for the very good reason that I frequently or habitually sense the contrast between my actions and the real right, in terms of which my actions are wrong. In like manner we must conclude that the objective moral law does not reside in the total human society, because one of the chief ways of making progress is to recognize that the group, as well as the individual, has sinned.

---

[9] Bernard Iddings Bell, *A Man Can Live*, New York, Harper, 1947, p. 36.

The only sense in which progress is possible is the recognition that there is a difference between what the generality of mankind approves and what is really right.

This means that the only locus of the moral law is a superhuman mind. That it must be a mind is clear when we realize that law has no meaning except for minds, and that it must be superhuman is clear when we realize that it cannot be ours. Therefore, the recognition of an objective moral law drives us to the belief in God, without whom that law would have no significant being. If we believe in the law we must also believe in the conditions which make the law possible.

Only a personal being can appreciate a moral law or be a moral lawgiver. Thus, the recognition of the moral law as objective leads to a personal understanding of what is deepest in reality. This insight is actually corroborated by the nature of moral experience at its highest and best, for it is a fact that the augustness felt is similar to that which is felt in connection with persons, but is not reasonable in other connections. We do not feel shame or pollution when we harm *things* or even when we transgress impersonal *laws,* but we do feel these when we violate the rights of *persons.* Why should men like Clifford and Huxley be so finicky about the "truth" if there is nothing in the world but matter and our feeble lives? Their carefulness becomes fully rational, however, *if there is One to whom their dishonesty becomes disloyalty.* The practice of the honest atheist frequently denies the conscious import of his words, because he is acting in a way which makes no sense *unless his conscious conclusions are untrue.*

The joy and wonder which men feel in the search for truth, including the quality of feeling of those scientists who think of themselves as materialists, is highly mysterious if the real world they seek to know is unconscious matter or force, for it is the *same kind of feeling we know best when there is real communication between two finite minds.* The joy that comes in the effort to know the truth and the reverence for it which makes good men spurn the temptation to deceit are not intelligible if the only consciousness is at one end of the transaction, but they are completely intelligible if truth is the meeting of mind with Mind. We act as though the latter were actually the case. We act as though there were an effort to communicate something to us, and that is why we say we understand. *It is hard to see how we can understand anything except another mind.*

It is crucial to the argument of this chapter that we make a clear distinction between a theistic *sanction* of the moral law and a theistic *explanation* of the moral law. The problem is not that of what will give the moral law power in men's lives, but that of a conception of the universe which will make the very existence of a moral law understandable. It is often supposed that the theistic emphasis on objectivity refers to sanction when, in fact, it refers to understanding. The following brilliant statement from the *Proceedings of the Aristotelian Society* is a case in point:

> They [the theists] claim that morality cannot be objectively valid without some sanction more fundamental than itself, and that the only possible sanction is the will of a personal or "super-personal" God, or universal spirit. To the argument that morality demands a sanction beyond itself, a sanction involved in the nature of the universe as a whole, I can only reply that I see no reason whatever to accept this view. Morality does indeed seem to involve a sanction beyond the particular individual mind that recognizes its authority, and even beyond the culture of any particular society, or of mankind as a whole. For these are themselves subject to moral judgment. But the sanction which lies beyond these is simply the judgment which *would* be passed in any particular moral situation by the ideally developed and unperverted mind, aware of all the relevant facts, and sensitive to all the relevant feelings and desires of all beings concerned in the particular situation. This is the sanction which we do blunderingly try to apply in actual living, according to our lights. So far as I can see, it is quite false to suppose that, unless such an ideally developed mind does actually exist, morality is without foundation. Equally false is it to hold that morality is groundless unless such an ideally developed mind is in fact almighty God, or the universal mind, and the creator and upholder of all things.[10]

What is significant to say is that Mr. Stapledon is quite right about the problem of sanction but that he does not even touch the problem of understanding, which is the chief philosophical problem in this connection. Practically, the good life might go forward even if it could be shown that God is not, but the theoretical prob-

---

[10] Olaf Stapledon, "Morality, Scepticism, and Theism," *Proceedings of the Aristotelian Society*, 1943-44, pp. 39-40.

lem would be almost intolerable for a thinking person. The mystery of life is always great, but if there is a moral order and yet no divine Mind as the locus of that order, the mystery is impenetrable, indeed.

It will be noted that the present segment of our study does not stand alone. We found in Chapter VII abundant reason to believe that nature is akin to mind and, therefore, most rationally understood if it is the product of divine Mind. We now find that moral experience is an absurdity and a delusion unless there is a Divine Mind to whom our moral obligation refers and to whom we are disloyal when we fail. Nature and moral nature are, thus, two witnesses who, without collusion, confirm one another's testimony. The relationship between these two is carefully stated by Professor Taylor as follows: "In Nature we at best see God under a disguise so heavy that it allows us to discern little more than that someone is there; within our own moral life we see Him with the mask, so to say, half fallen off." [11]

If God really is, in the sense defined earlier, i.e., if, in addition to all physical constituents, there is Ultimate Purpose, then the experience of self-conscious creatures, who are concerned with knowing what is right, becomes abundantly reasonable. "No man," as Cardinal Newman said, "will die for his own calculations; he dies for realities." When men go against some received opinion, standing alone like Luther at Worms, their action is difficult to explain except on the assumption that they have a genuine perception, however dim and faulty, of a supernatural order which is part of their total environment. *The experience is what we should expect to find if theism is true and it, therefore, constitutes part of the verification which scientific method demands.*

[11] A. E. Taylor, *op. cit.*

9

The Evidence of Aesthetic Experience

The teleology of the Universe is directed to the production of Beauty.

ALFRED NORTH WHITEHEAD

If we seek to make the cumulative argument for God's being as strong as possible we dare not omit any important area of evidence. The normal expectation is that we should be able to show what is implied in each of the major experiences which have to do with what are universally recognized as the fundamental ends of life. Therefore, we should consider beauty, just as we have considered knowledge and goodness. In spite of this obvious pattern, however, the consideration of beauty has often been omitted.[1] It is fair to assume that the chief reason for the omission is the extreme difficulty of the subject. Nearly everyone who thinks seriously about it is convinced that there *ought* to be an aesthetic argument correlative to the moral argument, but all agree that it is harder to state. The subject seems elusive. We tend to feel, in dealing with the experience of beauty, as Socrates felt at the beginning of Book VI of the *Republic*. "To declare the truth about matters of high interest which a man honors and loves among wise men who love him need occasion no fear or faltering in his mind; but to carry on an argument when you are yourself only a hesitating inquirer, which is my condition, is a dangerous and slippery thing." Difficult as the subject is it must, nevertheless, be tried. It seems a shame to use a rope of only three strands when there might be four or five of approximately equal strength.

[1] Thus, it is not included in the excellent marshaling of evidence provided by A. E. Taylor in *Essays Catholic and Critical,* in his essay "The Vindication of Religion."

A. The Experience of Beauty

It is difficult to see why we should attribute less validity to the experience of mind in art than we attribute to the experience of mind in science. The artistic experience is far older and more truly universal, being by no means confined to professional artists or critics. The oldest monuments to human genius indicate an early flowering of artistic ability. Since the same man may be an able scientist and an intense lover of beauty, there is no reason to suppose that one of these approaches to reality is less revealing than the other. Certainly they are not incompatible. This becomes especially evident when we realize that the two methods actually support each other in that they point in the same direction.

In the *Phaedrus* we are told that the Form of beauty, alone among all Forms, appears in this world as it really is. There is, says Plato in the seventh epistle, a final flash, entirely divorced from the logical and mathematical processes of thought which necessarily precede it. It involves both immediacy and separation from self. A man's most unself-conscious moments are those in which the apprehension of beauty occurs. This is the experience which poets and artists have recorded both voluminously and repeatedly. It is surely reasonable to pay attention to those experiences which are uniformly recognized as among the noblest.

Among the brilliant insights of the late Professor Whitehead, none was more striking than his conclusion about the relationship between truth and beauty. In view of his scientific and mathematical training, it might reasonably have been supposed that Whitehead would have held truth to be the more fundamental notion, but, in fact, he held that the notion of beauty was the wider and more fundamental of the two. Truth is, of course, important, but it is important in only one way, that of the relations of Appearance to Reality. Truth refers to propositions and only to propositions, but the scope of beauty is vastly wider. "Beauty," says Whitehead, "is the internal conformation of the various items of experience with each other, for the production of maximum effectiveness. Beauty thus concerns the interrelations of the various components of Reality, and also the interrelations of the various components of

Appearance, and also, the relations of Appearance to Reality." [2] This is why, he says, any part of experience can be beautiful. It is because the relations involved are so comprehensive.

Such an analysis supports powerfully the logical structure we are seeking to erect. We are trying to learn the truth about the world, and in doing so we ought to appeal to the most fundamental aspects of experience which we can find. Truth always requires corroboration, but beauty, wherever we find it, is self-justifying. A truth-relation does not necessarily lead to the promotion of beauty, but beauty always gives us more truth about the universe because it adds to the corroboration of a thesis. "Thus Beauty," concludes Whitehead, "is left as the one aim which by its very nature is self-justifying." There are few facts about our world more arresting and more revealing than that of the way in which this self-justifying and unnecessary beauty is spilled about with such prodigality. Our philosophical task is to try to see what this means.

We begin to get a hint of the acknowledged uniqueness of the experience of beauty when we recognize the essential chasm between art and utility. Most actions and most thoughts are deeply utilitarian. We do not, in ordinary life, see *things in themselves;* instead, we normally see them in relation to purposes to the fulfillment of which they may lead, sooner or later. The artist may be the only creature who sees an object, not as a means to something other than itself but as an end in itself. An artist, it has been suggested in modern philosophy, is a person whose feeling for natural objects is essentially the same as the feeling which the nonartist has for works of art. The artist sees significance in a scene which others cannot see, save through the instrumentality of his production, but this he accomplishes by the omission of the irrelevant. He allows the beauty to emerge!

In the appreciation of beauty the physical senses are involved, but they are by no means sufficient to the aesthetic result. Always there is a process of thought in which some are more gifted or disciplined than others. Something of this occurs not only in the mind of the artist who produces, but also in that of each person who truly appreciates what is there. Only a person who is to some

[2] Alfred North Whitehead, *Adventures of Ideas,* New York, Macmillan, 1933, p. 341.

extent a poet can know poetry when he hears it. Art is not a mere imitation of nature, but neither does it add something wholly foreign to it. The former would be mere photography, while the latter would be grotesque. The artistic task, in contrast to both of these enterprises, is that of revealing beauty by the use of that within the mind which is the aesthetic ideal. In the inspired words of Ernst Cassirer, art *"discovers* the beautiful in nature by measuring it with a new and independent standard."[3]

Though, as Cassirer suggests, the appreciation of beauty is closer to *discovery* than to *invention,* even discovery is not an adequate expression of what occurs, since this word suggests that the artist is active in relation to a wholly passive environment. It is, instead, as though the artist did not *choose,* but was *chosen.* The relation is not that of calm and deliberate choice, but of submission to a spell.

> He holds him with his glittering eye—
> The Wedding Guest stood still.

The beautiful is not primarily something which we seek, but something, rather, which claims us. A. C. Bradley's penetrating analysis of the poetic experience is illuminating at this point. "Pure poetry," he writes, "is not the decoration of a preconceived and clearly defined matter; it springs from the creative impulse of a vague imaginative mass pressing for development and definition. If the poet already knew exactly what he meant to say, why should he write the poem? The poem would, in fact, already be written. For only its completion can reveal, even to him, exactly what he wanted. When he began and while he was at work, he did not possess his meaning; it possessed him."[4] We may thus speak appropriately of "beauty possession."

The situation is similar to that described in Francis Thompson's *Hound of Heaven.* "He on whom Beauty has cast her spell is not his own master, though in his bondage he finds freedom. He must listen and gaze till his release is given."[5]

[3] Ernst Cassirer, *Determinism and Indeterminism in Modern Physics,* trans. by O. T. Benfey, Yale University Press, 1956, p. 206.
[4] A. C. Bradley, *Poetry for Poetry's Sake,* New York, Macmillan, 1909.
[5] William Temple, *Mens Creatrix,* New York, Macmillan, 1935, p. 128.

B. The Objectivity of Beauty

Though aesthetic experience necessarily involves the external world, in both art and nature, and though the ordinary observer supposes the beauty to reside in objects external to the observer's mind, there has been, especially in late years, a strong tendency to suppose that aesthetic experience tells us nothing about the nature of the world at all, but only about the shifting subjective feelings of certain people. The subjectivistic interpretation of aesthetics is similar to the subjectivistic interpretation of ethics and is based upon similar arguments, which we have already examined. This interpretation may be simply stated, in Professor Montague's words, as the conviction that "the adjective *beautiful* is nothing but a somewhat solemn and decorative synonym for the adjective *pleasant.*" [6]

The notion that the sense of beauty is wholly subjective, telling us nothing about ultimate reality or the nature of the universe, receives at least superficial support in the fact that standards of beauty seem to change according to fashion. That this is true of clothing is common knowledge, inasmuch as what seemed to be suitable apparel only a few years ago now seems comical. That such change is by no means limited to clothing is apparent when we think of the rise, in each generation, of some new school of art or of poetry. Once Tennyson was almost universally admired, but more recently it has been the mode to belittle him. No doubt the more enduring verdict will rest somewhere between these extremes, but in the meantime there is no stability of judgment.

The fact that fashion plays a part, and, indeed, a great part, in aesthetic enjoyment is generally admitted and needs little documentation. Those who hold that there is an objective factor in the sense of beauty have been as quick to admit the fact of change as have been their subjectivist opponents. Indeed, one of the best available statements of the effect of aesthetic instability is to be found in Lord Balfour's chapter, "Naturalism and Aesthetic," in *The Foundations of Belief.* But Lord Balfour, like so many other philosophers who have analyzed the experience of beauty, found

[6] W. P. Montague, *The Way of Things,* p. 226.

that there was a significant remainder which mere fashion could not explain.

It is evident that the same argument, used in the immediately preceding chapter concerning objective reference in ethics, applies here as well. If all experience of beauty is merely subjective, we find ourselves in a position in which some people like rice pudding and other people do not like rice pudding, which is then the conclusion of the matter. In short, it would mean that no two people have ever differed or ever can differ on a question of beauty. When one person says the Philadelphia City Hall is more beautiful than the Parthenon and another person denies this, they are not, on the subjectivist theory, arguing at all. One man is telling about his *insides* and the other is telling about *his* insides. If someone wishes to contend that the works of a contemporary leader of a dance band are aesthetically superior to the works of Beethoven, there is, subjectively speaking, no suitable rejoinder.

This situation, however, is too absurd to be accepted by thoughtful critics as the last word on the question. The fact is that people *do argue* about aesthetic judgments, and the subjectivists argue as much as anybody else. A theory so markedly at variance with practice, including the practice of the most critical and sensitive natures, is rightly under strong suspicion. Regardless of their philosophical position, those who take beauty most seriously tend to hold that those who fail to see what they see really *ought* to see it, and with sufficient clarification of sight *would* see it. The maxim *de gustibus non disputandum est* is apparently believed by nobody, and has lived only because it is a kind of joke. Far from taste being beyond dispute, it is the subject of endless dispute. Conversation would be dull, indeed, if the maxim were taken seriously, which fortunately it never is.

Kant goes beyond the mere rejection of the familiar maxim and points out the imperative note which is essential to aesthetic judgment, a note similar to that which we found in moral judgment. To assert that a thing is beautiful is to blame those who do not agree. If I am right, they are wrong. How seriously Kant's dictum should be taken is suggested by the estimate of a contemporary philosopher, the distinguished realist Professor Montague, who says, "It seems to me that Immanuel Kant, in his theory of esthetics set forth in *The Critique of Judgment,* dealt more justly and more penetratingly with the two aspects of beauty than any other philos-opher." [7] The relevant passage from Kant's pen follows the assertion that it would be laughable of a man to justify himself by saying, "This object is beautiful *for me."*

Many things may have for him charm and pleasantness; no one troubles himself at that; but if he gives out anything as beautiful, he supposes in others the same satisfaction—he judges not merely for himself, but for every one, and speaks of beauty as if it were a property of things. Hence he says "The *thing* is beautiful"; and he does not count on the agreement of others with this his judgment of satisfaction, because he has found this agreement several times before, but he *demands* it of them. He blames them if they judge otherwise and he denies them taste, which he nevertheless requires from them. Here we cannot say that each man has his own particular taste. For this would be as much as to say that there is no taste whatever; i.e., no aesthetical judgment, which can make a rightful claim upon every one's assent.[8]

When people dispute about questions of taste it is clear that they are not concerned with the statistical calculation of pleasure. At the present time it is possibly true that the number of Americans who find pleasure in singing commercials is greater than the number who find pleasure in the poetry of T. S. Eliot, but this is not generally regarded as settling the question. In other words, we habitually distinguish between what men actually think beautiful and what they *would* find beautiful if their area of awareness were deepened and broadened. This implies that the change of fashion is a change in the observer, but not a change in that which is observed, namely, the beauty itself.

Such an implication of our universal experience is greatly strengthened by the consideration that people actually do change in their tastes, with developing maturity, in ways which we can hardly interpret as other than progressive ways. It is a common experience for young people, as well as some older ones, to get their greatest joy in music from obvious tunes like "Home on the Range," but, with expanding interests, they discover a keener

---

[7] *Ibid.,* p. 132.

[8] Immanuel Kant, *Critique of Judgment,* trans. by J. H. Bernard, 2d ed., rev., New York, Macmillan, 1914, I, I, 7.

joy in musical productions which are far more complex and much less obvious. The same kind of development occurs in the other arts and in the appreciation of nature. If subjectivism is an adequate account of the sense of beauty, this is mere *change;* it cannot be interpreted as *progress* unless there is objective reference in aesthetic judgment. If there is any way in which the critic's appreciation of beauty is superior to that of the savage, subjectivism is thereby refuted and rejected.

A further relevant consideration is the fact that aesthetic judgment actually gives far more evidence of permanence than superficially appears. In spite of the constant arguments about contemporary works, there are many judgments which are not ordinarily disputed or doubted by persons who have given the matter serious attention. Though the contemporary poet is on trial, Shakespeare is not on trial. We debate contemporary art, but we do not seriously debate classic art. That is why there are any classics at all. If we take into consideration a long time span, there is far more agreement in aesthetics than there is in science.

The observation that great works of art are more nearly date-less than are great scientific conclusions seems startling at first, but the explanation is easily available. The explanation is that scientific conclusions are necessarily interconnected, each depending upon a host of former generalizations. If one of these generalizations is proved inadequate, as knowledge grows, the other generalizations dependent on it are thereby affected. All kinds of laws required radical restatement after the Copernican hypothesis was accepted. Art, on the other hand, is always individual and particular. It is not a generalization and, therefore, is not dependent upon the general context or world view. A change in astronomical theories does not affect Michelangelo's statues in the least. The nature of all art, and not merely painting, is symbolized by the frame which frees art from its setting, making it relatively independent of contextual change.

There is no serious dispute about the merit of Phidias or Rembrandt or Dante. These men are now practically free from the irrational changes of artistic fashion; their works move us as they moved the first to enjoy them. Sometimes the great work of art, if it is truly great, may need interpretation or translation, but it is never merely quaint. If it be said that this permanence of aesthetic judgment is to be explained by the prestige value of a long past, according to which men praise the work of the masters because they are ashamed not to do so, an adequate reply is that the famous works are often *rediscovered* with manifest excitement by successive generations, for whom lip service is changed into enduring gratitude. Such a rediscovery is the whole point of Keats's sonnet, "On First Looking into Chapman's Homer." Not only is the testimony of John Keats impressive, but this is augmented immeasurably by the experience of the thousands who have loved the sonnet because it has expressed what they also have known but have not been able to say so well. What Keats discovered about Homer, through the instrumentality of Chapman's translation, others have discovered about Bach or Velásquez or the anonymous architects of the Middle Ages.

In our modern society we are inclined to suppose that the scientific experience of men's minds really tells us something about the external order, because scientists corroborate one another, while we are inclined to suppose that the aesthetic experience of men's minds tells us nothing about the external order, because in this field there is no corroboration. Actually, however, the truth is the reverse of the popular opinion. It is one of the great merits of the philosophizing of Archbishop Temple that he has called attention to the point that science does not have the advantage over art which is so often alleged. "What scientific theory," he asks, "has the security of these works of art? The Newtonian Law of Gravitation seemed till yesterday to be assured beyond the risk of modification. Yet now, though the repute of Newton himself remains as well assured as that of Milton, his system is displaced by those of curvilinear space; while no amount of modern free verse displaces Milton's *Sonnet on His Blindness*. It takes longer for the aesthetic judgment to become stable than for the scientific, but when it reaches stability it also achieves finality as the other does not." [9] It is not maintained that there is ever *full* agreement concerning beauty, but there is far more agreement than is often supposed and there is far too much to be explained on purely

9 *Nature, Man and God*, p. 159.

subjective grounds, unless we are prepared to accept the miracle of coincidence.

The endurance of judgment about works of art is also illustrated in reference to natural beauty. There is really no argument about the beauty of the Grand Canyon of the Colorado or of the Yosemite Valley or the English Lakes, and it is difficult to believe that the mere desire to be fashionable has been sufficient to take so many to Switzerland again and again. That there should be something considerably less than perfect agreement on the subject of beauty is what we should expect, but the agreement is too great to neglect.

A further important consideration is that the appreciation of beauty is found outside the experience of man, playing a part in the lives of many animals. That men thrill to beauty in a thousand ways might, conceivably, mean nothing more than a human idiosyncrasy, something alien to the rest of reality and possibly pathetic, but if we find the response to beauty in various levels of nature, it is hard to avoid the conclusion that here we have a genuine insight into the nature of the real.

C. THE METAPHYSICAL SIGNIFICANCE

What is the metaphysical significance of aesthetic experience? In our effort to answer this question we are driven to the conception of the Divine Artist. How else can we account for the objective element in beauty? The heart of our contention is found in the recognition that aesthetic experience always involves a recognition of purpose. Let the reader consider what occurs when, in an art gallery, he is mystified by some unfamiliar work. It baffles him, but he cannot tear himself away. Finally, perhaps with the help of a friend, the picture ceases to baffle and the observer says, with satisfaction, "Oh, yes. I see." It is then that aesthetic pleasure, as distinct from mere sensuous pleasure, begins. It is not that the observer suddenly learns what the artist was trying to *say*, but rather what he was trying to *do*. Joy comes with an understanding of meaning and purpose. Mind, for a moment at least, matches mind.

As was mentioned earlier, the artist, as artist, is not utilitarian, but this does not mean that he lacks purpose. To have a purpose is not the same as to have an ulterior motive. Though he may be a successful propagandist, the man who tries to do us good or to modify our opinions has missed the aesthetic enterprise. The artist, on the other hand, is one who has seen something of such intrinsic worth that he must do something about it. He is as far from purposelessness as he is from mere interest in utility.

In his Gifford Lectures, *Theism and Humanism*, Lord Balfour considered the situation in which there is a purely accidental or purposeless combination of colors. Let us say we were to look at a color pattern produced by machinery, when this is something unintended by the maker of the machine. Or let us say that a dog's wagging tail dips into colors and splashes them on a nearby canvas. We might consider the result ingenious or striking, but we should not respond to it as we do to a work of conscious art. The reason is not the tiresome one that we must find a "lesson" in our art, but rather that there must be a matching of mind with mind, which is not possible when the cause of the production is accidental. "And this is not," says Balfour, "because we are unable to estimate works of art as they are *in themselves,* not because we must needs buttress up our opinions by extraneous and irrelevant considerations; but rather because a work of art requires an artist, not merely in the order of natural causation, but as a matter of aesthetic necessity. It conveys a message which is valueless to the recipient unless it be understood by the sender." [10]

To be akin is not the same as to be identical. As we come to understand something of the nature of reality we are increasingly conscious of our smallness and inadequacy, and yet we are made aware that we are not complete strangers. The lock is large while the human key is small, but sometimes the key fits, and it is difficult to believe that this is accidental. With the discovery that the counterpart of the principle of the mind's activity may be found beyond itself comes a sense of grandeur, but without bewilderment. Small as we are, we belong!

One of the best reasons for considering truth and beauty together, as both Whitehead and Temple do, is that the pursuit of each of these gives the same intimation of kinship, and thus a tentative conclusion is greatly strengthened. When a scientist, working in his

[10] Arthur James Balfour, *Theism and Humanism*, New York, Doran, 1915, p. 67.

laboratory, thinks *truly,* his calculations and predictions are matched by the actual events as apprehended both by himself and by others. This is what we mean when we say that truth is more an adverb than a noun. The fact that we can devise formulae which unlock secrets and facilitate new productions means that mind finds its counterpart in reality. The successful formula brings great delight, the same kind of delight we know when we master an ancient tongue and finally understand what the message is.

We already know, in dealing with human productions, that there is an artist responsible for the art, but whether there is an Artist responsible for natural beauty is what we are trying to determine. In this connection we are forced to rely on the reported experience of sensitive persons. How do those feel who have been greatly moved by the beauty of ocean and mountains and starry sky? Lord Balfour's own testimony is helpful:

> The feeling for natural beauty cannot, any more than scientific curiosity, rest satisfied with the world of sensuous appearance. But the reasons for its discontent are different. Scientific curiosity hungers for a knowledge of causes; causes which are physical, and, if possible, measurable. Our admiration for natural beauty has no such needs. It cares not to understand either the physical theories which explain what it admires, or the psychological theories which explain its admiration. It does not deny the truth of the first, nor (within due limits) the sufficiency of the second. But it requires more. It feels itself belittled unless conscious purpose can be found somewhere in its pedigree. Physics, and psycho-physics, by themselves, suffice not. It longs to regard beauty as a revelation—a revelation from spirit to spirit, not from one kind of atomic agitation to the "psychic" accompaniment of another. On this condition only can its highest values be maintained.[11]

If men do not feel this, it is hard to know what more is to be said, except that it has received the corroboration of other sensitive minds. Speaking of Balfour's testimony, Temple testifies as follows: "For what my own experience may be worth, it entirely confirms his interpretation." [12] As is well known, this is also the interpretation of Wordsworth as expressed in his *Lines Composed a Few Miles above Tintern Abbey.* Wordsworth was making his own

11 *Ibid.,* p. 90.
12 *Nature, Man and God,* p. 253.

testimony about natural beauty as genuine communion, which is not possible except between minds, when he wrote:

> And I have felt
> A presence that disturbs me with the joy
> Of elevated thoughts.

Here the poet, like the scientist, is not satisfied to rest with appearances; he delves deeper. The important fact about the testimony for our present purpose, however, lies not in Wordsworth's personal testimony, but in the response which his poem has elicited. *Millions have strengthened the testimony by their satisfaction in the poem, thus adding to the fellowship of verification.*

Since we are forced to start from where we are, we are wise to learn all that we can from the human production of beauty which occurs in all forms of artistic endeavor. It is a great advantage to know, at one point in the vast universe, how beauty is actually produced. We, thereby, have something comparable to the insight into creation which comes from the production of synthetics in chemistry. In both situations we have, as it were, an inside view.

What we learn is that the closest artificial approach to the beauty of nature, which painting provides, comes not at random, but by disciplined effort and by patient thought. The more the effort is truly thoughtful the better it reveals what is already existent, though not revealed to the unprepared. Thus, it is mind, not mechanism or accident or chance, that begins to unlock the secret beauty of the world. We know very well what random sound is, because we have it in radio jamming, and it is not beautiful by any standard. This is because it is a meaningless jumble of sounds. If we go to the other extreme and listen, as a trained choir renders Palestrina's *Missa Iste Confessor,* we begin to have a slight hint of how beauty is a self-justifying expression of *mind.* It could not be accidental; it comes from thought. If the world is the creation of Infinite Mind, the prodigious beauty of the world makes sense. In short, if theism is true, the aesthetic experience of natural beauty is what we should expect to find.

10

The Evidence of Historical Experience

All religion is history.

MARTIN BUBER

All four of the evidences for theism thus far presented are based on human experiences, but all of them are experiences in which the object is other than human. In science we study the natural order; in ethics we study the moral order; in aesthetics we study the beauty of the world, and when we come to consider religious experience we face the fact that God may be known directly. In the present chapter the logical structure is radically different, in that the object of interest is the total human story. That there is a teleological aspect of the natural order has long been affirmed. Is there, likewise, a teleological aspect of the historical order, an aspect which requires the being of God as its explanation?

A. The Logic of Events

The shift in emphasis from ideas to events is a striking feature of the contemporary theological scene. Once the greatest attention was given to the elaboration of a rational system, such as a man might develop in the privacy of his study, but this is the case no longer. Today the major tendency in Western religious scholarship is one which not only includes but accentuates the wonder of the story. This is chiefly because of the renewed appreciation of the Bible, an appreciation which has come in a way that could not have been predicted a few years ago. Respect for the Biblical message, far from declining as a result of literary scholarship, has grown remarkably in the recent past, and it has grown among those who are normally classified as intellectuals. The renewed interest in the Bible has led to a heightened respect for the Hebrew genius, for the Bible is largely Hebrew in tone. Even the New Testament books, which constitute a minority, are deeply influenced by the Hebrew pattern and include numerous quotations, particularly from the Psalms, from Deuteronomy, and from Isaiah.

Steeped as we are in the philosophical temper of ancient Greece, it comes as something of a shock to see how the Hebrew people, who had such a remarkable religious genius, upheld their faith. In the sense that Greeks philosophized, the Hebrews hardly philosophized at all. They produced nothing remotely similar to the cosmological and teleological arguments for the being of God, and they made relatively little reference to God in nature. The few references which they did make are well known, chiefly because they are exceptional. That is why we remember the admonition of the prophet Amos, "Seek Him that maketh the Pleiades and Orion." Psalm XIX, devoted partly to nature and partly to the moral law, is striking not because it is characteristic, but because it is rare. "It is a remarkable fact," wrote Pascal, "that no canonical writer has ever used Nature to prove God." Of major philosophical problems, only one, the problem of evil, is taken seriously by any Biblical writer. This problem is given careful treatment in the Book of Job, but such treatment is found in no other part of the Bible.

The relative absence of philosophical treatment does not mean that the Bible has no way of validating the faith which it espouses. It does have a way, and that way is the simple witness of historical events. The people of Israel early became convinced, not that they had chosen Yahweh but that Yahweh had chosen them and had personally led them all the way. If they were challenged they merely told and retold the story. How could you doubt the reality of Yahweh if you could see, through hundreds of years of history, what He had done for this chosen people?

The story, as told, is not always a pretty one. It is profoundly realistic, including, in the graphic account, unhappy and tragic as well as fortunate events. It abounds with the records of the lives of evil and imperfect human beings. Instead of suffering and failure being minimized, these are stressed as evidences of God's way of chastising even His chosen people. The bad kings far outnumbered the good ones, and most of the prophets took a gloomy view of their own times.

Though many contemporary thinkers have helped to draw attention to this aspect of Biblical theology,[1] no philosopher has understood better the reliance on history in the search for truth than has Martin Buber, who, in his distinguished academic career, both in Germany and in Israel, has always stressed the logic of events. "In the biblical religion, which is a history religion," writes Buber, "there is no nature in the Greek, the Chinese, or the modern Occidental sense. What is shown us of nature is stamped with history."[2] Buber's strong emphasis has been an important factor in popularizing the vivid theological term *Heilsgeschichte,* meaning "redemptive history." "History," says his editor, Will Herberg, "is the texture of reality, the texture of the divine-human encounter, the texture of revelation and redemption. It has stamped nature with its mark, and in the 'consummation' it will finally overcome and absorb it."[3]

The chief evidence for the existence of Yahweh, according to His worshipers, was not history in general, but their own history. "Look at the record, and see for yourself," they said over and over. They were a despised people in bondage in Egypt, but Yahweh helped them to go free. He raised up leaders while they were still a feeble folk, led them through the wilderness, helped them to cross the Jordan and set up their homes in a goodly land, in spite of violent opposition. Finally, He aided them in establishing a kingdom of their own, even against His own desire. Of all this development, the Exodus from Egypt, which, they were convinced, was a sheer miracle of deliverance, was the central symbol. Far from having recourse to arguments such as the Greek thinkers encouraged, the Israelites would have considered such arguments abstract or even tiresome.

---

[1] Christian as well as Jewish scholars have swelled the chorus. Thus, G. Ernest Wright's *God Who Acts* is subtitled "Biblical Theology as Recital." Alan Richardson has dealt repeatedly with this theme, while in Charles Clayton Morrison's *What Is Christianity?* the nature of the faith is identified, in large measure, with its story. The hymn "Tell me the old, old story" seems no longer quaint.

[2] *Moses,* Oxford, East and West Library, 1946, pp. 78, 79.

[3] *The Writings of Martin Buber,* New York, Meridian Books, 1956, pp. 32, 33. The idea of *Heilsgeschichte* is carefully explained by Will Herberg, "Biblical Faith as Heilsgeschichte," in *The Christian Scholar,* vol. 39, No. 1, March, 1956, pp. 25-31.

What was the need of arguing about your God if you could see that
He had helped you?

This historical appeal is perhaps the chief key to the understanding of the Old Testament. It is no accident that so many of the
books of the Hebrew Scripture are *historical,* since the entire com-
pilation was originally conceived as a history of Yahweh's dealing
with His people. The Bible as a whole is a Book of Acts. "The
crucial truths revealed in the Bible," writes President Mackay in a
remarkable chapter, "are not timeless truths about God and man;
they are rather historical truths, truths regarding events which took
place in time but which were invested by God with eternal significance." [4]

Eventually the story was made to reach back to the origin of the
earth and its inhabitants, but the most important part of the story
covers only a few hundred years, reaching its climax in the glorious
reigns of David and Solomon. Later events, dealing with exile and
restoration, were naturally added to complete the story, while the
books of the prophets furnished side lights on these events. The
poetical and wisdom works were thrown in for good measure, on the
supposition that they had been produced in the period before the
decline of prophecy.

The history of Israel, as understood by the Israelites themselves,
was far from a smooth progress to victory or to success. On the contrary, this history was full of backsliding, disloyalty and deceit. But
those who heard and retold the story for posterity thought they
could discern through it all the guiding hand of God, chastising
His people for unbelief and wickedness, giving ultimate reward for
faithful devotion, and always loving them. Thus, the Book of
Deuteronomy makes Moses say:

> . . . thou hast seen how that the Lord thy God bare thee, as a man
> doth bear his son, in all the way that ye went, until ye came to this place.
> Yet in this thing ye did not believe the Lord your God, who went in the
> way before you to search you out a place to pitch your tents, in fire by
> night, to show you by what way ye should go and in a cloud by day.
> And the Lord heard the voice of your words, and was wroth, and sware,
> saying, Surely there shall not one of these men of this evil generation see

[4] John Mackay, *A Preface to Christian Theology,* New York, Macmillan, 1941,
p. 93.

that good land, which I sware to give unto your fathers, save Caleb the son of Jephunneh; he shall see it, and to him will I give the land that he hath trodden upon, and to his children, because he hath wholly followed the Lord.[5]

This might do very well for a people who were in the midst of the deliverance, as the associates of Moses were, but what about succeeding generations? When they should become curious, what kind of interpretation or apologetic should be given them to convince them? The answer was a simple one: Tell the old story again.

Then shalt thou say unto thy son, We were Pharaoh's bondsmen in Egypt; and the Lord brought us out of Egypt with a mighty hand! And the Lord showed signs and wonders, great and sore, upon Egypt, upon Pharaoh, and upon all his household, before our eyes!
And he brought us out from thence, that he might bring us in, and give us the land which he sware unto our fathers.[6]

Here is a philosophy of history according to which events are shot through with meaning. History is a theater of moral judgment, and the entire process points to the presence of a Guiding Hand. It was too wonderful, they supposed, to have happened accidentally.
Partly, no doubt, because they were still so largely under Hebrew influences, the earliest defenders of the truth of Christianity emphasized events rather than abstract ideas, sometimes speaking slightingly of the latter. Thus, it is no accident that the book which holds a central and, in many ways, dominating position in the New Testament is the Book of Acts. This is the astonishing account of the victory of the early Church against incredible odds. The exciting fact is that it did not pass away, as Gamaliel said it might, but that it endured, as he said it would, if it were *of God*. The characteristic Hebrew logic of events was put in a single sentence by this wise Pharisee in the council when he said, "If this plan or this undertaking is of men it will fail; but if it is of God you will not be able to overthrow them." [7]
Some of the "acts" recorded were sermons in which the major appeal was to other acts. Thus, at Pentecost, Peter's sermon was

[5] Deut. 1:31-36.
[6] Deut. 6:21-23.
[7] Acts 5:38, 39. R.S.V.

largely a recital of events, and, since this was so, the natural response of the people was not "What shall we think?" but "What shall we do?" [8] The defense of the first Christian martyr, Stephen, began with the ancient story: "Men, brethren and fathers, hearken; the God of glory appeared unto our father Abraham, when he was in Mesopotamia." [9] And so the evidence is that of telling what God *did* for His people, ending with the coming of Christ and his rejection at the hands of the very people who constitute the martyr's audience. Paul of Tarsus, though obviously a well-educated man of the world, who could quote Greek poets, used the same narrative approach when he gave his great sermon at Antioch. "Men of Israel," he began, "the God of this people of Israel chose our fathers and exalted the people when they dwelt as strangers in the land of Egypt, and with an high arm brought he them out of it." [10] Again the story was brought to a climax with the life, death and resurrection of Christ.

Though this emphasis on events rather than mere ideas is seen more strikingly and abundantly in the Bible than anywhere else, it is not limited to the Bible. As the Apostles' Creed was developed in early Christian centuries, its major items of belief were not abstract ideas, but were, in large measure, a recital of what was said to have occurred. The characteristic terms of the creed are not nouns, but verbs, such as *born, suffered, crucified* and *rose*. From the point of view of most Greek philosophy, this is shockingly worldly.

Evidence of the truly shocking character of the new message is shown by the reaction of the Epicurean and Stoic philosophers to Paul's message on Mars Hill, as recorded in the seventeenth chapter of Acts. If Paul had argued systematically for immortality, his hearers would not have been surprised or repulsed. After all, Plato had done that very well four hundred years earlier. But Paul merely recounted, as a fact, that Christ had *risen*. It was then that, as the account says, "some mocked." Because we have been so deeply steeped in Greek mentality, many in the modern world also have mocked. Now, however, the intellectual change is so great that one of the ablest of modern scholars can say, "The gospel is good news

8 Acts 2:37.
9 Acts 7:2.
10 Acts 13:16, 17.

of God, good news not so much concerning God's eternal nature in the abstract, but concerning God's action in time through which His eternal nature is expressed and understood." [11]

One important result of this emphasis upon events as the heart of the apologetic effort is the current insistence upon the historicity of Jesus Christ. There was a time when, while a few hostile critics asserted that Christ was a mythical person who never lived at all, many more said that historicity made no difference. The teachings, it was commonly maintained, were eternally valid, regardless of who said them or what he did. We understand much of the change in mentality when we realize that it is, apparently, impossible to find a serious thinker who would make such an assertion now. Not only the *fact*, but also the *importance*, of Christ's historicity is affirmed today as seldom before. There is today abundant evidence that Christ really lived and a deep conviction that this is the heart of the good news.[12] A generation ago it was popular to think of Jesus primarily as a teacher, with little reference to his deeds, but the entire climate of opinion has changed in this regard. What impresses us now is something that occurred in the days of such men as Tiberius Caesar and Pontius Pilate. Mere teaching we may dismiss, but it is hard to dismiss an actual occurrence.

B. Religion and History

In a way not found in other forms of human experience the involvement of religion in history is intrinsic rather than accidental. Herein, for example, lies one of the greatest contrasts between religion and science. Science is not deeply concerned with history, because it can, without serious loss, be abstracted from its past, but a religion abstracted from its past would be practically nothing at all. The dependence of religion upon history is analogous to the dependence of science upon mathematics. In large measure this difference is the fundamental difference between ancient Palestine and ancient Greece.

Old science, even that of two or three generations ago, almost

[11] H. G. Wood, *Christianity and the Nature of History,* Cambridge University Press, 1938, p. 29.
[12] Cf. H. G. Wood, *Did Christ Really Live?* London, Student Christian Movement Press, 1938.

always seems to us to be bad science, but old religion may be good religion, indeed. Science seems to be engaged in the denunciation of its ancestors, while religion seems to be engaged characteristically in the support and confirmation of its ancestors. We can put this in another way by saying that religion has classics, as science does not. Augustine's *Confessions* and the *Private Prayers* of Lancelot Andrewes are quite as valuable in the twentieth century as when they were written, and are still widely used, because the reported experiences are independent of technological changes. These works are classics in the sense that they have universal appeal, not limited to one time, location or class. Science has interesting older books, landmarks on the way, but they are now outmoded and have, for the most part, only antiquarian interest. The characteristic ancient scientific treatise seems quaint, whereas the characteristic ancient religious treatise seems contemporary. Pascal, we may suppose, was equally intelligent in his scientific and his religious writings, but, whereas the former are *interesting*, the latter are far more than interesting, being quite as valuable now as when they were written three centuries ago, and far more widely read.

Such considerations lead us to suppose that science is subject to progress, with all the attendant advantages and disadvantages, whereas religion is not subject to progress. Yet this conclusion is not wholly true. There has been genuine progress in religion since the dawn of history, *but it is not the same kind of progress* that science presents. The scientific spirit cannot come to maturity except in a highly complex society, enjoying a well-defined division of labor, but the religious spirit can come to maturity in a life close to the simplicity of the desert. In fact, insight into eternal verities may be hindered by a busy modern society and greatly facilitated by relative simplicity of organization.

The progress in religion which is most striking and most instructive is that which has come in the Judeo-Christian stream of development. Here we have a record which, fortunately, has been kept with unusual faithfulness, and which tells the story of emerging theism from early nature worship to the maturity of the Christian faith. It is important to see the entire stream as one spiritual movement. The Hebrew development, standing alone, is an unfinished building, while the Christian faith, standing alone, is a structure without a foundation. Each needs the other. One of the most fortunate decisions made by the early Christians was the decision to retain the Hebrew Canon as part of their Holy Scriptures, along with the specifically Christian writings. Thus, they provided historical roots to what might otherwise have seemed to be a mere contemporary speculation. One result of this arrangement is that great numbers of Christians are far better acquainted with the deeds of Hebrew heroes than with the deeds of any of their own remote ancestors.

There was a time when it seemed preposterous to suggest that a series of events which once occurred in Palestine might be of cosmic significance. That time is now gone, precisely because we have been reawakened to the revelatory value of history. The very conception of historical progress is a creation of Christianity, strikingly different from the cyclical conceptions which were dominant in the Greek and Roman worlds before the formulation of Christian thought.

Religion differs from most other human pursuits in that it is constrained to make reference to the dimension of time. The leading of God which is apparent at the moment may be delusory, because it may be transitory, but the more we extend our temporal reference the more we enlarge our field of verification. This is why the appeal to prophecy and to its fulfillment is not obscurantist, but highly intelligent, for it is by such means that we can discern historical coherence. The combination, for example, of Isaiah 53 and Acts 8 is powerful. Though it would be unwise to neglect the single moment of ecstasy, we cannot depend wholly upon it when such ecstasy is abstracted from the temporal process. Western religion tends to stress the effort to discern a purposive pattern running through years and centuries of events rather than the isolated experience. Herein lies one great advantage of the Judaic over the Buddhic religious tradition. The Buddhist scriptures tell stories, particularly those which recount supposedly factual incidents in the life of Buddha, but they are for the most part separated stories. The people of ancient Israel, by contrast, were not interested in separated incidents, but were deeply impressed by an emerging pattern which, since it was certainly not of their making, they felt bound to ascribe to the Living God. They were not concerned primarily with the individual believer, but with the remarkable preservation of a people. That they were preserved is, indeed, astonishing, when we consider how they were surrounded by powerful and ruthless enemies and that the area which they occupied was seldom larger than Vermont.

The truth is that they *did survive* and have had a continuous existence to this day, whereas their contemporaries among the nations were lost, one by one. In view of the facts that it was through this people that the amazing development of prophecy took place and that it was among this people that Christ was born, the conviction that a special people was kept alive for a special purpose is far from absurd. When, in one of his famous conversations, Disraeli was asked what reason he had to believe in God, his reply was as brief as it was prompt. "The Jews," he said.[13]

An example of how providence may be seen in the long run, though it is not always evident in the short run, is seen also in the triumph of Christianity. That the Christian movement could have succeeded, so that the humble men who fished on the shores of the Sea of Galilee are today better known and more admired than the very Caesars who ruled the world of which their province was a despised part, is so amazing that it would be considered incredible if we did not know it to be the case.

Frequently, we can see a reason for events after they have occurred, though they are most baffling when we are in the midst of them. Even bad situations can serve good ends; good fruit *does* grow on evil trees. It is sobering to each succeeding generation of Americans, since the Civil War, to read the words in which Abraham Lincoln bore such eloquent witness to his own conviction that the hand of God can be seen in historical events.

If we shall suppose that American slavery is one of those offenses which, in the providence of God, must needs come, but which, having continued through His appointed time, He now wills to remove, and that He gives to both North and South this terrible war, as the woe due to those by whom the offense came, shall we discern therein any departure from those divine attributes which the believers in a living God always ascribe to Him?

[13] A similar story is told of the circle of Frederick the Great.

C. THE LARGER HISTORY

Though the Hebrew people, as the first to develop the historical argument for the being of God, confined their attention largely to their own particular history, there is no point in preserving that limitation now. The Hebrew story is a remarkable story, but it is only one out of many in the far-flung annals of mankind. Is there anything about the human story in general which can help us to universalize this kind of evidence so that it is more clearly valid? The God whose real or illusory status we are seeking to determine is not merely the God of a favorite people, but of all mankind. Is there anything about the entire story which requires us to postulate the reality of Divine Purpose in order for the process to make sense?

We are well on the road to an answer when we discern that there *is* a process, that it is moving in a direction, and that it covers an immense period of history. One allegedly miraculous incident, like that of the appearance of the gulls, which saved from destruction the precious grain of the Utah pioneers, or the change in weather, which permitted the escape of so many British soldiers from Dunkirk, might be explained as mere coincidence, but the wider the scope and the longer the process the less is coincidence an adequate explanation.

History is far greater than recorded history or even the *human* history. Today we are all convinced that the story is a very long one. We have reason to believe that matter existed for a long time before our infant earth was formed and that our earth went through many developments before even the simplest forms of life appeared. In a similar manner, there is good evidence that life existed on the planet for millions of years before the advent of man. The period of written records, relative to the whole process, is only one page in a very long book.

As a climax to this long story we have, today, not only pain and turmoil in human life, but an amazing amount of excellence in the search for beauty of all kinds, in the effort to establish justice, and in knowledge of the external world. We need not be sentimental or blind to human tragedy to recognize that, with the growth of learning and with the advances in the direction of equality of opportunity, there has been and is a great deal of good life in the human race. We *do* enjoy excellent music, we *do* respond to great ideas, including those of the distant past, we *do* succeed in scientific research, we *do* experience a great deal of affection. We have, sometimes, been so seriously impressed by the problem of evil that we have failed to notice the equally insistent problem of good.

We do not know that all of this remarkable development, finding its climax, for the present at least, in the possible cultivation of goodness, truth and beauty, is the direct result of an Infinite Purpose which has, all along, been working in this direction, but we do know that it is only by a most delicate balance of complex conditions that this result has been achieved. Judging by what we can observe, which is all that we can do anyway, there could not have been life apart from the long and tortuous development of the earth's surface with its particular combination of the atmosphere, the sea and the temperature. In like manner animal life depends upon the vast accumulation of vegetable life and human life depends upon the slow evolution of animal life up to the primate level.

The whole story is one story, and it looks as though it had a meaning. All of the slow development is justified if it is the necessary means to a wonderful end, the performance of a really good and unselfish deed. If the entire process has been one calculated to provide both the setting and the development of free personality, the process makes sense. It is hard to see how it makes sense in any other way. We cannot prove that the process has arisen by virtue of Divine Purpose, but we can show that the end, which we presently know, is one which is consistent with such a purpose.

The argument from history, when taken in its larger context, turns out to be the teleological argument in its valid form. The purpose back of creation is not to be seen so much in the individual product, such as the human eye, but rather in the total process, in so far as we can envisage it. In short, teleology appears not in objects abstracted from time, but in the entire sweep of events. Any particular moment might be the result of coincidence or of chance, but it stretches credulity too much to believe that the entire story is accidental.

II

The Evidence of Religious Experience

I have heard of thee by the hearing of the ear, but now mine eye seeth thee.

JOB

The four types of evidence found in the four preceding chapters are all on the same logical level in that all are basically inferential. All support each other by their cumulative effect, but all are limited, in the nature of the case, to what is at best a reasonable postulate. If we had nothing else, the case for theism would be strong, but the entire logical structure is immensely strengthened if there is also empirical verification of that to which they jointly point. This can give us a situation like that which obtained in the discovery of the planet Neptune. The existence of the planet was first inferred as a hypothesis which was required to explain observed phenomena completely mystifying on any other basis. Then, finally, the telescope was trained on the proper point in the heavens, and the inferred body was actually seen. What we want to know is whether any such corroboration is possible in the effort to know the truth in religion. The empirical argument, if it is valid, constitutes not only an added strand in the rope of evidence, but a verification of all the other strands as well.

A. THE EMPIRICAL ARGUMENT

The empirical approach to the being of God is so obvious and so straightforward that we should expect it always to be the major approach. The most convincing reason for believing that the moon is in the sky is not the inferential evidence concerning the existence of tides, but the direct evidence that men see it. Consequently, we should expect that thoughtful men would be more impressed by direct experience of God than by any other arguments.

The empirical argument must be clearly distinguished from the classical arguments, which have been used throughout most of the past two thousand years. It is not one of the five used by Thomas Aquinas, and is not one of the three examined by Immanual Kant in the eighteenth century. It must also be distinguished from the argument known as *consensus gentium*.[1] That the bulk of mankind has believed in supernatural beings is an interesting fact, although not more conclusive in this field than in any other, but it is very different from the assertion that many people have reported direct acquaintance with God. It is important to understand that we are concerned, in the present connection, not with belief, which has many different grounds, but with one particular ground of belief, namely, reported experience. There can be belief *because of* direct experience and there can be belief *apart from* direct experience. The point we are making is not that millions of men have believed in God, but rather that millions of men have reported and continue to report that they have known God with the directness and intimacy with which they know other persons and physical objects.

Though the evidence of religious experience has suffered great and surprising neglect, there are brilliant examples of its use. One of the best of these is that of Professor A. E. Taylor, of Edinburgh, who, in a brief but memorable essay, presents the cumulative evidence in three parts of approximately equal strength. The first part is called "From Nature to God," the second is called "From Man to God," and the third is called "From God to God." That is, he first points to the order of nature; he then points to human values; and finally he stresses the credibility of religious experience. "I have urged," he says in the conclusion, "that the suggestions of an eternal behind the temporal are derived from three independent sources, and that the agreement of the three in their common suggestion gives it a force which ought to be invincible." [2] In a similar fashion,

[1] The consensus argument, though mentioned by Plato, *Laws*, X, 886-888, was not given much weight by him, partly, it seems, because he was keenly conscious that atheism was not rare. "There have always been persons more or less numerous," he wrote, "who have had the same disorder." An excellent example of the modern and official use of this argument from universal consent by the Roman Catholic theologians is found in G. H. Joyce, *Principles of Natural Theology*, London, Longmans, 1934, pp. 179-198.

[2] A. E. Taylor, "The Vindication of Religion," *Essays Catholic and Critical*, ed. by E. G. Selwyn, p. 80.

C. C. J. Webb has used the evidence of religious experience to give content to the other forms of evidence. "It is true to say," he says, "that only in and through a religious experience have we any knowledge of God. And when there is religious experience present, the arguments which, apart from it, prove the existence of something which is yet not God, are informed with a new significance." [3]

The fact that a great many people, representing a great many civilizations and a great many centuries, and including large numbers of those generally accounted the best and wisest of mankind, have reported direct religious experience is one of the most significant facts about our world. The claim which their reports make is so stupendous and has been made in such a widespread manner that no philosophy can afford to neglect it. Since we cannot hope to build up a responsible conception of the universe unless we take into consideration every order of fact within it, the claim of religious experience with objective reference cannot be lightly dismissed.

The proposition that men have had genuine intercourse with God may be true, or it may be false, but the proposition is neither manifest nonsense nor an obvious truism. If it can be shown to be actually true that men do have contact not only with other persons and things, but also with the infinite Person, that is a fact of the greatest significance. The very possibility that anything so important *might* be true gives our researches into these matters a necessary mood of seriousness. Since the claim is conceivably valid, there is the heaviest reproach upon those who fail to examine it seriously. When the claim is cavalierly rejected, without a careful examination, this is presumably because of some dogmatic position.

Because the empirical argument is closely allied with the mood and temper of science, it ought to be especially attractive to scientific minds. The reasonable procedure is to look at religious experience with open-mindedness, as we look at any other datum. If we are truly scientific we approach any experience or report of experience without prejudice and with humility. The scientific temper demands neither that we *accept* the data of experience unreservedly nor that we *reject* it uncritically. We do not know what any experience,

[3] C. C. J. Webb, *God and Personality*, New York, Macmillan, 1918, p. 152.

whether sensory or nonsensory, is worth until we analyze it, sub-
jecting it to all the appropriate tests that are available.

In the light of the scientific approach we are naturally deeply
concerned with three major facts: the number of the reporters, the
character of the reporters, and the relative unanimity of their reports. This is how objective truth is known in any field. The crucial
point is that of the character of the reporters. If, for example, it
could be shown that all of those who report the experience of God
have been insane or unreliable in some other way, the whole matter
could be dismissed. No one seriously supposes that, out of the great
number who have reported the immediate experience of God, there
are many who are consciously fraudulent. Therefore, the only logical
position which remains for the unbeliever is to affirm that all of
those who make the report are deluded persons. It is important to
realize, in this situation, that only two genuine alternatives remain:
*either God is or all of those who have claimed to know Him have
been deluded.* This must include great prophets, as well as many
humble men, and it must include Jesus Christ. If God is not, then
Christ was the victim of self-delusion, for there is no serious doubt
about the immediacy of the experience implicit in his reported
prayers and of his sense of unity with the Father.

This puts the unbeliever in a position much harder than has
been usually recognized. The unbeliever is bound to hold that,
except for man's capacity to believe falsehood, much that is recognized to be best in civilization would not have existed. It is not
necessary for the positive believer in God to show that all reporters
are trustworthy and sound; without any harm to his position he can
admit that some are not.[4] All he needs to show is that *any* of them
are sound and trustworthy. If any man, anywhere, has truly met
God and continues to meet Him, then God is.

That this has occurred is the conclusion of a number of extremely
careful thinkers. Few are more careful than C. D. Broad, yet Broad
writes:

---

[4] A. E. Taylor is very forthright at this point. "We may readily admit, then,
that much which the experiencer is inclined to take for 'religious' experience is
illusion. He may mistake the vague stirrings and impulses of sex, or aesthetic
sensibility, or even pure illusions of sense or perception, for the self-revelation
of the divine, just as any of us may, in favourable conditions, mistake what he
has merely dreamed of for an event of waking life." *Op. cit.,* pp. 72, 73.

Finally I come to the argument for the existence of God which is based on the occurrence of specifically mystical and religious experiences. I am prepared to admit that such experiences occur among people of different races and social traditions, and that they have occurred at all periods of history. I am prepared to admit that, although the experience has differed considerably at different times and places, and although the interpretations which have been put upon them have differed still more, there are probably certain characteristics which are common to all of them and will suffice to distinguish them from all other kinds of experience. In view of this I think it more likely than not that in religious and mystical experience men come into contact with some Reality or aspect of Reality which they do not come into contact with in any other way.[5]

B. The Report of Experience

"There are two sorts of persons," wrote the late Professor Bennett, "who will not let you go without a definition: the wise man and the fool. The difference between them is that the latter demands one at the beginning of an investigation, while the former is content to wait until the end." [6] There are few subjects to which this epigrammatic wisdom may be applied more perfectly than to the one under discussion. It is, indeed, important to know, as precisely as is possible, what we mean when we speak of religious experience, since the subject lends itself easily to vagueness, but the most satisfactory way of arriving at a modicum of precision in understanding is to begin by the humble method of denotation. There are certain experiences of ourselves or of others which we should all agree in calling religious ones, just as there are others which we should all designate as borderline cases. It may be true, as has been ably argued, that both religion and the sense of "ought" are indefinable, inasmuch as the phenomena in question are wholly unique and cannot be explained in terms of anything else, but, even so, we can point and say, "This is what we mean."

There may be a sense in which all religious experience is ineffable. A close friend and associate of John Woolman said, "I may tell you of it, but you cannot feel it as I do." [7] Nevertheless, we can at least listen to what people tell of what they have known. In any

---

[5] C. D. Broad, "Belief in a Personal God," *Hibbert Journal*, vol. 24, p. 47.

[6] Charles A. Bennett, *A Philosophical Study of Mysticism*, Yale University Press, 1923, pp. 6, 7.

[7] *The Journal of John Woolman*, New York, Macmillan, 1922, p. 542.

case, we shall not know very much about the subject unless we listen to the reports as attentively as possible.

Not all religious experience is the same, but there are characteristic features which appear with astonishing regularity and which are not especially difficult to describe. Normally, it is not some experience wholly separated from other experiences, but a particular way in which all reality is apprehended. It comes about most naturally in the mood of prayer or worship, though it is by no means limited to stated times for these, either individually or collectively. Ordinarily religious experience has nothing to do with visions, ecstasies, raptures or other phenomena which are usually considered abnormal. It is true that some mystics have experienced these exalted states of consciousness or unconsciousness, but they are no part of *normative* religious experience.[8] On the contrary, such experience is as unspectacular as breathing or sleeping. For most men and women, religious experience has been a calm assurance of the reality of a relationship which gives meaning to existence.

Few in our time have expressed more clearly than has Martin Buber the idea that the fundamental religious experience is unspectacular, precisely because it is not an *exception*. He says that in his younger years he thought of religious experience as something apart from the normal course of events, but that, with more spiritual maturity, he changed his view. "I possess," he says, "nothing but the every day out of which I am never taken. The mystery is no longer disclosed, it has escaped or it has made its dwelling here where everything happens as it happens. I know no fulness but each mortal hour's fulness of claim and responsibility. Though far from being equal to it, yet I know that in the claim I am claimed and may respond in responsibility, and know who speaks and demands a response." Buber knows no ecstasy, but he knows what it is to be "willed for the life of communion." [9]

The sources of reports are varied, including many of the scriptures of the world and much of the devotional writings of mankind.

---

[8] Unusual mental states, such as "speaking with tongues," have frequently been minimized, even by those reporting them personally. Note, for example, the Apostle Paul, "I would rather speak five words with my mind, in order to instruct others, then ten thousand words in a tongue."—I Cor. 14:19.

[9] Martin Buber, *Between Man and Man,* trans. by R. G. Smith, New York, Macmillan, 1948, p. 14.

A great deal of the Bible is a report of religious experience, one of the most convincing of the reports being that recorded in the sixth chapter of Isaiah. In any case, the Biblical authors are chiefly concerned in telling not about their speculations, but about what they have known. The words of Job at the head of this chapter constitute a Biblical golden text.

Of modern collections of reported experience one of the most famous is that of Professor William James's *Varieties of Religious Experience*. In spite of its fame, the book suffers greatly from the failure of James to proceed seriously beyond the collection of accounts to the process of validation. His friend and student, Professor Rufus M. Jones, surpassed him in this regard, determining very early to make the emphasis upon religious experience and its validation what he called his "life clue." One result of the lifework of Rufus Jones is an impressive set of studies, not only of mystical religion in the classic sense, but of the kind of experience available to the rank and file of devout men and women.[10]

There are three special ways in which most of the reports of religious experience are made available. The first is by the direct testimony of the individual, as he tries to tell others what has occurred in the divine human encounter. This may be an oral testimony of the type that was developed voluminously in the early class meetings and the later prayer meetings of the Wesleyan Movement. The report may, on the other hand, be a written one—usually composed as a personal reminder to the author of what is felt to be superlatively precious.

The author of the *Imitation of Christ* [11] provides us with one of the most extensive examples of such personal testimony found in all literature. The book is a revelation, not only because of what one modest man experienced five hundred years ago, but also because of the way in which it has elicited a response from so many others in so many generations and cultures.

[10] See *Studies in Mystical Religion* (New York, Macmillan, 1923) and *Spiritual Reformers of 16th and 17th Centuries* (New York, Macmillan, 1928). Rufus Jones sought always to reinterpret the word "mysticism," so that it need not have a bizarre construction. He was, himself, a man eminent for his common sense and practicality. His best collection of testimonies is *Selections from The Children of the Light*.

[11] An excellent modern edition is the Whitford Edition, edited by Edward J. Klein, New York, Harper, 1941.

This small, old-fashioned book, for which you need pay only sixpence at a bookstall, *works miracles to this day,* turning bitter waters into sweetness. . . . It was written down by a hand that waited for the heart's prompting; it is the chronicle of a solitary, hidden anguish, struggle, trust, and triumph—not written on velvet cushions to teach endurance to those who are treading with bleeding feet on the stones. And so it remains to all time a lasting record of human needs and human consolations.[12]

Always the emphasis of the *Imitation* is on firsthand experience, which is declared to be superior to all indirect ways of knowing God. "Let not Moses nor any other of the prophets speak to me, but rather Thou, Lord, that art the inward inspirer and giver of light to all prophets; for Thou only, without them, mayst fully inform me and instruct me; they, without Thee, may little profit me."[13] Always the Fountain is more to be valued than anything which flows from the Fountain. The man who has known God face to face values the Giver more than the gift. The result of such immediate contact is a wonderful sense of joy. At no point is this said more vividly than in the following sentences:

Ah, my Lord God, most faithful lover, when thou comest into my heart, all that is within me doth joy! Thou art my glory and the joy of my heart, my hope and my whole refuge in all my troubles.[14]

The more we know of the background out of which such a testimony comes the harder it is to ridicule it. "No other book, except the Bible," says Rufus M. Jones, "has been a more permanent source of joy and comfort and hope."[15] Here is a witness which it is very hard to neglect or to disdain, because it is so obviously modest and sane.

Another excellent example of the written testimony is the record of Blaise Pascal, memorializing his keen sense of God's presence which came to him on November 23, 1654. Pascal sewed the report in his coat, where it was found by his servant after his death. He valued the memory of the experience so highly that it affected the remainder of his days.[16]

12 *Mill on the Floss,* Bk. IV, chap. 3.
13 *Imitation,* III, 2.
14 *Ibid.,* III, 5.
15 Rufus M. Jones, *Studies in Mystical Religion,* pp. 325, 326.
16 See Appendix C of this book for Pascal's account.

In trying to state faithfully what occurred, this brilliant man wrote what was essentially a string of interjections. The word "fire" was the most emphasized of all, probably in an effort to say that what was perceived had about it the same indubitable quality that we find in the flame which warms, lights, and even burns.

The importance of this witness is increased in our estimation as we remind ourselves of the kind of man Pascal was. He was one of the world's really great mathematicians, he was an excellent scientist, and he was a transparently good man. But, in spite of his learning, he was, in effect, repeating the famous judgment of the *Imitation of Christ*, "I had rather feel compunction than be able to give the most accurate definition of it." He valued his acquaintance with God far more than his knowledge about God.

A second source of reports is the specifically religious autobiography, particularly the journal of the inner life. Such an account is fuller than that of the separated report, often showing how an entire life has been guided by God's love. During the first hundred years of the Quaker Movement it was practically standard for leading Quakers to write their journals, and all of them were written with the same purpose in mind.[17] The beginning of the *Journal of George Fox* makes this purpose wholly clear. "That all may know the dealings of the Lord with me, and the various exercises, trials and troubles through which He led me in order to prepare and fit me for the work unto which He had appointed me, and may thereby be drawn to admire and glorify His infinite wisdom and goodness, I think fit briefly to mention how it was with me in my youth, and how the work of the Lord was begun and gradually carried on in me, even from my childhood." It must be understood that the best of this literature of witness has not come from those who can, in any sense, be called professionals, but often from modest people who have no reason to tell what their experience of God is except

[17] The abundance of this literature has made possible a very impressive anthology of religious experience in *Christian Life, Faith and Thought in the Society of Friends*, being the first part of the Christian Discipline of the Religious Society of Friends in Great Britain, adopted in 1921. Characteristic expressions in this volume are: "He Himself met with us, and manifested Himself largely unto us," and "The Lord appeared daily unto us, to our astonishment, amazement and great admiration." "When I was weak," said James Nayler (1616-1660), "Thou stayedst me with Thy Hand."

the natural desire to share with others what is precious. Our time
has been marked by a renewal of interest in the devotional classics,
a number of scholars giving us interpretations and fresh editions.[18]
Several good colleges offer courses in spiritual classics.

A third source of such reports is what is implicit in the use of
hymns and prayers, as well as the general sharing of liturgy. The
best-loved hymns are loved precisely because they express the experience of countless people who could not possibly make adequate
expressions of their own. Their joy in singing of how the Living
God has found them is a verification of the truth of what the authors
say. This means that the empirical basis of living faith is very much
wider than we usually suppose.[19]

Those who sing

> Sometimes a light surprises
> The Christian while he sings
> It is the Lord who rises,
> With healing in his wings . . .

are really verifying the experience of the poet Cowper, who knew
what it was to be sure of a "life-giving countenance." When we
think of all the reports through the years, both explicit and implicit,
we realize that the person who neglects this body of evidence is in
any case unscientific.

C. Criticisms of the Argument

The argument from religious experience is obviously so strong
that it is bound to stand *unless* it can be shown to have some serious
flaw. Certainly, it is the argument which is calculated to appeal
most persuasively to the ordinary person, who, though he is a bit
skeptical of speculation, trusts the man "who was there." The argument has so much in its favor that it ought to be accepted unless
really damaging criticism is forthcoming.

There has long been some criticism of the empirical evidence

---

[18] Reliable modern studies of this rich deposit are available in Gaius Glenn
Atkins' *Pilgrims of the Lonely Road,* and Willard L. Sperry's Lowell Lectures,
Strangers and Pilgrims. More recently Professor Thomas Kepler of Oberlin
College has edited a series in which the classics of devotion appear as convenient
separate volumes. See also the works of Professor Douglas V. Steere of Haverford
College.

[19] Judging by the use of hymns, it now includes Buddhists.

from those who assert that the experience cannot be genuine because it is not a matter of sensory perception. They limit the empirical to the sensory. All that is necessary in order to counter this criticism is to inquire concerning the ground of certainty on which the limitation rests. How could we possibly know that immediate contact between the Divine Object and the human subject, apart from the mediation of the senses, is impossible? As soon as we ask this we realize that the objection rests on nothing more substantial than a naturalistic dogma. Until this dogma is made credible, the criticism is not really worthy of consideration in any extended way. It is not self-evident that there is any antecedent impossibility about there being other data than those of sense.[20]

A more serious criticism is that of devout persons who fear that the acceptance of the credibility of religious experience will lead to spiritual presumption and special claims on the part of undisciplined individuals. The great Dr. Samuel Johnson was a devout believer in the Living God, but he feared religious movements which stressed the possibility of firsthand experience. That is why he denounced, with such vigor, his contemporary, John Wesley. In his famous *Dictionary* Johnson defined enthusiasm as "a vain belief of private revelation; a vain confidence of divine favour or communication."

With all respect to Johnson [21] we can point out his essential mistake. His mistake was that he interpreted religious experience as the reception of particular messages, and these have rightly been looked upon as suspect by many thoughtful observers. But this is not what religious experience usually claims. What is normally claimed, instead, is the sense of a Divine Power which brings new life. *What is revealed is not propositions, but a Presence.* What is so well attested by the agreement of a very great number of reporters is not primarily new *information* about God, but a vivid sense of acquaintance with God Himself. Johnson would have understood this if he had perused more carefully the Baskerville edition of Barclay's *Apology*, which we know he saw in Boswell's

[20] We need not mention here the criticism based on psychological explanation, since that is faced in the chapter "The Challenge of Freud."

[21] My own respect for him is indicated by the introduction to *Doctor Johnson's Prayers*, New York, Harper, 1947.

company at Lloyd's in 1776.[22] There he would have read one of the finest statements of religious experience that is anywhere available, a statement which stresses the new life rather than new information.

> For not a few have come to be convinced of the Truth, after this manner, of which I myself in a part am a true witness, who not by strength of arguments, or by a particular disquisition of each doctrine, and convincement of my understanding thereby, came to receive and bear witness of the Truth, but by being secretly reached by this Life; for, when I came into the silent assemblies of God's people, I felt a secret power among them, which touched my heart, and, as I gave way unto it I found the evil weakening in me and the good raised up.[23]

Among modern critics of the argument from religious experience none is more demanding of respect than F. R. Tennant, whose two-volume work, *Philosophical Theology,* is generally recognized for its thoroughness. Though Tennant is a vigorous critic, it is part of his merit that he understands the importance of the kind of evidence mentioned in this chapter. "No account of the universe," he says, "can be final, which leaves the mystical consciousness disregarded: its claims must be met." [24] Tennant considers that he meets these claims fairly and that he shows them to be incapable of providing the validation required. He has, however, been vigorously challenged in this regard, particularly by a thorough and detailed examination which constitutes Number XIII in the Yale Studies in Religious Education.[25] Tennant has also had his criticism severely criticized by some of his British colleagues in the philosophy of religion.

The heart of Tennant's contention is that, while the mystic is invulnerable in regard to his private conviction, he is "powerless to substantiate his claim." [26] Tennant realizes that he cannot, without begging the question, positively repudiate the claim of the man who, like Barclay, reports that he has been "secretly reached by the Life," for there is no way to prove that he has not been so reached, but he

[22] Mentioned in the *Life* under that date.
[23] Robert Barclay, *An Apology for the True Christian Divinity*, XI, 7.
[24] F. R. Tennant, *Philosophical Theology,* Cambridge University Press, 1935, vol. 1, p. 314.
[25] Delton Lewis Scudder, *Tennant's Philosophical Theology,* Yale University Press, 1940.
[26] Tennant, *op. cit.,* p. 319.

says that the person who makes this affirmation has no way of showing anyone else that his experience is more than subjective. The fact that he believes it to be more than subjective is not evidence, even when the reporter is superlatively certain. The experience, he says, may indeed involve a high degree of "certainty," but this may be nothing more than subjective psychological certitude. He may be confusing his inference with direct apprehension. Religious experiences, Tennant concludes, are so private, so exclusive, and so essentially autobiographical that they cannot be accorded evidential value at all.

This attack seems very convincing until we employ the dialectical method of asking how this same analysis applies to the validation of sense experience. I see what I take to be a planet in the sky. How can I be sure that I really do see it? I may find that others report a similar experience, and this we normally take as good evidence that my experience is not hallucinatory, but this is something of which I cannot be sure. The truth is that one man does not live through another man's consciousness. My objects are mine in a way in which they cannot also be yours. Moreover, no experience can be communicated to another person unless the other person has a capacity for the experience. I cannot force the other person to corroborate my experience; all that I can do is to tell him what to look for, in the hope that he may finally perceive it. Since some will not look or cannot see, universal corroboration does not occur in any realm of human experience.

The important consideration in all this is that the validating process, whether in religious experience or in sense experience, is identical. If Tennant's contention about the necessary privacy of an experience is an absolute barrier to validation in one field, it is an absolute barrier in another. "My external sensations," says F. H. Bradley, "are no less private to myself than are my thoughts and my feelings." [27] But Tennant accepts validation by agreement in sense experience; therefore, he ought not to reject it in religious experience. It is part of the merit of Professor D. L. Scudder's book that this insight is stated with helpful clarity.

[27] F. H. Bradley, *Appearance and Reality*, New York, Macmillan, 1893, p. 346.

The subjective processes by which the religious object is intuited are neither more nor less mutually exclusive from person to person than sense processes, and the method of communication in both cases is necessarily indirect. That is to communicate experience of the religious object the saint or the prophet can only arrange the circumstances under which another may "see God" for himself, and even then the other will not "see God" unless he has the capacity and desire to do so.[28]

We can be grateful to Tennant for his constant warnings. It is true, as he says, that the reporter may be attributing to the divine encounter what he has learned from other men. It is, unfortunately, a fact that "when the mystic believes he intuits God with sense-like immediacy, he is perhaps but causally interpreting his elation, peace, etc., by aid of a concept already to hand." [29] All that the warning means, however, is that the reporter *could* be wrong, and this we have admitted from the first. What is relevant to say is that we could, likewise, be wrong about anything else but that it is not profitable to reject all possibility of validation for that reason. We are no worse off, in this regard, in religious experience than we are in any other.

D. THE VALIDATING PROCESS

Tennant's criticism is valuable not only in the way in which it puts us on our guard against any tendency to take religious experience easily at its face value, but also in the way in which it demands that we learn to state, with some precision, what the validating process is. This process, similar to that used in sense experience, is as follows:

1. *The number of reporters* must be considered. What is reported by only a very few *could* be objective, but chances are against such a conclusion. In the case of firsthand experience of the divine the experience in question is reported, as we have already seen, by many people of many types in all ages of history. This is generally conceded by all who have studied the evidence.

2. *The character of the reporters* is, as in any experience, varied. This would be true of reports about the moon. What is significant, however, is that so many, like Blaise Pascal and Robert Barclay, who are generally accounted trustworthy on other matters, are in-

[28] Scudder, *op. cit.*, p. 164.
[29] Tennant, *op. cit.*, vol. 1, p. 318.

cluded in the reckoning. They cannot be discounted, because of insanity or credulity or general inability to judge the weight of evidence.

3. *The agreement of the reports* is not complete, but complete agreement is not required for validation. If it were, science would be destroyed. What is required is a substantial core of agreement, with increasing agreement in proportion to developed sensitivity. In countless cases the religious experience is one which combines ultimacy and intimacy and is distinguished from all other human experiences by this combination. The critic who claims that there is no substantial agreement achieves his end only by calling attention to the variety of the supposed information which religious experience yields. If, however, the heart of the matter is not such information, but the sense of new life which comes from the Divine Source of power, much of the alleged confusion and dissimilarity disappears. That it does not all disappear is shown by the fact that, with some, the Divine Object appears to be personal while with others it appears to be impersonal. In fairness we must say that C. D. Broad, while he held that the ascription of objective reference was required by a careful analysis of the empirical evidence, believed that this objective reference could not be claimed as personal. Professor A. N. Whitehead felt the same way. On questions of interpretation there is thus great divergence, but we should be foolish, indeed, to allow this fact to hide from us the more important fact that, on questions of contact with the Source of life and power and the consequent new life within, there is often remarkable agreement, especially among humble and saintly people.[30] No one in our time has seen this more vividly or has said it more persuasively than Dr. Inge:

It will be found that these men of acknowledged and pre-eminent saintliness agree very closely in what they tell us about God. They tell us that they have arrived gradually at an unshakable conviction, not based on inference, but on immediate experience, that God is a spirit with whom the human spirit can hold intercourse: that in Him meet all that they can imagine of goodness, truth and beauty; that they can see His footprints everywhere in Nature and feel His presence within them as

[30] I have presented evidence of this in *The Trustworthiness of Religious Experience* (London, Allen & Unwin, 1939) and *The Knowledge of God* (New York, Harper, 1939).

the very life of their life, so that in proportion as they come to themselves they come to Him.[31]

4. *The consequent change in lives* is the final step in this valida- tion. We naturally look for something sufficiently objective so that others can see it, as when we photograph a planet. We cannot, of course, have an imprint of God on photographic plates, but others might be able to see marks on human lives and changes in per- sonalities. This is what, to a remarkable degree, we do find, though we cannot claim, in all honesty, to find it in all. One of the most remarkable features of so much of religious life is its consequent joy in the face of pain and hardship. George John Romanes, the eminent naturalist and associate of Darwin, for whom the Romanes Lectures are named, was turned from agnosticism to theistic convic- tion, not because of his own personal religious experience, but be- cause of his observation of the lives of others who reported such experience. The crucial consideration to one who tried to be fully scientific was as follows:

Consider the happiness of the religious—and chiefly of the highest re- ligious, i.e. Christian—belief. It is a matter of fact that besides being most intense, it is most enduring, growing and never staled by custom. In short, according to the universal testimony of those who have it, it differs from all other happiness not only in degree but in kind. Those who have it can usually testify to what they used to be without it. It has no relation to intellectual status. It is a thing by itself and supreme.[32]

Here, in brief form, is the logical structure by means of which the testimony of religious experience ceases to be something purely private and becomes both the strongest and most direct of all evi- dences for the being of a Divine Reality in the universe. Though the argument has been severely challenged, it continues to stand.

[31] W. R. Inge, *Christian Mysticism,* New York, Scribner, 1899, pp. 325, 326.
[32] George John Romanes, *Thoughts on Religion* (a posthumous work edited by Charles Gore), p. 162.

Part III
CHALLENGES to FAITH

12

The Challenge of Dialectical Materialism

All contemporary religions and churches, all and every kind of religious organization, Marxism has always viewed as organs of bourgeois reaction, serving as a defense of exploitation and the doping of the working-classes.

LENIN

However good the older philosophies of religion may be, they cannot speak adequately to our time. This is not so much because of the inadequacies of their answers, but because, to a very great degree, they are not the answers to the right problems. Most of the ancient problems persist, of course, inasmuch as the fundamentals of the human situation have not been altered, but their modern dress makes them *seem* different. The greatest difference, however, appears in the enemies which the classic religious faith is forced to encounter in the modern world. Here is where a real measure of novelty has emerged in our tumultuous century.

It is chiefly because of these new enemies that the philosophy of religion must be partly recast. If those who seek a rational faith cannot answer the sternest critics, not many modern-minded people will listen, however valuable the rest of the material may be. It is right to begin with the Leninist challenge, because it is vociferous and numerically great. There are not many, in contemporary life, who have not felt this challenge in one way or another, even though it is true to say that often the precise nature of the challenge is grossly misunderstood.

A. The Marx-Leninist Attack

By Marx-Leninism we mean that philosophical, economic and

social system which received its first potent literary formulation in *The Communist Manifesto* over one hundred years ago and which has appeared in a successful political form for thirty-nine years. No single word is really adequate to denominate this system. Though originating, in some measure, in the mind of Karl Marx, it is certainly more than Marxism. On the other hand, to call it communism is not satisfactory, because it is much more than a system of ownership and, furthermore, there are forms of communism, particularly those represented by monastic orders in various religions, which are in sharp contrast to the system under discussion. On the whole, it is satisfactory to use the method of denotation and say that the system we have in mind is that which is now in operation in Russia and mainland China and partly in operation in what are called satellite countries.

If we have to use a single term to designate this system, Leninism is probably the least unsatisfactory among possible alternatives, because it is Lenin's thought which is most highly revered in Russia and because his is the mind which did most to adapt theory to practice. In the sudden and shocking popularization of the contemporary dogma of anti-Stalinism, the most potent appeal to authority has been the revelation of what is called Lenin's will. Marx is not neglected, but his writings are somewhat in the position of an Old Testament, whereas Lenin's writings constitute a New Testament. It was his function to *fulfill.* This combination of background and foreground has made it reasonable for many, particularly fanatical believers like those in China, whose devotion is passionate, to refer to their system as Marx-Leninism.

The reason why this system must be considered in any rational discussion of contemporary religious faith is twofold. First, as the chapter-head quotation indicates, the system has been untiring in its open attack on religion from the beginning and, second, the system has obvious religious features of its own. What we observe, therefore, is a civil war within religion, and this is a partial explanation of the ferocity of the conflict. Marxist or Leninist leaders oppose, and believe they are able to *expose,* all theistic religion, in spite of the fact or because of the fact that they have another commitment which is itself qualitatively religious. Instead of the Living God, they have the Dialectic of History and as a spur to endeavor, instead of the Kingdom of God, they have the classless society where government will have withered away because, in a truly ordered society, it is no longer required. As there is no zeal like that of the convert, so there is no antagonism like that of the defector. Dialectical materialism, the official philosophy of the Communist revolution, represents a mass defection from the classic faith of the West in favor of an alternative religion, one which is without God but not at all lacking in evangelical zeal.

Our century is the first for hundreds of years to witness the emergence of new and vigorous religions. One of these, the Fascist religion, of which the Nazi faith was a variant, is now in decay, partly because of military defeat, though remnants of it may still be found in various places and in various minds. The reasons for the greater success of fascism's first cousin, Leninism, constitute a significant subject of inquiry. Though the fortunes of war have been influential in this development, they do not appear to be the major factor, partly because it was ideological strength and weakness that helped to determine the military outcome in 1945. However successful Hitlerism was in arousing fanatical zeal and consequent strength sufficient to hold off a great part of the world's power for nearly six years, Leninism is far more successful. Though only a minority of the population espouse the fanatical faith, they espouse it with sufficient conviction and organization to be able to control the destinies and many of the thoughts of more than eight hundred million people.

It is important to face honestly the fact of just how successful the communist faith has been. The Bolsheviks have undertaken to carry on several revolutions at once, agrarian, industrial, social and intellectual, as well as political. Though they have failed at many points, their energy and audacity are really amazing. In so far as there is a deep strain of pragmatism in all of us, we cannot but be impressed by such a record of success in the face of outside hostility. Though part of the success of this system arises from its latent idealism, seeming to offer a chance to the poor and the exploited, its deeper appeal comes from the way in which it offers a unifying principle in life and culture. As Berdyaev and others have taught us, we have had, since the Renaissance, an increasing tendency to departmentalize all of our major interests. We, thus, separate business, law, religion, education and politics, each being allowed to make its own declaration of independence. The result is that, in the life of the West, we do not have a common faith or a common purpose inspiring our total social order, except fleetingly in wartime and then on a negative basis. A measure of negative unity has come more recently in our popular anticommunism. In both Russia and communist China all aspects of life, including even sports, are unified by the acceptance of a common conviction, which is largely positive.

It is a very important part of this common conviction that it should think of itself as radically antireligious. This, in the beginning, was partly an accident of history. Both Marx and Engels were deeply influenced by Feuerbach at the time that their ideas were taking on their permanent and crucial form, for Feuerbach's *The Essence of Christianity* appeared in 1841. Feuerbach attempted to explain religion as man's mistaken effort to project himself, as infinite, upon the universe. The religious error, then, is for man to mistake his own nature for external reality. What he thinks he sees in the universe is really what he sees in an enlarging mirror, but man, Feuerbach suggests, does not know this.

Marx accepted the essentials of this explanation, but went further in the attempt to show why man makes this projection. It is because man is frustrated in two ways, by nature and by society. The easy answer to frustration is pious imagination. Most men suffer terrible poverty, because of social injustice, but this poverty can be made bearable by dreaming of pie in the sky. Thus, the American slave, in pre-Civil War days, compensated for his bondage by the wonderful visions of heaven expressed in the composition of "spirituals." The conception of omnipotence is only a measure of human impotence. Marx put it this way: "The omnipotence of God is nothing but the fantastic reflection of the impotence of people before nature and before the economic social relations created by themselves." This doctrine is reminiscent of the saying which was current during the last war, that there are no atheists in foxholes. If the sailors are swearing, all is well, but if you hear them praying, put on your life belt!

The Marxist doctrine was thus, in its inception, not really something new at all, but a reasonably faithful reflection of nineteenth-century atheism. It simply picked up this theme, as it picked up other themes, such as militant feminism, and incorporated it in a larger system. As Jacques Maritain has pointed out, Marxism was, in this regard, "the heir of the stupidest thing the world has ever known, i.e. bourgeois free-thought." [1] In Lenin, however, we get less of conventional rationalistic and atheistic humanism and more of emphasis on social conditions. In his famous conception of religion as the opium of the people he was thinking primarily not of the hardships of nature, but of the hardships of society. His stress on the frustration produced by the social-economic order is illustrated by the following:

> In modern capitalistic countries the basis of religion is primarily *social*. The roots of modern religion are deeply imbedded in the social oppression of the working masses, and in their apparently complete helplessness before the blind forces of capitalism, which every day and every hour cause a thousand times more horrible suffering and torture for ordinary working folk than are caused by exceptional events, such as war, earthquakes, etc. "Fear created the gods." Fear of the blind force of capital—blind because its action cannot be foreseen by the masses—a force which at every step in life threatens the worker and the small with "sudden," "unexpected," "accidental" destruction and ruin, bringing in their train beggary, pauperism, prostitution, and deaths from starvation—this is the *tap-root* of modern religion which, first of all, and above all, the materialist must keep in mind, if he does not wish to remain stuck forever in the infant school of materialism. [2]

Religion is evil because it turns men's minds away from the real remedies. The real remedy is scientific socialism, which alone can insure, in large measure, against natural disaster and, in complete measure, against social disaster. The greatest threat to faith, these men rightly understand, is always a substitute faith. Religion, as they see it, is evil precisely because it is a substitute faith and wholly groundless and delusory in that it is not *scientific*.

Though the attack on religion and churches has been sometimes violent and sometimes subdued, during the past fifteen years, only the gullible see in this any real change. The apparent changes are occasioned by the need for friends outside the regime and by internal

[1] *True Humanism*, New York, Scribner, 1938, p. 612.
[2] Lenin, *On Religion*, p. 19.

dangers. As though to establish in all minds the permanent teaching on the subject and to counteract false conclusions, based on the policy of temporary tolerance, *Pravda* said on August 11, 1954, perhaps as a kind of preparation for the Second Assembly of the World Council of Churches: "The morality of devoted and convinced protagonists of progress demands a resolute and irreconcilable struggle against all kinds of religious survivals and superstitions which spiritually cripple and abase mankind." The reason given for the greater tolerance of religious bodies in recent years is that "under pressure from the believers themselves" the religious organizations had become more co-operative, but the basic fact, in spite of this, was that religion, as such, continued to be an antiscientific ideology. Though it was admitted that some still performed religious rites, there was cause for rejoicing in that the majority of the people had been "freed" forever from the bondage of religion.

When we listen to Radio Moscow we can hear frequently the elaboration of this line. The school and the family are urged to play their part in the struggle against religious survivals. This is particularly necessary because belief in God hampers the child in attaining complete mastery of the knowledge imparted at school. All loyal people are asked to discard "all idealistic invention to the effect that the world was formed by a spirit or God." A recent broadcast from Radio Moscow included:

In the struggle against idealism and religion, Marxist philosophical materialism bases itself firmly on scientific discoveries. Study of the natural sciences has convincingly proved that nature existed before man and before the origin of life. Great scientific discoveries have established the inherent link between various forms of matter in motion and the possibility of the conversion of one form of matter into another without interference by any supernatural force.

Emphasis is put increasingly upon the idea that liberation from religion is a slow process and fundamentally an educational process. Since "religious prejudices have become rooted in the minds of the workers over centuries," says an article in *Molodoi Kommunist (Young Communist)*, "it would be naïve to imagine that one can deal with them in a single swoop, by a sort of cavalry charge." Since the task is educational, and since believers are also workers, it is not permissible to insult the feelings of believers or to jeer at religious cults.

The fact that there are still some religious survivals only shows that full communism has not yet been established. The position has been put clearly by an article in the Soviet *Journal* of the Ministry of Education, which says: "Our Soviet society, where Socialism has been constructed, and the social origins of religion have been liquidated, is the first basically atheistic society in the world, a society in which religion already has no foundation and has turned into a survival of capitalism in the minds of a certain part of the population. Under Communism religion will vanish entirely."

B. The Philosophy of Communism

What the Western world sees of Communist life seldom reflects the inwardness of the movement. In the newspapers and in speeches we hear of clever political maneuvering, hard-drinking parties, ruthless domination of subject peoples, and Siberian labor camps. All of these occur or exist, but they belong to the realm of strategy rather than to the realm of faith. Discussion of these has a suitable place in some books, but not in a book devoted to the philosophy of religion. What we need to understand, in connection with our present subject, is how communism can be so successful as a rival faith. What is the set of primary convictions that can inspire such passionate earnestness as that of Karl Marx and hosts of his disciples? What is the belief that can produce such genuine self-sacrifice? Whatever this is, it is certainly something other than careful thought control at home and brilliant psychological warfare abroad.

The combination of elements, as we face them, is rather surprising. The surprise consists in the fact that each item of the creed seems uninspiring alone, while there is no doubt about the effect of the total scheme. As we analyze the current Communist creed we find that there are three dominant elements.

1. *The first element is Scientism.* From the beginning of the movement science has been a sacred word, superior to any other in the total system. In the internal fight between Communist camps a century ago, the chief line drawn by orthodox Marxists was the line between "utopian" communism and "scientific" communism. One of these referred to a dream world of ideas, but the other was simply

a realistic analysis of what was occurring in the historical process. In the current Leninist vocabulary the opposite of scientific is idealistic. Idealists may concern themselves with what ought to be, but scientists engage in no such foolishness; they are concerned with what is.

In large measure this conception is one which was borrowed by Marx and his immediate followers from the positivist movement of his day. The dates of Auguste Comte (1798-1857) help to make this clear. Positivism, as taught by Comte, meant the willingness to leave behind both the theological and the metaphysical stage of human development and to accept unreservedly the new day, which is the day of science. All prescientific explanations or descriptions are thus suspect in the very nature of the case. To be scientific is to be mature.

To those of the Western world who have learned something of the limitations of natural science, this simple faith in science, in the Communist creed, is so naïve as to be almost unbelievable. But there is no doubt that this is what is taught in the speeches and articles directed to the general public. God is a fiction because He cannot be discovered by laboratory technique. Prayer is futile because it cannot be proved by scientific method. Religion is unworthy of serious attention because it arose in the prescientific age. What we have here, of course, is not merely *science,* but a particularly unsophisticated philosophy of science, which deserves the epithet *scientism.*

According to this faith, which is official in Russia, there is only one set of causes, the natural set. Therefore, all supernaturalism is inherently false. Because the fundamental explanation of the physical world is to be found within it, not outside it, there is no Creator and no need for Him.

There is a real connection between naïve scientism and the day-by-day conduct of life in Communist countries. On the one hand, a very great emphasis is placed on scientific education and scientific development in general. This is one of the areas in which money is spent most lavishly. On the other hand, there is a thorough effort to handle the population in a fully scientific way, which includes attempted conditioning, according to scientific psychology. All nations do this to some degree, but in a Communist country it can be done more thoroughly because there is no difficulty engendered by the notion of the dignity of the individual as a child of God. If positivism is true, this is the way to act. Emil Brunner has put his finger on the central point by referring to the totalitarian state as "the dynamic heir of positivist philosophy." [3]

2. *The second item is Materialism,* because the fundamental order is the material order. This emphasis on the logical priority of the material basis of existence is given an added twist, in official communism, by what is called the materialist conception of history, with special reference to economic production and the class struggle. The class struggle is presented as a necessary outcome of the material structure. This wonderful combination was originally explained by Engels in a famous statement as follows:

The *Manifesto* being our joint production, I consider myself bound to state that the fundamental proposition which forms its nucleus, belongs to Marx. That proposition is: That in every historical epoch, the prevailing mode of economic production and exchange, and the social organisation necessarily following from it, form the basis upon which is built up, and from which alone can be explained, the political and intellectual history of that epoch; that consequently the whole history of mankind (since the dissolution of primitive tribal society, holding land in common ownership) has been a history of class struggles, contests between exploiting and exploited, ruling and oppressed classes; that the history of these class struggles forms a series of evolutions in which, nowadays, a stage has been reached where the exploited and oppressed class—the proletariat—cannot attain its emancipation from the sway of the exploiting and ruling class—the bourgeoisie—without, at the same time, and once and for all emancipating society at large from all exploitation, oppression, class distinctions and class struggles.[4]

The philosophical point of this is that the class struggle is the necessary outcome of the prevailing mode of economic production and exchange, and that these, in turn, are the necessary outcome of the material structure of the world. Thus materialism logically entails determinism.

3. *The third item of the Communist creed is the Dialectic.* His-

---

[2] Emil Brunner, *Christianity and Civilization,* New York, Scribner, 1949, vol. 2, p. 18.
[4] *Manifesto of the Communist Party* (Lawrence and Wishart), ed. 1941, p. 7.

tory follows a pattern, but it is not a pattern provided by Divine Purpose. Given our kind of world, with its land and its population, the formation of classes, with the consequent class antagonism, had to follow. It would be as idle to blame the capitalist for his greed as to blame the bull for his horns. Both come naturally and necessarily in evolution as means of survival. But such evolution involves a feature which, on the surface, seems to combine poorly with materialism: an inner dialectic of history which is working itself out with an inevitable logic by successive steps.

If this be materialism, it is an odd kind, for the very matter of the universe seems to obey what, in any other philosophical system, would be called mental laws. The combination of nineteenth-century materialism with Hegelian dialectic is an unlikely one, but there is no doubt that it is widely and officially accepted. The combination seems unlikely because, on the face of it, the adjective contradicts the noun, yet it is important to realize that it is in this very combination that the chief source of the power of Marx-Leninist religion actually lies.

It must be carefully noted that both Marx and Lenin made a sharp distinction between Mechanistic Materialism and Dialectical Materialism, definitely rejecting the former. Dialectical materialism asserts the temporal priority of matter and regards mind as appearing in matter, without supernatural creation, but goes on to assert that mind, when it has once appeared, acts by its own principles, which are not reducible to the categories of physics and chemistry. Mind is not regarded as identical with matter, though it is held to originate in and *out of* what is material.

Man cannot live well without some spiritual hope, and Leninism provides it in this way. The course of nature is inherently dialectical, moving from thesis to antithesis to synthesis. This is avowedly drawn from Hegel by a conscious inversion of the dialectic, which is his chief contribution to philosophical thought. But it always avoids a full idealism by insistence that mind is limited, in its activity, to reaction to situations presented by the material order, so that mind is always secondary and dependent.

It is the sense of a mental movement in history, working out a necessary logic of events, that gives the dedicated Communist a surrogate for religious faith. There is a wave of the future and he is on it! The decay of capitalist enemies, who are presently so bothersome and so hard to evangelize, is as sure as anything can be. Thus historical determinism brings real peace of mind and a sense of participation in something far bigger than the individual worker or even the individual state.

The careful student will realize that many of these features are similar to features of the Biblical faith from which the Communists have seceded. The rejection of mere unsubstantial ideals, without any rooting in reality, is something which all theists can understand and appreciate. The emphasis on the material order is not one with which Christians would argue, for it is often pointed out that Christianity is the most materialistic of all the world religions. It is not satisfied merely with the spiritual; it builds hospitals. The Leninist combination of matter and mind is even reminiscent of the sacramental theory of the universe in which material things can become means of grace. But the difference, though slight, is crucial. Christian theism and dialectical materialism lie close together on two sides of a cultural watershed.

C. The Beneficent Revelation of Leninism

As we face critically this amazing new religion we have many reactions, but the first is one of gratitude. Even the most hostile critic is bound to admit that some of the points made in Marx-Leninism are valid ones. For example, it is true that religion *can* be an opiate. "Men have been urged to pray," writes H. G. Wood, "when they would have done better to think, observe and act." [5] Even in modern America there is always the fear, based partly on evidence, that the well-to-do may try to pacify the less fortunate by encouraging their religious experience, and especially that kind of religious experience in which religion is a matter of peace of mind, with little attention to the righting of injustices. Among those who have pointed to this danger is Will Herberg.[6] It is not the whole

[5] H. G. Wood, *Christianity and Civilization,* New York, Macmillan, 1943, p. 61.
[6] Cf. Herberg, *Protestant, Catholic, Jew,* New York, Doubleday, 1955, especially p. 281. Mr. Herberg warns as follows: "Certainly, when we find great corporations such as U. S. Steel distributing Norman Vincent Peale's *Guideposts* in huge quantities to their employees . . . we are not altogether unjustified in suspecting that considerations of personnel policy have somehow entered into these good works of religion."

truth, but it is part of the truth that metaphysical and religious ideas have been used to justify systems of exploitation, as is glaringly true in the history of slavery. What is so difficult for the outsider to understand is the failure of those dedicated to Marx-Leninism to see that *their* metaphysical system is likewise used for exploitation. This is the case when present denials of freedom are justified by the conviction that the system is still in its intermediate stages. There is, indeed, an "ideological taint" in connection with most of our convictions, on either side of the iron curtain, and it is good to be reminded of this. Though Marx is now thoroughly out of date, he does put his finger on some of our weaknesses.

Our greatest gratitude must be reserved for the fact that Marx-Leninism provides an objective revelation of so many features of our own civilization. The really frightening thought is not the conventional and continually repeated one that we have *two worlds* on the planet, but rather that we have come so close to having *one*. In spite of the different labels, and in spite of the fervent anti-communism, we of the Western world are more similar to the Communists than we like to admit. This, unfortunately, includes a considerable part of our religious life.

Certainly we have a vast amount of scientism in the West, since every great university harbors many exponents of the first item of the Leninist creed. Economic materialism is not strange to the West, and particularly America, even though the contradiction between this and theistic faith is seldom recognized or openly avowed. "That economic values are the highest, the genuine reality," points out Emil Brunner, "is not an invention of Karl Marx, but of capitalist society of the 19th century." [7] If we, too, believe in our hearts that economic goods are the very substance of life, if we agree that "money rules the world," there is no fundamental disagreement on a major issue. This leads Brunner to conclude that "the dispute between Marx and the capitalists is merely concerned with the question who shall have money."

It is a little shocking to many Westerners to realize that dialectical materialism is religious in character, even though it rejects belief in God, creation and immortality. A religion without God seems very queer. But is it so queer? In the confessions of personal faith

[7] Brunner, *op. cit.*, p. 60.

of a hundred "thoughtful men and women in all walks of life," published in 1952 in a volume *This I Believe,* by Simon and Schuster, barely half even mentioned God at all. These supposed leaders of opinion in America declared their faith in brotherhood, service, idealism, reason, tolerance, democracy and faith, but not often or seriously in *God.* This is a more serious revelation than we have normally admitted. How many of these statements would be unacceptable in Russia? Apparently very few, granted the different meanings of some of the terms as they would be understood in another setting. Certainly Bulganin and Khrushchev went in strongly for brotherhood, tolerance and equality when they visited South Asia following the second Geneva Conference of 1955.

The Communist system is of great value to the rest of the world if it shows, in time, the damaging nature of some of the features of which we tend to be tolerant, but which we are now privileged to see, in the Communist experiment, in their naked ugliness. It is a help to see our own materialism in large letters, as it were, and without the softening effect of the various combinations into which it normally enters in the life of the West. Reinhold Niebuhr puts this with his usual vividness when he says, "The fact that Communists should adorn their more explicit dogma with the prestige of science provides modern liberal culture with a caricature of its own beliefs." Something of this was sensed very early by the erratic yet brilliant mind of Adolf Hitler. In *Mein Kampf* he wrote: "Marxist doctrine is a brief spiritual extract of the philosophy of life that is generally current today. And for this reason alone any struggle of our so-called bourgeois world against it is impossible, absurd in fact, since this bourgeois world is also essentially infected by these poisons, and worships a view of life which in general is distinguished from the Marxists only by degrees and personalities." [8]

D. NAÏVE SELF-RIGHTEOUSNESS

It is not very difficult for the person who is not embedded in the Communist religion to see that it involves many serious intellectual mistakes. The most important of these is the constant failure to

[8] Adolf Hitler, *Mein Kampf,* trans. by Ralph Manheim, Boston, Houghton Mifflin, 1943, p. 382.

apply to their own system the same standard of criticism which they apply ruthlessly to others. If all systems involve ideological taint, why does not Leninism involve that taint? Why is white colonialism "bad" while red colonialism is necessary and "good"?

It is to the credit of religious philosophers that they have been among the most persistent in pointing out the inner contradiction. Characteristic of such efforts is the following from Professor Harry Cotton:

> When the Marxists say that all systems of thought, including the most abstract mathematics and the most speculative metaphysics, are ideologies, they obviously intend to make an exception of their own statement. In this one case, at any rate, they succeed in getting beyond "ideology" to reality.[9]

The notion that the capitalist is essentially predatory, but that the workingman, when he comes to power, will not be equally predatory reflects a vast unsophistication concerning the human predicament and is constantly belied by events. When a strike occurs, the labor leader is not obviously more unselfish than is the representative of the company.

It is not wholly surprising that the most serious criticisms of dialectical materialism, both in theory and in practice, have come more from the religious standpoint than from the standpoint of economics or politics. Though the economics of the Communists are indeed vulnerable, their theory of man is far more vulnerable. Even during the war, when there was so much of a sense of comradeship in arms, Reinhold Niebuhr showed how trenchant basic criticism can be. In his West Lectures, *The Children of Light and the Children of Darkness,* he asserted, in January, 1944, that the future peace would depend primarily on three great powers, Britain, Russia and the United States. His analysis, written while the war was raging, deserves to be remembered for a long time:

> Of these three Russia will have the greatest difficulty in establishing inner moral checks upon its will-to-power. This will be the case, not because it is communistic or materialistic; but rather because it is informed by a simple religion and culture which make self-criticism dif-

---

[9] J. Harry Cotton, *Christian Knowledge of God,* New York, Macmillan, 1951, p. 41.

ficult and self-righteousness inevitable. Its creed assumes the evil intentions of capitalistic powers and the innocency and virtue of a nation which stands on the other side of the revolution. The naïve self-righteousness which flows from these presuppositions is more dangerous to a mutual accord between the nations than any of the real or fancied vices which are attributed to Russia. The tendency toward self-righteousness is accentuated in Russia by the absence of democratic institutions through which, in other nations, sensitive minorities may act as the conscience of the nation and subject its actions and pretensions to criticism.[10]

The Western nations have a culture which demands self-criticism, but this self-criticism stems, in large measure, from their religious heritage. It is because all men are sinners that no one, not even the dictator or the group of leaders, can be trusted with unlimited power. Thus "man's capacity for justice makes democracy possible; but man's inclination to injustice makes democracy necessary."

Both the strength and the weakness of the philosophy of communism stem primarily from the fact that communism is a religion and an oversimple religion. The strength arises because a powerful mood of dedication can be engendered, accentuated by the covert social idealism which is overtly denied. Its greatest weakness is not merely that it fails to face the evidence for the being of God, but that it lacks the human corollaries of belief in God. It has neither the belief in the inherent dignity of man as a child of God nor the belief in man's chronic sin, which is an antidote to self-righteousness. In short, it misses both sides of Pascal's famous paradox: it sees neither the essential greatness nor the essential misery of man.

In the light of these considerations, we may confidently affirm that Marx-Leninism as a religion will not survive. It does not have enough truth on its side. In its emphasis on religion as an opiate it has utterly missed the astounding fact that prophetic religion has been one of the major sources of social change. It simply is not true to say that theistic religion has always been a conservative force. Leninism claims to deny all values except economic values, but it introduces a glaring inconsistency by assuming "without acknowledging the assumption that it is good to be a Marxist." [11] Whatever

---

[10] Reinhold Niebuhr, *The Children of Light and the Children of Darkness,* New York, Scribner, 1944, p. 183.

[11] Samuel M. Thompson, *A Modern Philosophy of Religion,* Chicago, Henry Regnery, 1955, p. 14.

the basis of this judgment may be, it is not economic, for it is something in terms of which economic systems are judged. The lack of
concern for objective truth has made possible a radically changing
party line, with infallibility at each point, even when former positions are openly contradicted. This may suffice for a tyranny, but
it will not suffice for a religion. We cannot do better than conclude
with the dictum of Professor H. G. Wood: "The Marxist philosophy
cannot face a careful criticism." [12]

[12] Wood, *op. cit.*, p. 65.

13
The Challenge of Freud

Any conception of reality which a sane mind can admit must favor some of its wishes and frustrate others.

C. S. LEWIS

The challenge to objective realism in religion which arises in some forms of psychology is almost as serious as that which comes from dialectical materialism. It does not involve as many people as does Marx-Leninism and it represents no hardened orthodoxy, but it penetrates many minds. The fact that the challenge is not always explicit and clear, as it is in the Communist challenge, does not keep it from being effective. Sometimes it is even more effective in that way. The attack is difficult for the ordinary believer to answer because it tends to be condescendingly tolerant. The ordinary attack of psychologism does not say that belief in God is false; it says that belief in God can be "explained." The critic thus poses as the wise man who can see more deeply than can others into the foibles and pathetic faith of other men. Instead of being crudely antagonistic, as the orthodox Communist is, he may appear to be sympathetic, tender and helpful. Freud considered himself a humanitarian.

A. THE THEORY OF PROJECTION

The notion that all objective religious belief is groundless because it can be explained away by psychological factors has been entertained by many, but the one man who has most fully caught the imagination of the public in this connection is Sigmund Freud, whose teaching continues to enjoy widespread popularity, with added impetus in this regard from the efforts made to celebrate the one hundredth anniversary of his birth. Any philosophy which professes to deal with religious truth in contemporary terms must come to grips with Freud's teaching in regard to religion. Since any effective answer to Freud will involve an answer to less famous persons who have presented a similar position, it is right to concentrate on him. If Freud cannot be answered, the chance that an honest religious faith can be held by civilized men and women is slight. Intelligent faith must find some valid solution to the problem presented by Freudianism, as it earlier had to find solutions to the problems presented by Copernicanism and Darwinism.

The unwary reader might suppose from reading Tillich's *Systematic Theology* that he takes a less serious view of the Freudian challenge: "It is not the task of theology to protect the truth of revelation by attacking Freudian doctrines of libido, repression, and sublimation on religious grounds." [1] His point is that there is no revealed psychology, as there is no revealed physics, and, therefore, within revelation, the conflict does not arise. This may do very well for theology, but it will not suffice in the philosophy of religion, where we are inevitably concerned with all of the relevant evidence. The simple truth is that, if the Freudian position is fully warranted, there is no way, by either revelation or any other way, in which an honest and intelligent person can be a believer in God in any objective sense.

Though they differ at certain important points, the average man is not wholly wrong in associating Freud and Marx as belonging to the same chapter of intellectual history. The psychological relativism of Freud has seemed to buttress the sociological relativism of Marx. As a result of the former, as Will Herberg has told us, "ideas, values and standards are regarded as at bottom merely the expression of unconscious desires striving for fulfillment and of the various mechanisms by which these desires are diverted or checked." [2]

Another important connection is that both men drew heavily on the thought of Feuerbach, especially in regard to the concept of projection. We have seen, in Chapter XII, that Marx accepted Feuerbach's theory that man, in his frustration, projects himself on a cosmic screen, but this was only a small feature in the Marxian system. With Sigmund Freud, however, the conception developed into something of central importance. Feuerbach's words, "Man has given objectivity to himself, but has not recognized the object

<hr />

[1] Vol. 1, p. 131.
[2] Will Herberg, *Judaism and Modern Man*, p. 20.

as his own nature," can stand, even now, as a brief formulation of a crucial aspect of Freud's doctrine.

Ludwig Feuerbach (1804-1872) published his most important book, *Das Wesen des Christentums*, in 1841. Religion, this philosopher held, is only the imaginative projection of human needs and hopes. Man supposes, in his innocence, that he has immediate contact with superhuman Reality, but he is only communing with himself. What men worship as gods are nothing but *Wunschwesen,* "wish-beings." Gods are *personified wishes.* Since men, when they worship and pray, are not conscious of the projection of their wishes, all religious experience is delusory.

When religion—consciousness of God— is designated as the self-consciousness of man, this is not to be understood as affirming that the religious man is directly aware of this identity; for, on the contrary, ignorance of it is fundamental to the peculiar nature of religion. To preclude this misconception, it is better to say, religion is man's earliest and also indirect form of self-knowledge, as in the history of the race, so also in that of the individual. Man first of all sees his nature as if *out* of himself, before he finds it in himself. His own nature is in the first instance contemplated by him as that of another being . . . Hence the historical progress of religion consists in this: that what by an earlier religion was regarded as objective, is now recognized as subjective; that is, what was formerly contemplated and worshipped as God is now perceived to be something *human.*[3]

Feuerbach proceeds to his task by attempting to show that each item of religious belief or experience may be interpreted as man's effort to objectify some wish. Providence is the desire to believe we are important, the experience of God as personal is the effort to say that *our* personality is the highest form of being; prayer is our desire to converse with ourselves. Miracle is the very heart of faith, for, though natural modes of dealing with human wishes and needs are satisfactory, miracle "satisfies the wishes of men in a way corresponding to the nature of wishes—in the most desirable way." [4] We love a miracle because in it we get what we wish right away—without any tiresome waiting.

[3] Ludwig Feuerbach, *The Essence of Christianity,* trans. by Marian Evans, 2d ed., London, 1881, p. 13.
[4] *Ibid.,* p. 129.

Contemporary psychologists who have upheld theories similar to that of Feuerbach have not added materially to his evidence, but they have, by introducing psychoanalysis, appeared to give a scientific turn to the question. The chief contemporary advance, if any, has been made by researches into the phenomena of the "unconscious" and the "subconscious," providing new data thereby. The study of abnormality has undoubtedly progressed in recent years and in so far as this sheds light on religious experience we have new information.

An unfortunate aspect of the projection theory is that it lends itself very easily to use on the part of the half-educated, making them feel superior to their fellow men, who still believe in objective reference. The evidence of direct religious experience, part of which we have presented in Chapter XI, is obviously very strong, but it is countered today by such phrases as "psychological explanation," "father image," "conditioning" and "wishful thinking."

B. The Freudian Attack

Sigmund Freud (1856-1939) gave his long life to efforts to penetrate the human mind, with very substantial results, the most substantial of which was the development of psychoanalysis. Of psychoanalysis he said, "For it cannot be denied that this is my creation." His belief that he had discovered something of intrinsic and enduring worth receives some substantiation from the success which his method has achieved, particularly in the treatment of mental illness. He held that what he had discovered was a method rather than a doctrine and said explicitly, "In reality psycho-analysis is a method of investigation, an impartial instrument like, say, the infinitesimal calculus." [5] In spite of this methodological claim, however, Dr. Freud did not hesitate to engage in sweeping conclusions about the nature of the world and the nature of man. His teachings about the predominance of the sexual urge and the crucial nature of childhood experiences are well known. About religious experience and belief he was equally explicit. Because he was so much better equipped in psychology than he was in philosophy it is unfortunate that he tried so often to be a philosopher. The path of wisdom for us, accordingly, is to keep the grain and to dismiss the chaff, though

[5] *The Future of an Illusion,* New York, Liveright, 1953, p. 64.

there has, as yet, been no general achievement of this result. No doubt the ultimate judgment will agree with that of Lewis Mumford when he says, "But the practical gifts of analytical psychology, which derive unmistakably from Freud's genius, outweigh its ideological defects." [6]

Freud's serious convictions about religion are found in three important books: *Totem and Tabu, The Future of an Illusion,* and his final work, *Moses and Monotheism.* The middle one in this series is the most significant for our present purposes, partly because it is Freud's most philosophical effort in this connection. *Totem und Tabu* was written to explain the origins of totemism, with strong emphasis on the son-father relationship and with little or no direct reference to contemporary or developed religious belief, but the *Future of an Illusion* proposes to deal with religious experience in general, including contemporary faith.

Freud's approach to the subject is, on the surface, a very plausible one, so plausible, indeed, that the reader may easily be led along by a line of thought which seems reasonable and fair. It begins with the incontestable fact that life is very hard for man to endure. There is always some measure of privation; there is the suffering which is occasioned by the animosity of other men; there are the evils of nature; and always, in the end, there is "the painful riddle of death." This is really an intolerable situation and man, naturally, seeks a solution of his perennial problem. "Man's seriously menaced self-esteem craves for consolation, life and the universe must be rid of their terrors, and incidentally man's curiosity, reinforced, it is true, by the strongest practical motives, demands an answer." [7]

The first step toward a solution of man's intolerable problem is the "humanization of nature." If there are personal forces in nature, we can do something about them, perhaps by appeasement or bribery. Freud calls this a substitution of psychology for natural science. Because this development is strictly analogous to infantile experience, in which the father is an object of both fear and dependence, man tends to make the forces of nature not merely human, but fatherlike. "And so," concludes Freud, "a rich store of

[6] Lewis Mumford, *The Conduct of Life,* New York, Harcourt, Brace, 1951, p. 249.
[7] Freud, *op. cit.,* p. 28.

ideas is formed, born of the need to make tolerable the helplessness of man." [8] Thus, at one stroke man protects himself in two directions, against the dangers of nature and fate, on the one hand, and against the evils of human society, on the other. The mystery is explained and the cruelty of men toward other men is curtailed by the invention of the idea that the superhuman Person is the arbiter of moral justice.

One would suppose that all this would be obvious to men, particularly because there is no valid proof for religious ideas, but, unfortunately, people in this enlightened age are still believers. This is a keen disappointment to Freud. He sadly admits that "in spite of their incontrovertible lack of authenticity, religious ideas have exercised the very strongest influence on mankind." [9] This, he says, presents a fresh psychological problem and leads to his clearest statement of his position in the following important paragraph:

These, which profess to be dogmas, are not the residue of experience or the final result of reflection; they are illusions, fulfilments of the oldest, strongest and most insistent wishes of mankind; the secret of their strength is the strength of these wishes. We know already that the terrifying effect of infantile helplessness aroused the need for protection—protection through love—which the father relieved, and that the discovery that this helplessness would continue through the whole of life made it necessary to cling to the existence of a father—but this time a more powerful one. Thus the benevolent rule of divine providence allays our anxiety in face of life's dangers, the establishment of a moral world order ensures the fulfilment of the demands of justice, which within human culture have so often remained unfulfilled, and the prolongation of earthly existence by a future life provides in addition the local and temporal setting for these wish-fulfilments.[10]

Since Freud's answer to the continuing strength of religious ideas is his doctrine of illusion, it is necessary for him to clarify the meaning of the term. It is not the same as error, for error may arise in many ways; it is *belief based on wish*. "Thus we call a belief an illusion when wish-fulfilment is a prominent factor in its motivation, while disregarding its relations to reality." [11] Of religious doctrines

[8] *Ibid.*, p. 32.
[9] *Ibid.*, p. 51.
[10] *Ibid.*, p. 52.
[11] *Ibid.*, pp. 54, 55.

he says, categorically, that "they are all illusions, they do not admit of proof." [12] Some of them *could* be true, of course, since they cannot be refuted, as they cannot be proved. The reason is that they do not lend themselves to scientific method, and "scientific work," Freud says, "is our only way to the knowledge of external reality." It is no wonder that Will Herberg can write: "Feuerbach's skepticism did not keep him from a gross idolatry of Man, nor did Freud's keen insight into the mechanism of rationalization and 'wish-fulfilment' save him from the incredible banalities of nineteenth-century science-worship." [13]

C. The Inaccuracy of the Data

When the above line of reasoning has been given there is no more, in Freudian terms, to say. The rest of the argument is merely repetitive, adding nothing fresh. In Freud's other writings, not specifically devoted to the analysis of religion, there are religious references, but they add nothing substantial to the argument just presented. Some of them, however, remove the mask of scientific impartiality and reveal a virulent opposition. For example, in *Civilization and Its Discontents*, published two years later than *The Future of an Illusion*, Freud wrote of the experience which includes prayer and faith in providence: "The whole thing is so patently infantile, so incongruous with reality, that to one whose attitude to humanity is friendly it is painful to think that the great majority of mortals will never be able to rise above this view of life. It is even more humiliating to discover what a large number of those alive today, who must see that this religion is not tenable, yet try to defend it inch by inch, as if with a series of pitiable rear-guard actions." [14] Earlier he had written of approaching the subject with "diffidence," but there is no diffidence here. It is conceivable, indeed, on Freudian assumptions, it is likely, that such a frenetic attack requires an explanation in terms of the unconscious. Was Freud illustrating his own thesis?

Since Freud has elevated science almost as much as the Russian

[12] *Ibid.*, p. 55.
[13] *Op. cit.*, p. 39.
[14] *Civilization and Its Discontents*, Sec. II, *The Major Works of Sigmund Freud*, Encyclopaedia Britannica, 1952.

Communists have, it is fair to examine his analysis of religion on
the level of scientific method. Whatever else science demands, it
demands a fair view of the available data, rather than an unrepre-
sentative selection. Freud's selection of religious data is almost as
unfair as could be arranged. All of his major illustrations are of
three related kinds, the pathological, the primitive and the infantile.
The great religious tradition of the Western world, according to
which men, acting under a sense of God's sovereignty, are able to
stand against the conventional morality, even unto death, is not so
much as mentioned. One would never suspect, from reading Freud,
that there ever were any Hebrew prophets or early Christians at all.
No reader could suspect the existence of great religious minds, of
the stature of Pascal's, who have wrestled mightily with the effort
to be both devout and intellectually honest. Imagine describing the
work of William Temple as a pitiable rear-guard action. All that
Freud says of religion is represented by the following:

> Religion circumscribes these measures of choice and adaptation by
> urging upon everyone alike its single way of achieving happiness and
> guarding against pain. Its method consists in decrying the value of life
> and promulgating a view of the real world that is distorted like a delusion,
> and both of these imply a preliminary intimidating influence upon
> intelligence.[15]

At the time that Freud wrote these bitter words such giant minds
as those of Reinhold Niebuhr, William Temple, Karl Barth, Jacques
Maritain, Albert Schweitzer and Martin Buber were vigorously at
work, but all that Freud could see was "the forcible imposition of
mental infantilism" and "mass-delusion." We see, even more vividly,
how far from accurate Freud is in his scientific data, when he men-
tions the ways in which the validation of religious ideas is attempted.
"If we ask," he says, "on what their claim to be believed is based,
we receive three answers, which accord remarkably ill with one
another. They deserve to be believed: firstly, because our primal
ancestors already believed them; secondly, because we possess proofs,
which have been handed down to us from this very period of
antiquity; and thirdly, because it is forbidden to raise the question
of their authenticity at all." [16]

[15] *Ibid.*, Sec. II.
[16] *The Future of an Illusion*, p. 45.

The most important thing to say about the above account is that no deeply concerned religious person of the twentieth century would recognize his efforts in this at all, for this is a caricature. Freud's only references to further methods of intellectual validation are to the ancient formula *Credo quia absurdum* and to the "as if" philosophy of Hans Vaihinger, according to which religious ideas are fictions, but useful fictions. Where is Thomism? Where is neo-orthodoxy? Where is *I and Thou?* Where is the theistic evidence represented by the very existence of science?

If there is one thing clear about the great religions it is that those who have, within them, striven most vigorously for intellectual integrity have, over and over, expressed their serious doubts. Even Christ, upon the cross, could say "My God, my God, why hast thou forsaken me?" That such doubt is not unique is shown by the fact that Christ was quoting the Twenty-second Psalm. Thousands of reverent men have been tortured by doubt and have said so openly. But Freud seems never to have heard of this aspect of religious life. "Let no one think," he says, "that the foregoing remarks on the impossibility of proving religious doctrines contain anything new. It has been felt at all times, assuredly even by the ancestors who bequeathed this legacy. Probably many of them nursed the same doubts as we, but the pressure imposed on them was too strong for them to have dared to utter them." [17] But they did utter them!

There is a widespread belief that Freud's researches seriously undermined current religious belief, but the shocking truth is that he apparently never understood current religious belief and certainly never mentioned it. His attack seems serious until it is examined at first hand and then it is not formidable at all, because it is not scientifically sound. We must always listen to the hostile critic, providing he knows what it is whereof he speaks, but there is no reason to pay attention to one who has no real comprehension of his subject. We must remember here what was said in an earlier chapter about disciplined insight. There is no good reason to respect the judgment of the alleged music critic who has not listened to music. In every area the question is whether the person who utters his critical dicta has engaged in the kind of examination which makes his observations potentially trustworthy. It is especially er⁴

[17] *Ibid.,* p. 47.

roneous to give supine credence to a man in one particular field because of his eminence in another, but this is really what has occurred in the reputation of Sigmund Freud. For a balanced judgment of his religious importance we cannot improve on the following sentences from Professor Thompson:

> Many of the things which Sigmund Freud had to say about religion were true enough. He had unusual insight into some of the psychological uses of religious belief, and he saw the frequent close relation of religious ideas with neurotic syndromes. But nowhere in Freud's principal writings is there the slightest indication that he ever dreamed of what religion at its best means to men and women whose religious faith feels itself completely at home and entirely secure in the company of their own highly developed critical intelligence.[18]

In many ways the most accurate sentence in *The Future of an Illusion* is that in which Freud writes: "The one person this publication may harm is myself."

D. THE CONFLICT WITH EXPERIENCE

Freud's greatest mistake, from the point of view of scientific objectivity, is his assumption that in all religious experience belief is in accord with wishes. As we read religious history we find that this is glaringly untrue. "We say to ourselves," says Freud, "it would indeed be very nice if there were a God, who was both creator of the world and a benevolent providence, if there were a moral world order and a future life, but at the same time it is very odd that this is all just as we should wish it ourselves." [19] The task of the psychoanalyst would be very easy if the situation were as simple as that, but, fortunately, it is not. The sober truth is that, in mature and critical religious experience, *conviction is frequently at variance with wishes.* "For the authentic decision of faith," Herberg reports, "is not something that is pleasant to natural man or flattering to his ego; on the contrary, it challenges the self in all its claims and voids it of all its pretensions." [20] The more we read of the great journals of worshiping men the more we conclude that religion is not so much a comfort as a disturbance. We have here the great word

[18] Samuel M. Thompson, *A Modern Philosophy of Religion*, p. 135.
[19] *The Future of an Illusion*, p. 58.
[20] *Op. cit.*, p. 37.

of Professor Whitehead when he said in his highly quotable style, "Above and beyond all things, the religious life is not a research after comfort."

The great response to Francis Thompson's poem, *The Hound of Heaven*, shows how deep the experience of unwanted encounter is in human life. We try to *escape* Him, but still He reaches us. Jonah tried to escape because his religious experience *forced* him to believe what he did not *want* to believe. The demands which the experience involved were too hard.

Far from helping men to have a good opinion of themselves, normative religious experience makes them despise themselves. When they see themselves in the light of God's presence they realize that their supposed righteousness is filthy rags. Note that in the classic account of the prophetic experience in the sixth chapter of Isaiah, the prophet, having "seen" the Lord, says "Woe is me." It is not, therefore, surprising that Pascal, who knew the spiritual life so deeply and so well, could write, "Men hate and despise religion, and fear it may be true." [21] Life would be so much easier and simpler if there were not the moral demands which religious commitment involves.

Religious experience in its simpler forms often gives a certain comfort, but as it becomes more advanced the note of tragedy enters. The maturity of Christianity, as a religion among other religions, is indicated by its stress on this tragic note. If the haunting words, "Let this cup pass away from me; nevertheless not as I will, but as thou wilt," can be interpreted as expressing a desire for comfort, the word "comfort" has become so ambiguous as to lose whatever explanatory value it ever had.

Not only has the nature of God, as revealed in religious experience, been different from what men have *desired;* it has likewise been different, in many cases, from what they have *expected.* Paul's experience on the Damascus Road is a vivid illustration of a revelation which was *neither* desired nor expected. The prophets were taught to expect one kind of experience, but they actually had another. Therein lies the possibility of progress. The whole prophetic movement reaches its climax in the words, "Ye have heard it said . . . but I say unto you."

[21] *Pensées,* 187 (Brunschvicg).

It is likewise erroneous to suppose that men invariably think of God as a larger exemplification of themselves. That there is some anthropomorphism no one doubts, but with the development of insight devout men recognize that God is "other" than themselves. The classic expression of this conviction is the sentence put in the mouth of God: "My ways are not your ways, nor my thoughts your thoughts."

The blunt truth is that the upholders of the doctrine of *Wunschwesen,* from Feuerbach to Freud and beyond, do not know what they are talking about. They have spun a theory without bothering to check the evidence, most of which is never seen in clinics or laboratories. That there have been men whose alleged religious experience has been highly comforting, wholly in line with their desires, none doubts, but to assert that this has been the universal experience or even the characteristic one is to reveal gross ignorance. If this dogma were true, we should expect all prayer to be self-seeking; instead, we find the recognition of a demand for the most rigorous self-denial and self-sacrifice. Those who have claimed to know God best have found that He demands things almost impossible to perform. How, on the hypothesis of *Wunschwesen,* did the notion of the *Cross* ever enter the world? Pascal seems to be addressing men of our time when he says, "Let them at least learn what is the religion they attack, before attacking it." [22]

[22] *Ibid.,* 194.

14

The Challenge of Logical Positivism

The doctrines of Logical Positivism are embraced with some of the fervour appropriate to a new religious creed.
C. E. M. JOAD

The threefold attack on the credibility of objective religious belief, which we are examining in this section of the book, appears in the form of a series, with increasing sophistication in the nature of the attacks. The intended blow which is included in the philosophy of Marx is wholly direct; it asserts blankly that belief in God, immortality, and an objective moral order is plainly *false* and superstitious, and this is the orthodox doctrine in Russia to this day. The attack which stems from Freud is much less crude and contents itself with showing, to its own satisfaction, that all such belief can be explained psychologically. The attack which stems from Logical Positivism does not bother to *deny* or to *explain,* but seeks to undercut much more radically by showing that all convictions about these matters are strictly meaningless. Since propositions about religious and moral truth are neither true nor false, they are *nonsense.*

It is obvious to the careful student that this is as far as it is possible to go along this particular line. Furthermore, it must be taken seriously, for the chief upholders of contemporary positivism are not men who can be neglected. Some of them occupy chairs of philosophy in some of our best universities, and thousands of thoughtful people, half consciously in some cases, have been influenced by them. Herein lies the contemporary residue of the once-vigorous struggle between science and religion. It is not that the cudgels are today taken up, for the most part, by practicing scientists, but far more by men, outside the laboratory sciences, who have a reverence for science. What is necessary to consider, therefore, is not science, but a particular philosophy of science which seeks to be universal in its scope of application. If the positivist attack cannot be met and answered, we may as well give up all talk about an intelligent faith.

A. THE DEVELOPMENT OF LOGICAL POSITIVISM

Positivism, as a philosophical influence in the Western world, has appeared thus far in two chief stages. The first stage was ushered in by the French thinker, Auguste Comte (1798-1857), who believed that he was producing, or at least recording, a revolution in human thought. He saw all history as a development through various stages, reaching at last to the scientific, or positivistic, stage, in which men are finally wise enough to refuse to speculate about what is beyond their experience, but limit themselves to what is observable, measurable and verifiable. Thus, they come, in the maturity of the race, to eschew both religion and metaphysics as worthless and idle undertakings. It is neither possible nor necessary to explain; it is sufficient to report and to describe.

Contemporary positivism uses some of the same terminology as that used by Comte and his associates, but it seeks to go much further in the attempted revolution in philosophy. It shares with nineteenth-century positivism an extremely high regard for science; it puts an equal stress on empiricism, and it rejects all metaphysics, but the grounds of these conclusions are different. The modern phase began with the brilliant work of C. S. Peirce of Johns Hopkins University, who was a pioneer in what has been called the modern *meaning of meaning*. He found a ready listener and, in some ways, a disciple in the person of William James. Peirce's most important work was an essay called "How to Make Our Ideas Clear." [1] This emphasis was carried further by the help of modern symbolic logic, in the so-called Vienna School of the nineteen-twenties. It rests heavily upon the foundations provided by the *Principia Mathematica* of Russell and Whitehead and by Ludwig Wittgenstein's *Tractatus Logico-Philosophicus*. The common element of all positivism is the effort to set

---

[1] First published in 1878 in the *Popular Science Monthly*.

limits to philosophical inquiry and thus to avoid fruitless discussion. It must not be supposed, however, that Professor Whitehead, though he helped provide some of the tools of this movement, was ever involved in positivism, even to the slightest degree.[2]

The study of what is fruitful and not fruitful has led to much discussion of language, so that much contemporary positivism seems almost wholly devoted to the problems of semantics. In this form it has become a cult, with a rigid orthodoxy of its own and a strong sense of belonging to the initiated circle. No one has founded a semantics church, as George Eliot and other followers of Comte formed a positivist church in London in the nineteenth century, but the marks of a cult are obvious to the outside observer even if they are not obvious to the faithful.

Of those who speak most authoritatively for logical positivism today the chief names are Alfred Jules Ayer, among English philosophers, and Herbert Feigl, among Americans, as well as some remainders of what was once the Vienna School. Professor Ayer has achieved a certain unchallenged eminence as a spokesman, partly because of his unqualified conviction that nearly all of his philosophical precursors have been wrong. The problems which occupied the minds of great men from Plato to Aquinas to Whitehead are curtly dismissed as unworthy of the attention of sensible men. The beginning sentence of Ayer's major book is "The traditional disputes of philosophers are, for the most part, as unwarranted as they are unfruitful." [3]

It is confidently asserted that, by means of logical analysis following the new principles, problems which have bothered mankind for centuries are now settled. The disputes between rationalists and empiricists, we are told, are among those "of which we have now finally disposed." This claim, it will be noted, is closely similar to the claim of Marxism to have settled once and for all a number of

[2] Cf. *Adventures of Ideas,* pp. 147-151. Whitehead's criticism of contemporary positivists was strong and forthright. "They canalize thought and observation within predetermined limits, based upon inadequate metaphysical assumptions dogmatically assumed."

[3] The book was first published in 1936. A new printing with a new Introduction came out ten years later. Though Ayer is quoted more than any other contemporary positivist, he does not and cannot have a position comparable to that of Marx or Freud in the other movements considered in the immediately preceding chapters.

ancient disputes. Positivism shares with Marxism both intolerance
and dogmatism.

Logical positivism, as it appears today, is a combination of the
older empiricism and the newer formal logic. The empiricism involved is that which restricts all knowledge of fact to *sense* experience. There are other propositions than factual ones, namely, necessary propositions, but they turn out, upon analysis, to be either
(1) mere tautologies or (2) conventions of language. Thus, when we
say that blue is a color we are not making a factual statement at
all, but merely repeating in the predicate what was already involved
in the subject. Many statements turn out to be nothing more than
definitions, and all definitions are arbitrary linguistic conventions.

If we want to know whether a statement has meaning we must ask
whether it can be *verified*, and the only terms in which we can verify
are those of sense experience. The proposition "There is gold in
Colorado" is meaningful, definitely either true or false, because it is
possible to go to Colorado and find out. Either we find metal which
can be weighed in a pan or we do not. Even statements about the
other side of the moon are meaningful, because we could verify them
if we were there.

Many of the discussions of the past, we are told, have been a
complete waste of time, because the opponents were not really arguing about anything that made sense. Thus, to ask what was the
purpose of God in the creation of the world is, according to positivist doctrine, the same as to make absolutely empty sounds. It is
not only that we do not know and cannot know the divine purpose,
because of our finitude, but that any propositions on the subject are
utterly devoid of meaning for the simple reason that there is no way
by which they can be tested. What difference is observable, if the
proposition is true? Meaning is fundamentally *operational*. If two
apparently conflicting propositions do not involve any operation
which would make a difference in human experience, the supposed
conflict is purely illusory.[4] Such propositions are worse than false;
they are strictly meaningless.

That this represents an attempted revolution in philosophy is
clear, since the inquiries of most of the great thinkers of human

[4] Cf. Percy Bridgman, *The Logic of Modern Physics,* for a full discussion of
the operational theory of meaning.

history are simply analyzed out of court. Their very statements about God, the Absolute, the soul, good and evil, justice, necessity, freedom, and a world beyond our experience are now seen to be meaningless, because none of these is verifiable by sensory experience. Freedom makes no marks on rotary graphs; God cannot be found in the laboratory; the good cannot be observed by means of sensation. Historically, philosophy has been a search for truth on important problems of human life and destiny, but, if logical positivism is to reign, all this is outmoded, along with the flat earth and phlogiston. Philosophy is thus restricted in its efforts and approaches the position of grammar. "It lays down the conditions under which propositions have meaning, lists the more useful of the arbitrary definitions that people employ in their thinking, and exhibits, through the new techniques, what these definitions formally imply." [5]

The effort of contemporary positivists to save their fellow men from profitless discussion is highly commendatory. There is no value in arguing about matters where no evidence is available. This is what is wrong, we may be sure, with the alleged science of astrology. So far as the outsider can see there is no astrological evidence at all, so that the statements made can be neither upheld nor refuted. The entire system may be coherent within itself, but it is not checked by reference to fact; therefore, it is a silly waste of time and effort.

But most positivists of our day are not willing to rest their efforts after such modest and beneficent contributions to society as those just mentioned. The standard procedure is to try to eliminate, at the same time, all moral judgments. When I say that slavery is wrong, how can my proposition be meaningful at all? "Wrong" does not have to do with weight or measurement or sound or taste or sight or touch or smell. What operation can be performed? I could, conceivably, make an experiment in modern slavery, as the Russians have done in the Siberian camps, but this would not produce any *wrongness* that could be observed empirically. We might observe lacerated backs and emaciated bodies, but to observe them is not to observe wrongness. Therefore, when I say that slavery is wrong I am not, says the positivist, making a factual proposition at all. I

---

[5] Brand Blanshard, *The Nature of Thought*, New York, Macmillan, 1940, vol. 2, p. 403.

am not saying anything about the world, but only giving expression
to my inner emotion. Statements about wrongness are strictly comparable to expressions of disgust over bad-smelling food.

> But in every case in which one would commonly be said to be making
> an ethical judgment, the function of the relevant ethical word is purely
> "emotive." It is used to express feeling about certain objects, but not to
> make any assertion about them.[6]

The point is made in a slightly different way by holding that
moral propositions are not propositions at all. Not all statements
are propositions, i.e., affirmations or negations capable of being true
or false. Consider the statement "Pass the bread." It can neither be
affirmed nor denied. In like manner "God is," "God loves," and
"man is immortal" are not real propositions, but only pseudo propositions. We do not need to be very astute to realize that this philosophy, if it is sound, makes all theology impossible; theology is
bracketed with astrology and, though kept up for a while by the
faithful, eventually fails to interest any first-rate minds. Some challenges are trivial and some crucial; this one is crucial.

Though the attack on religious knowledge of the kind claimed
in this book is widespread, we do not need to draw upon many
authors in order to illustrate it. We may, for example, read the relatively mild essay of John Wisdom of Trinity College, Cambridge,
called "Gods." [7] As we finish it we are reminded of Wittgenstein's
final dictum, "Whereof one cannot speak thereof one must be silent,"
and wish that the master's advice had been followed. But it is in
Ayer's major pronouncement that we get the clearest statement of
what the system involves for religious knowledge. At least it can be
said for this writer that he does not lack self-confidence. Consider,
in this connection, the following dictum: "This mention of God
brings us to the question of the possibility of religious knowledge.
We shall see that this possibility has already been ruled out by our
treatment of metaphysics." [8]

The belief "that all utterances about the nature of God are nonsensical" does not, says Ayer, support either atheism or agnosticism,

[6] A. J. Ayer, *Language, Truth and Logic*, rev. ed., p. 108.

[7] *Logic and Language*, 1st. series, Basil Blackwell, Oxford University Press,
1952, Essay X.

[8] Ayer, *op. cit.*, rev. ed., p. 114.

both of which make the foolish mistake of taking religious propositions seriously. We are told that "the atheist's assertion that there is no god is equally nonsensical since it is only a significant proposition that can be significantly contradicted." [9] And why is a religious proposition nonsense? Because there is no sensory experience by which the proposition can be verified. The fact that it is intelligible is not sufficient.

It might be supposed that religious experience, such as we have examined in Chapter XI, would be honored by one who calls himself an empiricist, but not so. Indeed, the tremendous claim of millions of thoughtful people whose reported experience of God is such that it meets the tests of scientific knowledge is dismissed in seventeen lines of print. The lines begin:

> We conclude, therefore, that the argument from religious experience is altogether fallacious. The fact that people have religious experiences is interesting from the psychological point of view, but it does not in any way imply that there is such a thing as religious knowledge, any more than our having moral experiences implies that there is such a thing as moral knowledge. The theist, like the moralist, may believe that his experiences are cognitive experiences, but, unless he can formulate his "knowledge" in propositions that are empirically verifiable, we may be sure that he is deceiving himself.[10]

B. THE SELF-CONTRADICTION OF POSITIVISM

Vigorous and even arrogant as the positivist onslaught has been, it has not lacked careful and vigorous critics. Among the most able and persistent of these is Professor Brand Blanshard of Yale University, who has subjected the positivist claims to careful logical analysis, both in his major work, *The Nature of Thought,* and in several subsequent articles that have appeared in the learned journals. Since positivists claim to depend largely upon modern logic, Professor Blanshard, who is himself a skilled logician, accepts battle on that ground. But in this he is by no means alone. There are many brilliant contemporary criticisms, one of the ablest being that of

[9] *Ibid.,* p. 115.
[10] *Ibid.,* pp. 119, 120.

Morris Weitz, who writes on "Philosophy and the Abuse of Language." [11]

Perhaps the most thorough of the criticisms is that of C. E. M. Joad, who turns the sharp weapons of the positivists against them with telling force. He points out their intolerance and their dogmatism, but he does not end there. He goes on to show in detail the way in which positivists are involved in the very nonsense they so vehemently decry.[12]

The chief way to deal with logical positivism is not to defend ethics or religion, but to examine critically the position of the attacker himself. Perhaps logical positivism, in spite of the confident tone of its proponents, is vulnerable. This is exactly what we find to be the case. The positivist is most vulnerable at his basic starting point, which is supposed to justify his restriction of meaningful propositions to a special class. His basic proposition is "No statement of fact is meaningful unless it can be verified in sense experience." Now, the major question is: How does the positivist arrive at the truth or credibility of *this proposition?* According to his own doctrine, there are only two types of statements that make sense, (*a*) those which are strictly logical and (*b*) those which record sense experience. But which of these is his basic premise? Certainly it is not an analytic proposition in the Kantian or any other sense, and we may say, with equal certainty, that it has not been revealed in sense experience. Which one of the senses could provide us with such a universal? It must be a mere matter of taste, in which case we do not need to pay serious attention to it, or it may be sheer dogma, but those who rest in dogma are poor critics of dogma. Few of those who have faced the positivist challenge boldly have been more trenchant than has Will Herberg in the following succinct sentences:

It is based on the premise that, aside from the rules of logic, only scientific statements, only statements of fact, have any meaning. This premise is a gratuitous assumption affirmed as a dogma; it is, moreover, self-destructive. Not only does it sweep away as so much nonsense virtually all human thinking—all, that is, but what has been devoted to logic and

[11] *Journal of Philosophy*, vol. 44, No. 20, Sept. 25, 1947.
[12] C. E. M Joad, *A Critique of Logical Positivism,* University of Chicago Press, 1950.

empirical science; in the end it turns upon and destroys itself. For the basic doctrine of positivism, as thus defined, is itself obviously neither a principle of logic nor the conclusion of any empirical science; it is, therefore, by its own criterion, nonsense.[13]

When the positivist is challenged to show why he makes an arbitrary limitation upon human inquiry, all that he can say is that he prefers to begin that way. Sometimes, when hard pressed on this point, the positivist says he is not making a dogmatic statement about reality, but is merely giving a definition. But, in that case, all of the revolutionary results, which are supposed to follow from the method, disappear. A man cannot eliminate whole areas of human experience merely by a definition of his own making. Actually, of course, the positivist is merely demonstrating a pathetic kind of *scientism,* the common faith of Marxism, Freudianism and logical positivism. The success of one particular method is so impressive that in spite of differences on other subjects, all of these groups have decided that any approach to truth other than that of natural science is to be discarded.

Such scientism is really disloyal to science, for science at its best is very humble in the face of nature and the ultimate mysteries. Science asks questions and accepts evidence of all kinds without judging the situation in advance. To say that we cannot know objective reality except by means of sense experience is clearly to prejudge the case. It is, therefore, *unscientific.*

The major defect of logical positivism is that it is not truly empirical, since empiricism is intrinsically humble and open-minded, rather than arbitrary. Partly because of this, many logical positivists today want to be called simply empiricists, but they cannot arrogate this term to themselves without begging the question. They are not empiricists for the simple reason that they rule out whole areas of experience, especially the ethical, the purely intellectual and the religious. All of the good arguments that positivists propose are merely arguments for empiricism in general and not for their party line in particular. The attempt to disguise positivism as empiricism does not succeed, provided the reader is truly critical, for there may be countless experiences open to living creatures which

[13]*Judaism and Modern Man,* p. 90.

do not come by means of what we call the physical senses. It is certainly not self-evident that our contact with reality is so meager that the only valid contact comes in ways which can be tested in a laboratory of physical science. It is part of the experience of every person to engage in a multitude of experiences which are not sensory at all. Here Professor Joad helps us greatly with his common-sense approach.

> I can do mental arithmetic, working out sums in my head without the aid of pencil and diagram, paper and blackboard—without, that is to say, having sensory experience. I can mentally add up a set of remembered figures, make a calculation on the basis of the sum I have arrived at, wonder if I have added it up wrong, and check it by adding it up again. Moreover, I can do all this in my mind. Once again, the processes involved are undoubtedly experienced; I can reflect upon them, remember them and dislike them. But, they are not sensory.[14]

It is important to realize that the positivist is propounding theories which go beyond the facts of science to which he claims to limit himself. This is the point of the following criticism from the pen of Erich Frank:

> The Positivist is right in saying that it is not merely the logic of the theoretical arguments which directs the argumentation of the metaphysician, but rather a certain preconceived conviction which has been borne out throughout his life. Yet the same is true of the Positivist himself; for it cannot be merely on the strength of the logic of his argument that he offers theories far transcending the mere facts of science. Instead, it must be an irrational belief, this selfsame belief in the perceptible world and in natural life which, to him, is the ultimate truth upon which he has decided to stake his whole existence once and for all.[15]

The self-contradiction of positivism is put in a slightly different way by Professor Blanshard when he says that "it is hard to believe that this theory about conventions figures in the minds of its advocates as just another convention." [16] But it is in the analysis of logical relations that Blanshard is most penetrating:

[14] C. E. M. Joad, *op. cit.*, pp. 52, 53.
[15] Erich Frank, *Philosophical Understanding and Religious Truth,* Oxford University Press, 1945, p. 39.
[16] *Op. cit.*, p. 417.

And what of the proposition itself that all necessary propositions are conventions? Which of the two classes does it fall in, the class of empirical probabilities or the class of tautologies? If the former, then at any moment a necessary proposition may turn up that is not tautology, and hence the sweeping statement above is illegitimate. If in the latter, the theory is self-contradictory again, for having laid it down that no necessary proposition says anything about the facts, it lays down a necessary proposition about propositions; and since a proposition is described as "a class of sentences," and sentences are facts, we have a necessary statement about facts after all.[17]

In the light of such analysis we have a right to conclude that logical positivism fails to undermine religious belief, because it undermines itself in the effort. In its attempt to fix the limits of rational inquiry, by fiat, it uses the natural sciences unjustifiably as the basis of a new authoritarian orthodoxy, but this means that criticism of other orthodoxies comes with poor grace. The criticism of sectarianism comes oddly from those who themselves constitute a sect.

C. VOLUNTARY POVERTY

Though the fact that logical positivism is internally inconsistent constitutes its most serious defect, sufficiently serious to remove it as a threat to objective belief, there is another defect that must be mentioned: it involves a signal impoverishment of human thought. It may be described as a form of extreme poverty of the intellect, not a poverty forced upon the philosopher from the outside, but one which is self-inflicted. By the very nature of the positivist self-limitation we have a kind of modern monasticism, in which the fullness of life is renounced. The limitation is such that the only subjects which can be discussed are relatively trivial.

Professor Samuel M. Thompson ends his long and careful work on the philosophy of religion on this important note. Theism may have difficulties, as any position has, but it at least sees the mystery and deals intelligently with it. But the positivists "do not even see the mystery. Because they do not see it they cannot even consider the greatest themes of human thought and experience. The themes of life and death, of God and the world, of good and evil are the

[17] *Op. cit.*, pp. 416-417.

themes of great art and great literature. They are the issues for which men bleed and die." The miserable fate to which positivists have condemned themselves is that they "cannot think on such things; for them the ultimate preoccupations of a life lived at maximum intensity are things which are mentioned only to be dismissed." [18]

One of the most paradoxical elements of this intellectual poverty is the fact that the consistent positivist cannot deal meaningfully with either the past or the future, being imprisoned necessarily in the specious present. How, on the grounds of a strict sensory empiricism, can we say that Caesar fought in Gaul? Certainly, we cannot now achieve a sensory record of Caesar *fighting* in Gaul. That is gone forever. How, then, is historical science possible? Of course, we can see evidences *now,* such as marks on stone or paper, but that is a sensory experience of a present and not a past event. We cannot conclude from them anything about the past except by some kind of postulate, which is precisely what the positivist disdains. In regard to propositions about the future, the methodological difficulty is even more clear. It is, therefore, not surprising that a highly percipient editorial writer in the *Times Literary Supplement* of London should write as follows:

> To the layman at least it seems clear that in so far as any scientist makes statements about either the future or the past he is making statements which, strictly speaking, can never be verified by observations, the principle of causality itself plainly comes into this category, and if a scientist should say that he regards the general truth of the theory of causality merely as a hypothesis, he will not be believed.[19]

What can the logical positivist say about the possibility of the annihilation of the human race and the consequence that the earth goes on spinning without men on it. He is forced to deny that the idea of the continuation of the earth without men is a meaningful statement, because it would not be experienced in sensation. But a doctrine which leads to such absurdity is itself absurd.

Another striking limitation of content is that which rules out not only other times, but other consciousness. By what scientific evi-

---

[18] Samuel M. Thompson, *A Modern Philosophy of Religion,* p. 529.
[19] "Relativity," *Times Literary Supplement,* March 2, 1951, p. 133.

dence, such as the consistent positivist will honor, do I know anything about the mind of any other human being, let alone the Divine Mind? Certainly mind is not seen in test tubes. That such a serious impoverishment is involved is one of the chief observations involved in Blanshard's keen analysis of the analysts. "All statements," he says, "about the consciousness of other people are meaningless, since none of our own sensations can verify its existence; the best we can do is to observe their bodily behavior; and hence, when we speak of their experience, it is their behavior that we mean. As regards everyone but himself, the positivist is, therefore, a behaviorist." [20]

The most serious self-limitation which is imposed by the superstitious reverence for science which is called scientism is that, in dealing with appearance and reality, the only possible object of attention is *appearance*. Ontological discussion is, by definition, ruled out. This is made necessary by limiting logic to the logic of extension. This can, of course, be attempted, but there is always the question whether the attempt succeeds. This is the question which Professor Tillich asks in the following passage:

The question is whether the elimination of almost all traditional philosophical problems by logical positivism is a successful escape from ontology. One's first reaction is the feeling that such an attitude pays too high a price, namely, the price of making philosophy irrelevant. But, beyond this impression, the following argument can be put forward. If the restrictions of philosophy to the logic of the sciences is a matter of taste, it need not be taken seriously. If it is based on an analysis of the limits of human knowledge, it is based, like every epistemology, on ontological assumptions. There is always at least one problem about which logical positivism, like all semantic philosophies, must make a decision. What is the relation of signs, symbols, or logical operations to reality? Every answer to this question says something about the structure of being. It is ontological. And a philosophy which is so radically critical of all other philosophies should be sufficiently self-critical to see and to reveal its own ontological assumptions.[21]

Man as a would-be knower is in a difficult position. On the one hand, he faces the danger of naïve simplicity in which he is not sufficiently aware of his liability to error. On the other hand, there is the danger that, fearful of making conclusions which outrun experience, he accepts a virtual nihilism in which there is no recognition of any important knowledge at all. Positivism falls into the second peril in its drastic endeavor to avoid the first. Modern man, poised between his faith in objective reality and his keen sense of the relativity of all human perceptions about it, must walk carefully, as on a tightrope. This involves a certain tension, but it can be a beneficent tension. The deepest mistake of the positivist is to give up the struggle to maintain this tension.

Part IV
ENDURING PROBLEMS

15

Naturalism and Supernaturalism

It is fashionable to state that religion and science can never clash because they deal with different topics. I believe that this solution is entirely mistaken.

ALFRED NORTH WHITEHEAD

Modern man is, for better or for worse, scientific man. From this there is no retreat. Scientific mentality has influenced our judgments on almost all matters which we examine. On the whole, this is as it should be, particularly if we see science as a process of inquiry and not as a set of fixed doctrines. Because ours is one world, religious concepts must make their peace with scientific experience and scientific concepts must make their peace with religious experience. Peace cannot be made by the superficial solution of allocating separate and autonomous realms. If we hold convictions with one part of our minds and deny them with another, life is finally intolerable. Though the problem of intellectual consistency may be felt with especial sharpness today, it is really a very old problem and has been inherent in the life of the West from the time of the first Milesian philosophers.

A. THE CENTRAL DIFFICULTY

Whatever the problem regarding the conflict of science and religion may be, it is not the old problem of geology and Genesis. The dogmatism on both sides of that controversy is gone now, with a greater humility on the part of all, because it is wholly possible, without contradiction, to appreciate the profundity of the Biblical account and, at the same time, to follow loyally whatever evidence we have about the age of the earth and the slowness of the process by which life developed upon it. One exciting feature of peace in this particular intellectual struggle is that the Genesis story of the garden is now seen as providing an especially sophisticated account of the basic human predicament. The conflict has ended, not by contempt for the Biblical account, as some nineteenth-century scientists supposed it would, but by a vastly enlarged recognition of the importance of that account.

The deepest difficulty appears in the open conflict between conceptions which are intrinsic to the two experiences under consideration. The essence of the problem is that science seems to require naturalism, whereas advanced religion requires supernaturalism, the two conceptions being superficially incompatible. If these conceptions were peripheral or tangential, the problem might be simple, but they are not. Science, as we know it, would not be possible were it not for the idea of natural law. The intellectual temper from which modern science has arisen is that of the Greek thought of the classic age, which developed the conviction that there is an intelligible order and system throughout nature. "Science has been built up all along on the basis of this principle of the 'uniformity of nature' and the principle is one which science itself has no means of demonstrating." [1] No inductive conclusion has any validity at all unless there is some sense in which the objects of limited observations constitute a "sample," not only of the vast unexplored present, but likewise of the past and the future. The very idea of *sample* is a profoundly revealing one.

It is important to realize that this entire scientific enterprise would be impossible if the actions of the various constituents of the universe which we study were arbitrary. Only upon the supposition that the natural world is fundamentally orderly is science possible at all. Unless there is some dependable pattern, some "law" which is illustrated in one case of diabetes as well as in another, the kind of research which led to the production of insulin would not be

---

[1] A. E Taylor, *Does God Exist?* p. 2. Cf. also Whitehead's dictum to the effect that "the order of nature cannot be justified by the mere observation of nature." *Science and the Modern World,* New York, Macmillan, 1948, p. 73.

either possible or sensible. Apart from natural law the entire practice of medicine is nonsensical.[2]

A world in which we could not say "because" could not be studied.[3] But is such a world one in which religion is possible?

The level of serious conflict is not primarily that of speculation, but the level of practice. There is no serious doubt that prayer is intrinsic to religion as the uniformity of nature is intrinsic to science. Nearly all public religion is public prayer and nearly all private religion is private prayer. This is more evident today than in many years, one of the chief marks of our current religious vitality being the spontaneous development of countless prayer groups organized by modest people, often without any help from those who are professionally religious. It might have been predicted that the practice of prayer would diminish in a highly scientific age, but the exact opposite has occurred. On all sides spring up "schools of prayer," and the books on prayer are so numerous that no one can keep up with all of them. The increase in daily prayer as a part of the discipline of the ordinary person has been phenomenal. If

[2] Few statements concerning this point have been as illuminating as that of Claude Bernard in his famous book, *An Introduction to the Study of Experimental Medicine.* This valuable French work is now available in the translation of Henry C. Greene, published by Henry Schuman, New York, 1949. Bernard's statement of the faith which science requires is worth quoting as follows:

"The first condition to be fulfilled by men of science, applying themselves to the investigation of natural phenomena, is to maintain absolute freedom of mind, based on philosophic doubt. Yet we must not be in the least sceptical; we must believe in science, i.e., in determinism; we must believe in a complete and necessary relation between things, among the phenomena proper to living beings as well as in all others" (p. 35).

[3] It is well known that some contemporary scientists have sought to give the impression that the idea of natural law is now outmoded and that causality has no significance. This movement is neither impressive nor convincing. In essence, it means the acceptance of the philosophy of David Hume, who understood very well that his philosophy *undermined* science. A. E. Taylor has pointed out in *Does God Exist?* that "on Hume's own assumption that all events are entirely 'loose and separate,' the holding-up of my finger is just as likely to be followed by the extinction of the sun as not. Unlike Mill, Mach and others who have tried to combine the principles of Hume with a belief that the results of the sciences are true, Hume himself saw the difficulty. It is because he saw it so clearly that his earliest and greatest work ends in scepticism in the proper sense of the word, i.e., in suspense of judgment and in refusal to commit himself to *any* 'philosophy of the sciences' " (p. 17). It is not now as popular as it once was to say that the Heisenberg principle of indeterminacy requires a revolution in philosophy.

prayer were removed from religion, not much worthy of attention would be left.

Here, then, we have two conceptions, one intrinsic to science and the other intrinsic to religion, but apparently in direct and serious conflict. On the surface, at least, the two ideas are strictly incompatible. When a child is stricken with polio, what shall we do? If prayer is sufficient, there is no need of prayer. It is easy to say that we ought to use *both,* but what are the intellectual grounds for this remark? The principle of parsimony is obviously a valid principle; there is no point in two cures if one is effective. It is the shame of many religious writers that they neglect or minimize this difficulty, going gaily forward as though no serious barrier were in the way. The consequence is that such writers make no more appeal to many scientifically minded persons than if they were talking about astrology. Intelligent people must earn the *right* to believe in prayer, and they cannot earn it except by careful thinking.

The greatest difficulty is felt in connection with petition and intercession. Men have long prayed for rain, but how can this be done with intellectual honesty when we realize something of the nature of meteorology? Men have long prayed for the restoration of the health of their loved ones, but how can this be done by honest persons who know something of the action of germs? When a patient has pneumonia what is needed, it would seem, is not prayer, but antibiotics. Such considerations do not, of course, prevent recourse to prayer, but they hinder it. Most parents, it is probable, pray for a child who is in danger of contracting infantile paralysis, but many wonder, in doing so, if they are acting rationally.

The difficulty is most clear when the time factor is involved. If a person receives a letter and, before opening it, prays that the letter may not contain bad news, the prayer has no justification. Whatever is in the letter is there already, and nothing under heaven will change it. In other words, such a prayer is self-contradictory. It asks that what is be something other than what it is. But the same difficulty remains in less obvious situations. Prayer about the contents of the letter is pointless at any time after it is written.

Much of our uneasiness in regard to other areas, such as the physical and the biological, arises from the conviction that the situation is already as fully determined by natural laws as the contents of the letter are already fixed by the writer. Whether there will be rain is already in the cards. But if this is true for one day, why not for a million? In the same way, the ravages of a disease seem to be already determined by the introduction of germs. In short, it is always too late. Perhaps, then, prayer is merely an irrational survival of a superstitious and anthropomorphic age. In that case, it will eventually cease with the growth of critical intelligence or continue as a sentimental gesture, but nothing more.

A second specific belief which the concept of natural law seems to rule out is the *belief in miracles*. Miracles, in the sense of striking evidences of Divine Power in the ordinary course of the world, have been reported from the earliest times, and the reports have been widely believed. Many miracles have been extremely well attested, and have been accepted as valid by thoughtful persons. The life of Christ, for example, has been considered miraculous by countless millions. This refers not only to his supposed deeds, but to his very existence and to his triumph over death. Even when we make due allowance, as we must, for the unreliability of oral transmission and the natural human desire to enlarge upon stories, there remains a core of historical evidence for such a miracle as the resurrection which meets adequately the tests used in historical research. But an increasingly large number of people find that they cannot believe such a miraculous account, not because the historical evidence is inadequate, but because they have a conception of natural law which rules out such events as *impossible*. From what we know of natural laws, they say, a body *could not* come to life after it had been dead more than two days. In the same way, they say, the physical amount of food *could not* be increased as it was alleged to have been in the story of the feeding of the five thousand. It is admitted that apparently miraculous *healings* might occur, since so many diseases have a psychical basis, but actual physical changes are, they suppose, in a different category.

This rejection of miracle, which often seems inevitable, is very serious for theism. If we find ourselves unable to believe in miracle, we may still think of God as the Author of the universe, including its natural laws, but such belief is almost valueless for practical religion. There does not seem much reason for worshiping a God who has made a world such that He is effectually shut out from participation in its management.

The widespread belief in *providence* is undermined along with the belief in miracle, because providence is nothing but a continuous evidence of miraculous care, either in the career of an individual or the career of a people. If miracle is impossible, the ancient Israelites were wrong in their crucial belief that God led them out of Egypt. They were merely lucky. The people of England prayed jointly during the battle of Dunkirk, but the safe arrival in England of so many survivors of that battle may have been a mere coincidence in the weather, which would have been the same if the people had not prayed. In short, if the conception of natural law which science seems to require is the true conception, then the experience of so many who feel the guiding hand of God in the events of their own lives is sheer self-delusion. Whatever the answer to this difficulty may be, it is one that cannot be neglected or answered lightly.

B. The Nature of the World Order

If the only alternative to belief in that kind of ordered sequence which seems to be incompatible with religious practice were *whim* or *caprice,* the choice of thoughtful people would necessarily be in favor of the faith required by science, rather than the faith required by religion. Unless ours is an orderly system, it seems difficult to know how we could proceed with anything. If the only choice is between orderly science and disorderly religion, science must win. But we are saying one of the most important things that can be said when we suggest that these two choices do not exhaust the logical possibilities. There is a third way, and it is a way which provides a working solution of the problem.

The great question before reflective thought is not *whether* ours is an ordered system, but *what kind of order* it represents. Though many different kinds of order may be imagined, there are two which have been presented with especial conviction, one of these being a *mechanical* order and the other an order of *purpose.*

(1) *The belief in a mechanical order,* fixed and uniform, has been at the heart of most of our difficulty about prayer and natural law. It can be stated simply without distortion. The thesis is that there

is fundamentally one kind of causal sequence in the world, that found in mechanical systems. This may be illustrated by the weather. The impact of air currents on one another is fully describable in mechanical terms, providing we have the time and patience. Wishing obviously does not affect the motion of the clouds nor are they self-moved. There are orderly ways in which material aggregates move, ways which we can learn but cannot alter. If the weather is determined already, as most of us suppose, for the next twenty-four hours, why is it not determined for the next million years? We chiefly assume that the official forecasters, when their predictions fail to come true, have overlooked some determinants and that, with more care or more skill, they could have succeeded.

It is customary to speak of this alleged system of nature as a "closed" system, and Professor Whitehead shows, with admirable conciseness, why this is the case. "We cannot wonder," he says, "that science rested content with this assumption as to the fundamental elements of nature. The great forces of nature, such as gravitation, were entirely determined by the configurations of masses. Thus the configurations determined their own changes, so that the circle of scientific thought was completely closed." [4] That there is such a closed system has been the orthodox creed of a great part of modern science since the seventeenth century. It has appeared to have a full justification by the pragmatic test, for it has actually worked and produced results. But grave intellectual difficulties have long been apparent in the system.

(2) *The belief in a purposive order* is the belief that nature cannot be explained except as the activity of Mind expressing itself through process. Nature, when interpreted in terms of purpose, is not a self-running mechanism, an enormous perpetual-motion machine, but a subsidiary system created and sustained for a *reason*. This *reason* gives dependability, since purpose is as strongly opposed to chance or caprice as mechanical determinism can possibly be. The purposive conception of law does all that the mechanical conception does, in that it points to the regularities of nature, but it also does more, in that it presents a rational explanation of the regularities. The world, according to this hypothesis, is not rational because it is a system of

---

[4] Alfred North Whitehead, *op. cit.,* p. 71.

natural law; it is, rather, law-abiding because it is the expression of a transcendent Reason.

Whereas the mechanical conception of natural law is entirely monistic, the purposive conception is dualistic or pluralistic in that it admits the existence of both minds and bodies, though both are part of the same creation. Purpose is the larger conception, since it can include mechanism, and mechanism cannot include purpose. The purposive systems we know best, i.e., human beings, include mechanical levels which operate alongside the levels of consciousness and, though they follow different laws, can be used in the service of purpose. In short, a purposive system is a personal system and our hypothesis involves the frank effort to understand the universe in personal terms.

When we suggest a way in which an ordered whole may follow laws and yet be dominated by purpose, we are not suggesting something unfamiliar to our common experience. The best illustration of how experience can be orderly and yet nonmechanical is found in moral experience, where we see the self-expression of a *constant* and constantly developing character. In character we observe an order which is flexible, but not capricious. We cannot predict the details of a man's moral actions as well as we can predict the weather, but we can do something far more important, we can predict the general character of his actions. When a man has a well-developed and trustworthy character, we do not know *which* of several particular alternatives he will choose, but we can be reasonably sure that he will *not* choose something ignoble. The reason for this is that moral actions are determined, not by efficient causation, but by the good as apprehended. The guide to conduct is not any one of several particular actions proposed, but something permanent which finds expression in them. In short, the conception of an ordered system in which the causal sequence is nonmechanical is not some wild speculation, but is already known in the moral experience of all men.

What is required is a conception of order which, while involving a certain degree of regularity, is flexible enough to include the emergence of real novelty. How necessary this is, Whitehead has made clear by his recognition that "nothing ever really recurs in detail." Ours is, indeed, in some sense an open universe. "No two days are identical, no two winters. What has gone has gone forever. Accordingly, the practical philosophy of mankind has been to expect the broad recurrences, and to accept the details as emanating from the inscrutable womb of things beyond the ken of rationality. Men expected the sun to rise, but the wind bloweth where it listeth." [5]

Not only Professor Whitehead, but many other contemporary philosophers, including Lloyd Morgan and Arthur O. Lovejoy, have called for a conception which is rich enough to give adequate expression to the variety of the world as experienced. Why, they ask, should we not pay as much attention to the kind of order found in organic wholes and the kind found in purposive behavior as we do to the kind found in merely material aggregates? Professor Lovejoy represents this entire revolt against the oversimplification of reductive naturalism when he writes:

> The union of the conception of evolution with the conception of reality as a complex of which all the parts are theoretically deducible from a very small number of relatively simple laws of the redistribution of a quantitatively invariable sum of matter and of energy—this union the "emergent evolutionist," if I may so call him for short, now declares to be a *mésalliance,* of which the progeny are hybrid monsters incapable of survival.[6]

It is important to ask what kinds of novelty there might be, which, if they should appear, would make the hypothesis of reductive naturalism invalid and would, accordingly, uphold the contentions of the emergent evolutionists. Professor Lovejoy has analyzed these for us as follows:

> They would consist in the appearance at certain points in the history of some system of (a) *qualities* not previously found anywhere in that system; or (b) *types of objects or events* not previously existent therein, not merely combinations of anything previously existent, and characterized by new qualities; or (c) *laws,* i.e. modes of uniform action, not previously exemplified by any entities in the system.[7]

That such kinds of novelty do appear in the evolutionary process, the studies of Lloyd Morgan, Jan Smuts, and others have shown. The chief point to stress now, however, is that the third kind of novelty mentioned by Professor Lovejoy is fully as important as the others

[5] *Ibid.,* p. 7.
[6] Arthur O. Lovejoy, "The Discontinuities of Evolution," *University of California Publications in Philosophy,* vol. 5, p. 177.
[7] *Ibid.,* p. 178.

and even easier to substantiate. Without arguing the question whether the new "objects," such as organisms, are merely combinations of previous existents or are genuinely novel, it is at least clear that there are new laws. The question whether mind and matter are fundamentally the same, substantially, seems beside the point when they so obviously follow different modes of action. The distinction between the "mental," as that which is private to consciousness, and the "physical," in the sense of an independent system of entities or events having those causal relations which physical science seeks to describe, was one of the first of man's philosophical acquisitions, and one which is still necessary for rational thought and action. Whether nature is bifurcated is a debatable question, but that experience is bifurcated is not a matter of reasonable doubt. Dualism, both psychophysical and epistemological, has been the main intellectual tradition in the Western world since the time of Plato, and modern attempts to discredit this tradition have not been conspicuously successful.[8]

Many men have set their hands to the task of showing the radical difference between the two kinds of being whose existence is almost universally admitted, *bodies* and *minds,* but few have done better service in this connection than Professor Webb of Oxford, who insists that all men do, in practice, distinguish between one set of qualities, such as extension and motion, which we attribute to bodies and another set of qualities, such as those of thinking and feeling, which we attribute to minds.[9] If we are going to be empirical, accepting the world as we find it, we must somehow find room for both sets of qualities. The truth is that a rigidly mechanical system cannot account for the second set of qualities, except in an epiphenomenal sense. Contemporary rejections of monism are based on the observation that the one-level conception of natural law does not cover all the facts. Since we actually find different levels of law in the experienced world, our notion of natural law must be enlarged and enriched to include phenomena radically different from those observable on the mechanistic plane.

[8] Professor Lovejoy's book, *The Revolt Against Dualism,* is an account of the attempt to dislodge the dualistic tradition, along with his defense of both kinds of dualism.

[9] C. C. J. Webb, *Religion and Theism,* New York, Scribner, 1934, pp. 100, 101.

Among the modern analyses of the problem of natural law as related to the philosophical basis of theism, that of F. R. Tennant is especially thorough. This is found in the first two chapters of the second volume of his *Philosophical Theology*. Professor Tennant's chief contribution is his insistence that the mechanical view of natural law is wholly abstract. It deals with "inert identicals" and these are separated from actuality. Metaphysically speaking, an abstraction is nothing. "Mechanism," Tennant writes, "is not a phenomenal aspect; it is abstractive description: and, as such, it is neither universally applicable nor in any single instance exhaustive." [10]

C. The Working Solution of the Problem

When we turn to the alternative principle of order, that which is produced in the interests of an enduring and unfolding Purpose, we find what we seek. Not only is this conception free from the strong criticisms which have long been felt in regard to a mechanistic order,[11] but new positive advantages are involved. Above all, it accounts for the delicate combination of regularity and novelty which experience reveals. The *regularity* of natural laws is explained if God is self-consistent in character and His actions not capricious. The *novelty* is explained by the fact that an intelligent motivation is always adapting itself to changing situations.

If the purposive order already described is really the order of the universe, it is reasonable to suppose that events in the world show thoughtful adaptation to circumstances, something that cannot be expected if the mechanical conception of universal law is the true one. Constancy of purpose must often exhibit itself by a *change in procedure*. The parent may have the constant purpose of the advancement of the child's real welfare, but loyalty to this purpose entails apparently contradictory behaviors at different times in the life of the child. The order which comes from Purpose has, thus, a unity of aim and variety of method.

Exceptions to the general rule would be fully consistent with a

10 F. R. Tennant, *Philosophical Theology*, vol. 2, p. 50.

11 The criticisms have been made by laboratory scientists as well as by philosophers of science. See R. A. Millikan, *Evolution in Science and Religion*, Yale University Press, 1928, especially pp. 13, 14.

purposive order though the reality of the Purpose would ensure that exceptions would be rare. Exceptions for a good reason, such as the welfare of the human race, would not be "breaks" in a purposive order, but would, instead, be demonstrations of such an order.

If the system of laws studied in physics and chemistry is only one system in a larger whole concerned with the carrying out of the purpose of God, it is wholly reasonable that the subsidiary system should be dependent and that, at times, its ordinary procedure should be superseded. If the world is really the medium of God's *personal* action, *miracle is wholly normal.* What we call a miracle *is a situation in which constancy of purpose makes necessary a conspicuous adjustment of means.* "When there is no sufficient reason for variation," writes Temple, "none will appear. And for the vastly greater part of Nature's course there is, so far as we can tell, no reason at all for variation, and much reason for uniformity." [12] A miracle is an event in which there is a *reason* for variation. In short, a miracle, far from being a mysterious event, as is popularly supposed, is really *an occurrence which can be understood.*

Such a conception makes miracles a reasonable feature of the world system. This is a distinct intellectual gain, since there has long been evidence for the existence of miracles, but many have found themselves forced to reject the evidence *a priori,* solely because of a belief in natural law which made belief in miracles impossible. The notion of a purposive order sets minds free from the bondage of such dogmatism. Unless we have a superstitious reverence for natural law as an independent entity, we do not decide in advance the question of the actual occurrence of apparently miraculous events, such as the resurrection of Christ, but decide on the basis of the available evidence. Reverent agnosticism keeps us from talking easily about what *cannot be.*

When we first begin to think about them, prayer and miracle seem to involve separate and distinct problems, but as we consider them more fully we see that they all refer to the same problem. The chief reason for the difficulty in each case has been a "block universe," a closed system of nature to which men's minds as well as their bodies belong and which permits no teleological adaptation. That such a rigid system is the actual system of the world does not appear to be

[12] William Temple, *Nature, Man and God,* p. 268.

self-evident and the arguments which many have advanced against the proposition make it appear improbable.

If, on the other hand, the order of the world is accounted for by reference to the constancy of Divine Purpose, the obstacles to belief in both prayer and miracle are removed. Prayer and providence are merely special kinds of miracles, obvious evidence, that is, of the direct effectiveness of purposive causality. Prayer means conscious participation in the purposive order in particular situations; providence means the continual evidence of Purpose, both in the lives of individuals and in the whole world. It is a corollary of belief in providence that history, instead of being a mere sequence of events, has a meaning.

In a wholly mechanical order prayer could not be efficacious, *even in the life of the individual who prays.* Not only would it be impossible for A to influence B's action or destiny by prayer; it would be impossible for A to influence A's action by prayer. Even the crude conception of autosuggestion is ruled out, since a fully mechanical system involves *epiphenomenalism,* either consciously or unconsciously. By this term we mean that thought, if it exists at all, exists as an impotent observer and not as a causal agent. Certainly mechanism cannot admit God as a causal agent. Countless people have comforted themselves with the thought that their prayer might be privately effective even though it had no intercessory value, but there is no rational justification for such a faith. Apparently there is no halfway house between belief in a purposive order, which makes any noncontradictory prayer a reasonable procedure, and the rejection of such an order, which rules out *all* prayer as delusion.

We come here to one of the most important decisions that men can make about their theory of reality. The essence of the mechanistic view is that it is totalitarian, seeking to embrace all of reality in a system of mechanical determinism. It is undermined whenever we can point to experience which cannot be understood on the mechanical level. But the experience of prayer is part of the evidence which shows the inadequacy of the closed system. It begins to look as though we must finally decide between what is only a metaphysical prejudice, on the one hand, and a living experience, on the other, an experience tested by the testimony of countless persons whom there is reason to trust.

Part of our reason for honoring the memory of the late Professor Whitehead is that it was he who most insisted upon the debt of science to religious faith, a debt which he summarized when he asked whence this unique scientific development comes, and answered: "It must come from the medieval insistence on the rationality of God, conceived as with the personal energy of Jehovah and with the rationality of a Greek philosopher." [13]

The persecution of Galileo and others does not disprove this. Galileo, Newton, and the other founders of modern science were able to assume confidently the thoroughgoing coherency of the pattern of natural events because they accepted the belief that nature had its origin in One who is Himself perfect intelligence and naturally reflects the character of its source. In the concluding scholium of his *Principia,* Newton wrote: "This most elegant system of suns, planets and comets could only arise from the purpose and sovereignty of an intelligent and mighty being. . . . He rules them all, not as a soul of the world, but a sovereign lord of all things."

The right relationship between science and religion is that of teamwork. Religion becomes superstition unless it accepts the rigorous methods of inquiry which science demonstrates, and science becomes superficial or dangerous without careful attention to its moral and religious roots. Both naturalism and supernaturalism are needed, and they are needed together. The joint light they can shed on the mystery of existence is far more revealing than any single light can be.

[13] *Op. cit.,* p. 18.

16

The Existence of World Religions

There are anticipations of Christianity in all history. This insight is deadly for ecclesiastical and theological arrogance.

PAUL TILLICH

Seeds of serious doubt about the truth claims of any one religion are sown in many minds when first they become deeply conscious of the fact that there are *several* religions in the world, as well as several versions of each particular faith. The child is undisturbed, because all that he knows, usually, is the faith of his fathers, but the modern world is such that this situation cannot long endure. Eventually the child will grow up to meet missionaries of other faiths or to study about those which are far away or which existed long ago. Though only a minority may actually engage in a scientific study of the history of religions or in the careful examination of comparisons and contrasts between living religions, something of the results of such studies inevitably contributes to the general mentality of our age.

The idea which is bound to arise, as a certain degree of religious sophistication appears, is the idea that truth and falsity in religion rest on nothing more substantial than geography or local culture. Some think of God as *one* and others think of God as *many*, so what? Perhaps "true religion" merely means *my* religion and "false religion" merely means *yours*. Is there, then, any justification for sending foreign missionaries to the "heathen"? The real problem is not that of too little religion in the world, but that of too much. What if the various faiths and insights merely cancel each other?

A. The Cruel Dilemma

Several helpful classifications may be made of world religions, one of the most useful being that of the separation of faiths into the limited and the universal. Only three are truly universal in their aspirations and claims—Buddhism, Christianity and Islam.[1] All of these seek to present a faith completely free from racial or local limitations, so that any person anywhere may belong. Though Buddhism has practically died out in the land of its birth, its inherent universality makes this an unimportant feature of its history. The universality of Christianity and Islam is indicated by their vigorous missionary activity, that of Christians being carried on chiefly by professional missionaries and that of Islam being carried on primarily by persons of secular occupation, such as the traders in Africa, who carry their faith aggressively wherever they go.

The other religions are largely restricted to particular places or peoples and seldom engage in attempted proselytizing. Thus, Hinduism is essentially limited to India and to Indian people who have migrated, while Shinto is a local Japanese phenomenon. Judaism has included converts from the Gentile world, but they come chiefly by intermarriage, most Jews being Jews by cultural inheritance. The ancient faiths of China today appear to be negligible in view of the way in which the convictions of Marx-Leninism have taken the center of the stage in that great land.

Whether they seek to be universal or not, all living religions claim that their chief assertions are true. But the difficulty is that they cannot all be true. Where there is a clear difference, how can it be settled? We appear to be faced with two alternatives, both of which are intolerable.

(1) *The first alternative is that of the assertion of exclusive claims.* Since we belong to the Western tradition, it is easiest to see this in the light of the exclusive claims of Christianity, the dominant religion of the West. The essence of the answer is that Christianity is true and that the other religions are consequently false. It is not really surprising that there should be a variety of views on religion; there are various views on everything that is important. We have different views about whether Mars or Venus or both are scenes of life, but this is no serious difficulty because one view is right and the

---

[1] We are not considering here Marx-Leninism because it is still only a quasi religion. It does, however, make universal claims. If it ever becomes a full-fledged religion, there will be at least *four* which claim universality.

contradictory view is wrong. There may be a hundred different judgments about the exact size of the earth, but one is the right judgment, presumably that which is arrived at by careful measurement in the geophysical year.

The false religions, then, are evil temptations, designed to draw us away from the truth, like false roads that lead us away from the straight and narrow path. Error, says Aristotle, is of the nature of the infinite, but truth is of the nature of the finite. There may be a million ways of *missing* the target in archery, but only one of hitting the bull's-eye. If Christ is *the way,* all other proposed ways are delusions. There is no other way by which men may be saved.

There is no doubt that this conception of exclusive claims provides a powerful incentive to engage in foreign missions, and it is the incentive that has sometimes been employed in actual practice. It is the major point of the well-known hymn, "From Greenland's Icy Mountains." If other peoples are condemned to darkness and superstition now, as well as to eternal damnation hereafter, *unless* they hear and accept the message of Christ, almost any person who cares about his fellow men will engage in the missionary enterprise either by active participation or by the provision of financial support for those who are sent.

Powerful as this conception is in its motivation, it leads, if pressed with consistent logic, to really terrible consequence. It means, for one thing, that Socrates is in hell! But if Socrates is thus eternally damned, so is most of the human race that has been on this earth for hundreds of thousands of years. The great bulk of mankind is "lost" because most of them never had any opportunity to know the saving message. Only by a specious trick does this exclusive theological scheme avoid consignment to hell of a transparently good man like Jeremiah. It is possible to differentiate between his fate and that of Socrates only by the provision that Jeremiah saw Christ from afar. By this device all the ancient Jews, up to the time of Christ's earthly appearance, may have been saved from damnation, but this does not apply to other Jews, however devout, who have remained outside the fold of Christ, since his coming. It does not help contemporary Jews at all.

Such a scheme is neat and simple, but it is morally shocking and consequently not a live option of belief for truly thoughtful or

sensitive persons of *any* faith. What kind of God is it who consigns
men and women and children to eternal torment, in spite of the fact
that they have not had even a remote chance of knowing the saving
truth? What sort of God would create men and women in love, only
to punish, irrationally, the vast majority of them? A God who would
thus play favorites with His children, condemning some to eternal
separation from Himself while admitting others, and distinguishing
between them wholly or chiefly on a basis of the accidents of history
or geography, over which they had no control, would be more devil
than God. In any case He would not even remotely resemble Jesus
Christ, and thus there is a contradiction at the heart of the system.
In the effort to glorify Christ as the only true revelation of God, it
presents a conception of the divine which is incompatible with the
picture which Christ himself gives.

(2) *The second alternative is that of religious indifferentism.* Since
we are all in the finite predicament, no one religious conviction is
more dependable than any other. Instead of there being one true
way, there are many ways, just as there are paths on different sides
of a mountain, but all point to the top. Consequently, we must be
tolerant of everybody and of every view that is presented. There is
nothing wrong with a situation in which there are many religions,
for one religion is as good as another. Shinto is good for the Japanese
peasant and Judaism is good for the Israeli farmer, so why argue?
Let each have his own religion and there will be no controversy.

Pleasant as this sounds, and popular as it undoubtedly is in some
quarters, this proposed solution of the problem raised by the existence of many world religions is one which leads to absurdity. Since
the notion that one opinion is as good as another will not work in
any other area of human experience, why should it work in the area
of faith? Consider an application to medicine. Some think polio
serum is valuable and some don't, so let's leave the matter there! Of
course, we shan't do this. Realizing the inadequacy of our present
stage of knowledge and experience, we press on to try to know *which*
of the competing views is sound. To rest content with indifferentism
on any serious medical problem would be vicious and callous. One
medicine may be better than another, even though none is wholly
evil. Things may be better and worse, even though none is perfect.

The principle of indifferentism would be fatally destructive if it were applied to science. Science cannot go forward except upon the assumption that some answers are more true than others. If not, why try at all? But if our religion refers to the real world, it ought to be amenable to the same laws of logical procedure. It is absurd to deny real differences in religion. This is obvious when we consider the fact that some religious practices are self-centered and even grossly immoral, while others lead to personal sacrifice for the common good and to the elimination of injustice or other social evils. Dr. Albert Schweitzer has told us how the people who are native to his section of Africa have a primitive religion which makes them afraid of demons on every side, but that with conversion to Christianity the terrors go away, because they become convinced that, in God's world, there are no demons. To claim that this is not progress is to be manifestly perverse, but if there is progress, the notion that one religion is as good as another is untenable.

The religious neutralism which refuses to see differences of higher or lower or more true and less true, necessarily destroys completely the missionary motive. But if the missionary activity were eliminated from the world something marvelous would be lost. The fact that millions of people in the West have given sacrificially, especially during the past hundred years, to bring new life and light to needy peoples whom they have never seen is really something wonderful. Evils there have been and are in the missionary movement, but the balance in its favor is tremendous. One of its most creative results is the development of technical assistance, popularly known as Point Four. Any doctrine which undercuts so much that is of value is suspect.

Thus, we find that the second horn of our dilemma is as bad as the first. Arrogance in religion is evil, but indifferentism is completely destructive of respect for truth. Tolerance is as serious an evil as exclusiveness if it cuts the nerve of effort to try to distinguish between the more true and the less true. The very cruelty of our dilemma thus drives us to a deeper analysis. Perhaps these two alternatives, which seem to exhaust the possibilities, do not really exhaust them. We shall see.

B. The Idea of Fulfillment

There is, fortunately, another possibility, in addition to the two unlovely ones just considered. The third possibility is a way of recognizing that there is some truth in *many* religions but that there is the highest truth in *one* religion. In a series of mountains there is, normally, one higher than the others, but this does not deny the existence of many peaks. The clue to this extremely satisfactory idea lies in the words of Jesus: "I came not to destroy, but to fulfill." Though there is a remarkable finality about the revelation of Christ, this has been foreshadowed by many insights among many peoples in the long past. Here is a thesis which it is possible to defend by careful marshaling of the evidence and one which does not bring moral revulsion. It avoids both the arrogant exclusiveness of one alternative and the impotent neutralism of the other.

This solution of what is, undoubtedly, a real problem in many minds is one which has received valuable contributions from a number of first-rate thinkers, including Principal John Caird, Baron von Hügel, Archbishop Temple and, most eminently among contemporary writers, Professor Paul Tillich. Von Hügel suggested the very helpful figure of the ladder. There are, of course, great differences among religions, but they are comparable to the differences of rungs on a ladder. Thus, there is no essential competition. Shinto represents the round of nature faith, combined with aspects not greatly different from those of the dominant religion of ancient Rome. Buddhism and Hinduism involve valid insights, but insights that are conspicuously incomplete. For example, neither has developed the church, with its richness of life as known in the Judeo-Christian tradition. Islam represents a relatively high rung on the ladder, with its emphasis on a strict monotheism, but it has not proceeded to the fullness of the idea of God in the trinitarian conception nor has it been able to inspire a truly social conscience in its adherents. Absence of service organizations in Moslem lands is striking. It is possible to make a good case for the proposition that, in the life, teaching, death, resurrection and living Church of Christ, each of the great major ideas found at various stages is carried further to completion.

One of the chief reasons for believing that the doctrine of Christ is the final rung on the ladder is its remarkable capacity not only to borrow and assimilate, but to develop with the times. Christianity has been able to develop because it is, *par excellence,* the religion of history and, as such, cannot be fixed. "The intrinsic greatness of Christianity," wrote a great religious scholar of a generation ago, "is revealed in this capacity of development by which it advances with the advancing life of humanity, and, in the spirit of its Founder, continues to minister to the ever growing and ever changing needs of an aging world. Only a religion which develops can be a truly Universal Religion." [2]

The germ of this idea was in Christianity from the beginning, by virtue of its exceedingly fortunate relationship to the Jewish faith. Not only were the first Christians steeped in the Jewish tradition; the early Gentile converts were soon introduced to the story of the patriarchs and prophets. Judging by the preaching recorded in the New Testament, the usual approach was to tell the ancient story, to show its manifest lack of completeness, and then to show that the *completion* had finally come. Paul's powerful sermon at Antioch of Pisidia, a sermon which had the effect of arousing the entire city, reached its climax with the words, "and we bring you the good news that what God promised to the fathers, this he has fulfilled." [3]

It has been one of the most fortunate elements in Christianity, as a potentially universal faith, to have a *background.* It came at the end of a historical series. The New Testament might be valuable alone, but it is many times more valuable when attached to the Old Testament. Hitler and the so-called German Christians were manifestly wrong in trying to rid themselves of the Hebrew Scriptures, because the top rung of the ladder is almost meaningless without those which lead to it.

The presence of the Hebrew background was bound to suggest to bolder minds that there were *other* backgrounds, some of which may have been equally preparatory. If Isaiah pointed the way, why did not Socrates or Zoroaster? That this conception was actually entertained is suggested by the opening of the Epistle to the Hebrews: "In many and various ways God spoke of old to our fathers by the

[2] George Galloway, *The Philosophy of Religion,* New York, Scribner, 1922, pp. 146, 147.
[3] Acts 13:32 R.S.V.

prophets; but in these last days he has spoken to us by a Son, whom he appointed the heir of all things." But why should it be assumed that the only prophets were *Hebrew* prophets? This developing universalism is indicated by the employment of the logos idea and especially by the sentence referring to the light "which lighteth every man." [4]

The answer of the early Christians began, apparently, from a hint dropped by Jesus himself, when he said, "Other sheep have I which are not of this fold." This theme is developed in the prologue to the Fourth Gospel in pursuance of a most remarkable idea. It is only by the Light of Christ that men may find the way, says the prologue, but this Light is not limited to those who, by good fortune, have known Christ in the flesh or even known *about* him in the flesh. Though this Light is seen in Jesus in its full and complete manifestation, it appears in a measure in every son and daughter of earth. It is the Light that lighteth every man who comes into the world. Thus the Christ of experience is identical with the Christ of history, though not limited to particular historical events and particular places. It is still true that Christ is the Way, but God, in His mercy, has made the knowledge of this Way open to men in countless fashions. The enormous advantage of this conception is that it keeps the uniqueness of Christ while avoiding the blasphemy of supposing that God condemns men for mere ignorance. This makes it possible to believe that there were many Christians before Christ because they saw something of the very Light which he *was*. There is no contradiction between the idea that God has been revealing Himself, in sundry times and sundry places, and the other idea that God has revealed Himself fully in one time and one place. Such, in any case, is the faith which is neither so vague as to be meaningless nor so narrow as to be blasphemous.

That this solution of the problem is not limited to contemporary thinking we realize when we note that John Caird published the essence of such an answer in his *Philosophy of Religion* seventy-five years ago. The eminent Scottish philosopher ended his volume with these words: "Thus, whatever elements of truth, whatever broken and scattered rays of light the old religions contained, Christianity takes up into itself, explaining all, harmonising all, by a divine

[4] John 1:9.

alchemy transmitting all, yet immeasurably transcending all—'gathering together in one all things in heaven and earth' in its 'revelation of the mystery hid from ages,' the revelation of One who is at one and the same time Father, Son and Spirit; above all, through all, and in all." [5]

In Caird's fruitful idea we have an adequate, but by no means condescending basis for missionary work. The task is to walk with each man as far as he is able to go and then, by joint effort, learn to walk further. "In the light of this idea we can perceive these imperfect notions yielding up, under the transforming influence of Christianity, whatever element of truth lay hid in them, whilst that which was arbitrary and false falls away and dies." [6] In the same way Christianity may divert itself of much that is arbitrary and false. This is not at all the same notion as the syncretistic one that "Christian doctrine is a mere compound of Greek, Oriental and Jewish ingredients." The least unsatisfactory figure of speech is that of the organism. That which is organic grows out of the ingredients, but it is not the same *as* the ingredients.

In our day Professor Tillich has put great emphasis on his conviction that "there are anticipations of Christianity in all history." His major instrument of analysis is a theory of types.[7] Thus the historical type of interpreting history first appeared, albeit in a mixed way, in Zoroaster. The major thesis is stated as follows:

Without preparation in all history, without what I later have called the "church in the latency" the "manifest" church could never have appeared at a special time. Therefore grace is in all history.[8]

Because Tillich does not doubt that the Christian theologian must criticize much that he finds in other religions, he is saved from the danger of undiscriminating tolerance, but there is a middle ground between tolerance and intolerance. "It is regrettable, and altogether unconvicing," Tillich writes, "if Christian apologetics begins with a

[5] John Caird, *An Introduction to the Philosophy of Religion*, New York, Macmillan, 1881, p. 358.

[6] *Ibid.*, p. 355.

[7] "Types are ideal structures which are approximated by concrete things or events without ever being attained." *Systematic Theology*, vol. 1, p. 219.

[8] Paul Tillich, *The Protestant Era*, p. xxi.

criticism of the historical religions, without emphasizing the element of universal preparatory revelation which they carry within them." [9]

C. THE DIALECTIC OF DEVELOPMENT

Once this fruitful idea of "universal preparatory revelation" is deeply embedded in our minds we are prepared to see genuine dialectical development in religious history. This is well illustrated in three strikingly different stages of the idea of God. The thesis, in this dialectic, is polytheism. This is the natural position of the natural man, who is bound to observe the richness of the concrete spirituality of the world. Man feels the pull of love, but he also feels the pull of justice. That ancient men could reverence both Hermes and Minerva and many more is an evidence that they were keenly sensitive to many aspects of the spiritual life. Polytheism is not a reasonable place to end, but it is a reasonable place to begin. It was far better than nothing.

The thesis ultimately gave way to a rigorous monotheism, because men were bound to see that there was an absolute element underlying all of the concrete manifestations. We find this partially understood by Plato; we find it the very heart of Judaism; we find it the object of fanatical devotion in Islam.

That the antithesis is an advance over the thesis we cannot doubt, for it is required by the manifest inadequacies and inner tensions of polytheism. But the strict monotheism of Islam also is a stage, and one that requires both transcendence and fulfillment. The negative moment in the dialectic is both necessary and important, but it cannot provide the adequate answer that is required. Though the antithesis corrects the errors inherent in the thesis, the basic insight of the thesis, to the effect that the religious object involves richness and variety, is still sound. As is usually the case, we are driven to a synthesis, which restates the central insight of the thesis, but with the benefit of the purging which the antithesis provides. Thus, we are brought to the idea of the trinity, three in one and one in three, as something truer than either profuse polytheism or restrictive monotheism. The trinitarian structure of thought is the result of the need for balance between the concrete and the absolute elements in religious experience. On the one hand, there cannot be a

[9] Paul Tillich, *Systematic Theology*, vol. 1, p. 221.

relapse into polytheism but, on the other, exclusive monotheism must be seen as inadequate. It is inadequate, says Tillich, because "it excludes the finite against whose demonic claims it has protested." [10]

Once we look at the development this way, there is no doubt which is the highest rung on the ladder, as known. It is self-evident, when we see it, that the trinitarian formula includes more of what demands inclusion if we are to grasp, as fully as possible, the truth about our world. But we do not grasp it if we are mere literalists. "Trinitarian monotheism," says Tillich, "is not a matter of the number three. It is a qualitative and not a quantitative characterization of God. It is an attempt to speak of the living God, the God in whom the ultimate and the concrete are united." [11]

Such a conception ennobles the various stages in religious history and takes most of the sting out of religious controversy. There are many stages on the road. As in sailing, we have to tack against the wind. Not all stages are equally advanced, but there are few from which we cannot learn. That this combination of realism and respect was the position of Archbishop Temple is indicated by the following sentences:

> One great gain that the scientific use of the comparative method in religion has brought us is the duty of genuine reverence for other men's beliefs. To reverence them is not at all the same thing as to accept them as necessarily true, but whatever thoughts any human soul is seeking to live by, deserve the reverence of every other human soul.[12]

We do not know how large and inclusive the church of tomorrow will be, but we can be certain that it will be more truly catholic than any existent church now is. No one has fully arrived, though some steps on the stairs are obviously higher than others. Humility is required of all who have any real notion of what it is to be in the finite predicament, but such humility need not cut the nerve of either intellectual or practical effort. There need not be an end to missions; far from it. What is required, instead, is a new mood for many missions. So far as Christians are concerned, it looks as though

[10] *Ibid.,* p. 228.
[11] *Ibid.,* p. 228.
[12] William Temple, *The Universality of Christ,* London, Student Christian Movement, 1921, p. 22.

they will be forced to adopt a system more like that of Islam, in which the chief missionary work is done by those who earn their living in following secular pursuits. Already this is partly necessary, so far as India is concerned, because the government of India will no longer permit the entrance of the *mere missionary*. Each one must have some secular task, such as medicine, agriculture or teaching. More and more it is seen that the best method is to use men and women who are employed in business or governmental enterprises, but who also have a deep religious sense of concern. If we eliminate both professional religion and the arrogance of exclusive claims, the missionary movement may continue to thrive. Certainly a person must seek to spread what appears to him as ultimate truth. About genuine religion there is always a mood of urgency. If the analysis of this chapter is correct, there is no good philosophical reason why this sense of urgency should not find practical expression.

17
The Problem of Evil

Nothing which implies contradiction falls under the omnipotence of God.

THOMAS AQUINAS

So far as rational faith is concerned, the most serious contemporary difficulty is also the oldest. Very early in human thought came the recognition that an obstacle to the argument from design exists in the recognition of unmerited suffering.[1] The essence of the positive evidence for the objective being of God has always been the occurrence of many experiences which are not understandable *unless* God is; the essence of the negative evidence, i.e., the evidence for atheism, has always been the occurrence of many experiences which are not understandable *if* God is. The chief negative evidences constitute the problem of evil.

A. How the Problem Arises

The problem of evil is not a necessary problem; it does not even exist for the unbeliever. Though the unbeliever has other problems, he is utterly free from this one. To one who does not believe that the world is ruled by a Loving Mind, the existence of pain in nature, and the wanton cruelty of man to man, is not in the least surprising. There is no reason why he should expect anything else. If there were no God, if reality should be shown to consist of a series of events wholly devoid of meaning and purpose, we might be perplexed, but the presence of evil in the world would be in no way alarming and would demand no special explanation. Even the mild believer need not be deeply concerned. Only when belief is intense and urgent does the problem arise in a really demanding fashion. It would seem

[1] C. S. Lewis translates a couplet from Lucretius as follows: "Had God designed the world, it would not be, a world so frail and faulty as we see." Cf. *Surprised by Joy*, p. 65.

that this is the reason why, in spite of the Greek genius for philo-sophical inquiry, the classic statement of the problem of evil should have appeared, not in the Hellenic tradition, but in the Hebraic. The Greeks could speculate, but the Hebrews cared.

Since the problem of evil cannot exist, logically, for the unbeliever, the widespread concern over the problem is an impressive piece of evidence. The fact that the demand for an adequate explanation is so nearly universal is one of our best indications of how widespread theism really is. This evidence is made far more impressive by reason of the fact that it is largely unconscious and indirect.

The problem of evil is that which arises in any rational mind when the widespread tendency to believe in the goodness of God is challenged by the patent fact that the world is imperfect. The world has in it, not only knowledge and heroism and love of beauty and saintliness, but also a vast amount of negative value. We have no interest in minimizing this or neglecting it. The advance of religious experience, instead of solving the problem, seems to make it harder. There are, let us say, twelve men in a concentration camp. Outsiders pray for six of them, but nobody prays for the others. The first six live and are released while the others die by torture. Is this fair? If prayer makes a difference, it seems only to add to the injustice.

The amount of sheer physical suffering at any moment, even in the human family, is staggering to contemplate, though this is only a tiny fraction of the pain constantly being borne on this planet. Thousands are daily dying of cancer and other thousands are so crippled that they must be carried wherever they go. Not all have suffered equally, but any loving parent can imagine what it is to see his happy child stricken with infantile paralysis, with the expecta-tion that he will never run again. The loss of lives in war is terrible to contemplate, particularly in its wastefulness of what we cannot afford to lose, but the maiming of the bodies and the shattering of the minds of those who survive the conflict may be even worse. Though there is a profound sense in which it is true that all men are created equal, as the Declaration of Independence says, in nearly all of the less profound senses they are created strikingly unequal. Men are not equal in talents, in intelligence, in strength, in op-portunities. Some seem to have a magic carpet laid in front of them, but millions of others seem to be born to misfortune, even in the most favored lands. They begin with frail bodies and they are doomed to struggle all their lives with grinding poverty. For great numbers of the human race such a possession as a fountain pen or a gold watch is manifestly impossible. And we must never forget, as we discuss the state of the world, while we sip our after-dinner coffee, that many of our fellow men are actually hungry and many more live near the hunger line.

If we are to be honest in our thinking we must never fail to look directly at such facts as these or try to explain them away. Even those philosophies which hold that all pain is illusory must nevertheless deal with the fact that all of us share the illusion and that the illusion is quite as difficult to explain as the reality could ever be. Ours, whatever the explanation, is a world in which there is not only happiness, actual and potential, but also a vast amount of sorrow. Ours is a struggle in which many lives are undoubtedly fortunate, but it is also one in which misfortune is real. It is not without reason that most popular songs are sad.

Even the most unphilosophic mind, when aware of the widespread presence of evil in the world, which there is reason to believe is the workmanship of a loving and omnipotent Spirit, recognizes a dilemma. Either God wills to remove the evil and is not able or God does not will to remove it. If we accept the first horn of this dilemma, God cannot be considered omnipotent and there is some doubt whether we have a genuine monotheism, for other powers, equal to God or superior to Him, are recognized. One way of accepting the first horn is to hold, as Hume suggested, that God is *incompetent*. Perhaps this world is the work of a mere amateur. This world, for all we know, says Hume, "is very faulty and imperfect, compared to a superior standard; and was only the first rude essay of some infant deity, who afterwards abandoned it, ashamed of his lame performance; it is the work only of some dependent, inferior deity; and is the object of derision to his superiors; it is the production of old age and dotage in some superannuated deity; and ever since his death, has run on at adventures, from the first impulse and active force which it received from him." [2] Thus, the first alternative is unacceptable, but if we accept the second alternative God is no longer

[2] David Hume, *Dialogues Concerning Natural Religion*, Pt. V.

worthy of our love and trust. He would, indeed, be morally inferior to some of His creatures, a situation which is hardly credible.

Since both of these alternatives have been widely recognized as unsatisfactory, there has been a continual effort to find a third alternative, logically consistent with the facts as known, which will make it possible to believe in One who is both all-powerful and all-good. The effort to find this third alternative is an enterprise which fills many volumes and even has a special name, originated by Leibnitz. Such an effort to vindicate the justice of God in permitting natural and moral evil is a *theodicy*. The first mature theodicy was the Book of Job.

The problem of the justification of evil after it has appeared is closely connected with the problem of its origin. If God is the Creator of the world, He would seem to be responsible for everything in it. But sin and suffering and other forms of evil are in it. Therefore, God must be the author of sin and evil. On the other hand, if there is something in the world which God did not create, how are we to account for it? As we have seen above, Mind is the only ultimate explanation of anything. Must we therefore posit an eternal Evil Mind as well as an eternal Good Mind? If Personality in the world is evidence for God, perhaps evil in the world is evidence for the existence of an evil power. If so, we are landed in the intolerable difficulties of ultimate dualism.[3] We are not greatly helped by adopting the Manichaean heresy.

All this suggests that the reasonable procedure is one in which we try to choose the path of least difficulty, realizing that no path is wholly clear. In this connection it is important to remember that giving up the problem does not provide an easy path either. That would mean a retreat to the naturalism which is so unsatisfactory because it is unable to account even for its own truth. In addition, the formidable problem of good would be quite unsolved. To overcome a difficulty about the meaning of the world by adopting a

[3] It should be noted that, though we have some reason to support both epistemological dualism and psychophysical dualism, consistency does not demand that we accept metaphysical dualism, which deals with another question. The convictions that the "knower" and the "known" are independent entities and that "minds" and "bodies" have different qualities and follow different laws are wholly consistent with the thesis that God is the ultimate bond of unity and that there is a single comprehensive order in which all find their place.

hypothesis according to which nothing has meaning is a bold step, but it has not seemed to most men a reasonable one. The adoption of pantheism likewise does not diminish, but actually increases, the theoretical difficulty "since the world as it stands, and not an Ultimate Reality behind it, is here held to be perfect." [4]

Our predicament, then, is this: the problem of evil cannot, so far as we know, be wholly solved, but it, likewise, cannot be avoided with intellectual self-respect. One way is open—to see how much of the problem can be whittled away.

B. Proposed Solutions

It is worth while to list, in outline form, the chief solutions of the problem which have been put forward seriously. In this we shall limit our list to those proposals which are supposedly consistent with theism, since the other proposed "solutions" merely give up the problem instead of solving it. Though hosts of suggestions have been put forward, many have no novelty other than the novelty of terminology. Consequently, the fundamental proposals may be reduced to five:

(1) *The first proposal is the wholly naïve suggestion that suffering is a direct result of sin and a just recompense for it.* This is the theory presented by Job's friends and is the chief metaphysical foil in the wonderful dialogue which is named for the man who rejected this view. The theory may be either that the suffering is visited directly on the sinner or that it is visited on others, especially his descendants. Both forms of the theory were rejected by Christ.[5]

How widely this theory is held it is impossible to know, but there are frequent indications that it is never quite discarded, especially in the popular mind. Each great earthquake brings out some pronouncements about the wickedness of the city that has been shaken, pronouncements reminiscent of Sodom and Gomorrah. But in any case the theory is wholly unsatisfactory, and that on three counts: (a) In the first place, it does not account for the sin, which is a far

---

[4] Baron Friedrich von Hügel, *Essays and Addresses on the Philosophy of Religion,* p. 94.
[5] Luke 13:1-5; John 9:1-3.

greater evil than the suffering it allegedly causes. We are no nearer
a solution of our fundamental question, which is how we can avoid
making God the author of sin. (b) In the second place, the theory
is not in accordance with observed phenomena. The Psalmist may
say that he has never seen the righteous forsaken, but most other
men have seen that deplorable sight. With the modern revival of
the strategy of terror and the widespread employment of physical
as well as mental torture the evidence for a disparity between what
men deserve and what they get is particularly abundant. Natural
evils, such as earthquakes, do come to "wicked" cities, since all cities
are wicked, but why do they not come to the other wicked cities? Are
we to suppose that San Francisco was especially wicked in 1906 and
Tokyo especially wicked in 1923? (c) In the third place, the theory
is not consistent with the goodness of God. Not only does it, in its
usual form, involve suffering to wholly innocent children, but also
its only virtue is an abstract justice, with no suggestion of love.

(2) *A second proposal is that all evil is really illusory.* Such a
doctrine is popularly represented by the teachings of Christian
Science and is academically represented by certain versions of absolute idealism. The theory gets its chief factual support from the
observation that what *seems* like evil often turns out not to *be* evil,
especially when viewed in a larger context. The upshot of this is the
essential identification of evil and error. Frequently it includes the
notion that all evil experience is purely subjective and, since it exists
only in the mind of the observer, is not part of the objective reality.

Though this suggestion is less inadequate than the first proposal,
it is gravely unsatisfactory as a solution of our problem. Even if the
hypothesis be accepted as true, we are still faced with the question
of how the *appearance of evil* is to be explained and how it
originated. The illusion of pain is undoubtedly almost as unpleasant
as "real" pain, whatever that may be. Why is not illusion itself a
genuine evil? A world in which so many persons are made so that
they are "deceived" about anything which seems as real as unmerited
suffering needs a vast amount of explaining. A world of dupes is
hardly preferable to a world of suffering sinners.

The hypothesis of illusion is upheld philosophically only by what
we are forced to call metaphysical hocus-pocus. We are told that all
evil disappears in the Absolute, just as temporal sequence is some-

how transmuted into eternality or timelessness.[6] But this kind of dialectic is increasingly unconvincing. It is not even religiously satis-factory, since the Absolute thus arrived at is utterly different from God as known and worshiped.

A still more formidable objection to this theory, from the practical point of view, is that it would cut the nerve of moral effort if it were taken seriously. If all evil, whether moral, natural or intellectual, is truly illusory, we are foolish indeed to *fight* it; it would be far preferable to *forget* it. Accordingly, it is hard to think of God in moral terms if there is no genuine evil to fight. If there is no genuine evil, if there is nothing in the universe that has *negative* value, our only moral task is to realize that this is the case. In the face of such notions there is something wonderfully refreshing about the words of L. P. Jacks, when he asks the question, "How shall we think of evil?" and answers it by saying, "We shall think ill of it." But we cannot think ill of it if it doesn't exist. "For my own part," writes Dr. Jacks, "I would rather live in a world which contained real evils which all men recognize than in another where all men were such imbeciles as to believe in the existence of evil which has no existence at all." [7]

A similarly impressive note is struck by Whittaker Chambers in his tortuous book, *Witness,* a book which includes more philosophy than might be expected. In the final chapter he tells what he wants for his son, as he becomes a man.

I want him to see for himself upon the scale of the universe that God, the soul, faith, are not simple matters, and that no easy or ingenuous view of them is possible. I want him to remember that the God who is a God of Love is also the God of a world that includes the atom bomb and virus, the minds that contrived and use or those that suffer them; and that the problem of good and evil is not more simple than the immensity of worlds. I want him to understand that evil is not something that can be condescended to, waived aside or smiled away, for it is not merely an

[6] For example, F. H. Bradley says that "since in ultimate Reality all existence, and all thought and feeling, become one, we may even say that every feature in the universe is thus absolutely good." *Appearance and Reality,* p. 412.

[7] L. P. Jacks, *Religious Foundations,* Rufus M. Jones, ed., New York, Mac-millan, 1923, p. 105.

uninvited guest, but lies coiled *in foro interno* at home with good within ourselves. Evil can only be fought.[8]

It is more profound to fight evil than to explain it. Whatever else we do we must avoid any supposed solution of the problem of evil which makes men think well of it or in any way "reconciles" them to its existence so that they do not seek to overcome it.

(3) *A third, and far more important, proposal is that which sees evil as a necessary defect in a good plan.* This does not deny the reality of evil, but it does hold that some forms of evil enter into the formation of a larger good or are the necessary concomitants of a good prócess. The strength of this solution lies in the fact that it can be illustrated abundantly from many levels of experience, some of which will be mentioned more fully later in this chapter.

Evil is a necessity in high moral endeavor, since a world which had no evil in it would not present the moral decisions which are the necessary means of developing moral strength. Though suffering sometimes crushes the sufferer, there are many times when the final result is more glorious than would be conceivable in any other kind of world. It is our duty to rid the world of disease and persecution and many other evils, but we must admit that some of the grandest chapters in human life are made possible by these very evils which men learn to bear nobly or to fight bravely. It is hard to avoid the conviction that any other kind of world than an imperfect one would be an everlasting tea party, and that its inhabitants would inevitably be soft. John Bennett has wisely said that, if there were no evil, "the very absence of evil would constitute a problem since there would, then, be nothing to jar us out of an attitude of self-sufficiency." [9]

It is the truth that many of the goods we value most highly are those a part of whose excellence we owe to the difficulty of attaining them. We like that which costs something, but how could any goods be costly and dangerous apart from the presence of evil in the world? Temple has provided a brilliant illustration of such a good in his discussion of victory, which is a conspicuous form of good. "A world in which there was no victory," he writes, "would be, so far, an inferior world. But if there is to be victory, there must be opposition.

---

[8] Whittaker Chambers, *Witness,* New York, Random House, 1952, pp. 797, 798.
[9] John Bennett, *Christian Realism,* New York, Scribner, 1941, p. 164.

To demand the good of victory without the existence of an antagonist is to demand something with no meaning." [10]

Persuasive as are these arguments to uphold the theory of evil as a necessary condition of the good, the theory is easy to lampoon. The form in which it was most widely held in the eighteenth century was savagely lampooned, as is well known, by Voltaire in *Candide.* The notion of which Voltaire was making fun was not, it should be emphasized, a notion that minimized evil. Far from it. The philosophical optimist frankly recognized the reality of evil, as well as its wide distribution, but *the point was that the world contained the proper amount of evil.* It was this, and not the entire absence of evil, as is popularly supposed, which made distinguished men speak of ours as the "best of all possible worlds." It was a world, many contended, which had just enough pain to make possible the good of patience, just enough danger to make possible the good of courage. If there were any less evil, it would be a worse world rather than a better one.[11]

In practice this doctrine has not actually tended to cut the nerve of moral effort, but this is because the logic of the situation is not followed to the bitter end. If it is really true that there is *exactly* the right amount of evil in the world, it would be a great mistake to remove any of it and thus make the world worse.

Because the theory we are now presenting has some superficial resemblances to the theory that all evil is illusory, the two have sometimes been identified in popular thought, but they are fundamentally distinct. According to this third proposal, the evil in the *part* must be real, else the good of the *whole* is impossible. One does not develop great virtue by combating *fancied* ills. The theory has much to commend it, and the basic insight on which it rests must be part of any moderately satisfactory view of the matter; but it has a serious fault in regard to the *amount* and *distribution* of evil. That *some* evil is the condition of the highest good seems clear, but why should there be so much of it? Would not a more modest amount suffice? Moreover, the evil does not seem to be spread in such a way as to achieve the highest moral ends. Some people have too much

---

[10] William Temple, *Mens Creatrix,* p. 268.
[11] See A. O. Lovejoy, "Optimism and Romanticism," Publications of the Modern Language Association of America, vol. 13, 1927.

suffering and some too little. And the theory seems to be most
earnestly espoused by fairly comfortable people who point out to
others how much worse their lives would be if they had less to
combat.

> The toad beneath the harrow knows
> Exactly where each tooth-point goes;
> The butterfly, upon the road,
> Preaches contentment to the toad.

How easy it is to lampoon the argument L. P. Jacks shows in the
following passage:

> I read the other day a book intended to justify the ways of God to man,
> which argued that if men are to have teeth at all they must have teeth
> that can ache. There must therefore be such a thing as toothache. Quite
> so. But what if the number of aching teeth in the world at this moment
> is a hundred times as great as it need be? And why should the aching
> be as violent as it is? Would not a milder and more endurable form of
> the malady satisfy the requirements of the argument? And why should my
> teeth ache rather than yours? [12]

(4) *The fourth fundamental way in which men have sought to
solve the problem of evil is by a frank admission that God's power is
limited.* This proposal admits that the popular dilemma presented
above is genuine and therefore inescapable. If we must conclude
either that God is not wholly good or that God is not wholly powerful, almost any sensitive mind will choose the latter hypothesis.[13]
Rashdall has shown us the rational justification for such a choice of
belief. To believe that there is a limit to God's goodness would be to
deny utterly the notion that the Good is our ultimate principle of
explanation, whereas to believe that there is a limit to God's power
is only to continue a line of thought which no person really escapes.
All admit that God cannot change the past, and this, says Rashdall,
is wholly consistent with a really intelligent conception of omnipotence. "God possesses all the power there is." [14]

[12] L. P. Jacks, *op. cit.*, p. 103.
[13] Some readers may wonder why we do not list the notion that God is not
completely good, i.e., the first horn of the dilemma, as one of the proposed
solutions. We do not because it is not really a "live option." Suggestions of it
appear in primitive religion, but it is not seriously proposed in advanced thought.
[14] Hasting Rashdall, *Philosophy and Religion*, New York, Scribner, 1910, p. 83.
See also *The Theory of Good and Evil*, Oxford University Press, 1924, vol. 2,
pp. 287-288.

The notion that God is limited and thus, in some sense, *finite* has received strong support from various quarters, but it has likewise received strong criticism. L. P. Jacks's brilliant essay, "How Shall We Think of Evil?" an essay which seems to have attracted surprisingly little notice, accepts the notion of the limitation of divine power with gusto. Jacks refuses to recognize as God any being with whose "goodness" evil can be "reconciled," but he can recognize as God the Source of all opposition to evil. God *opposes* evil and we, in so far as we oppose it, have a point of contact with Him. Though Jacks does not say so explicitly, he is bound to hold, as truly as did the standard eighteenth-century optimists, that ours is *the best possible world,* though he may have a different reason for upholding the proposition. Our world, according to the limitation doctrine, is the best world possible, because God has made it as free from evil as He could. There is something about evil, it is suggested, which even God cannot conquer at will. Hastings Rashdall, as intimated above, gave to this doctrine the backing of his great name.

Among American writers who have declared themselves as convinced of the limitation of God are men as representative of different metaphysical systems as E. S. Brightman, William James and W. P. Montague. Professor Brightman's ambitious work, A *Philosophy of Religion,* receives its distinctive flavor, in contrast with other volumes on the same subject, by the careful treatment of the question "Is God Finite?" Theistic absolutism and theistic finitism are carefully analyzed and contrasted, but Professor Brightman accepts the latter as the more satisfactory explanation of the facts, particularly the facts of evil. In distinguishing between God and the Given, Brightman reminds his readers that he stands in the tradition of Plato, for God, as depicted in the *Timaeus,* is not the omnipotent Creator, but the Demiurge or Cosmic Artisan. When faced with the criticism that theistic finitism, according to which God is *potent,* but not *omnipotent,* is inconsistent with the spirit of true religion, Brightman defends his position by pointing to five specific religious values which finitism safeguards:

(a) There is greater assurance of divine sympathy and love.
(b) There is something awe-inspiring about the magnificent cosmic struggle.
(c) Finitism furnishes incentives to co-operative endeavor.

    (d) Belief in a finite God affords ground for belief in cosmic advance.

    (e) It is more natural to pray to a finite God, who may be moved by our infirmities.[15]

Professor Brightman's well-known thesis has been brilliantly defended by his pupil and successor, Professor Peter A. Bertocci, of Boston University, especially in Bertocci's *Introduction to the Philosophy of Religion.* Like Brightman, he holds that, on the basis of what we know, God must be infinite in most ways but is finite in two ways, knowledge and power. Both philosophers agree on the inference that there must be an aspect of God's mind, which they call *The Given,* which God must take account of in all His activity. "God is finite," writes Bertocci, "because he cannot completely control the Given." [16] The argument in favor of this conclusion is worked out by an analysis of the minds we know intimately, i.e., our own, and by an extension of what we know to the divine scale. "In basic structure, God's experience does not differ from ours. There is form and content in God's mind, and there is challenge, enjoyment and struggle in his life." [17]

The thoughtful student of religious truth is bound to examine this proposal with respect. He is impressed by the courage of the proposal and by the intellectual integrity of the men who have made the proposal. There is real courage in the decision to throw oneself boldly on one of the horns of the dilemma, which is what all proponents of divine finitude are doing. They think they see an irresolvable conflict between God's power and God's goodness, so they sacrifice the power. This means, literally, that, if these philosophers are right, we cannot any longer speak, as did Newton at the climax of his *Principia,* of the Lord God Almighty. Whether the resistant power is outside God's mind or in His mind makes no essential difference.

Admirable as are the men mentioned above, it is highly significant that the great weight of opinion in philosophical theology is critical of the doctrine of divine finitude. The opposition includes all of the

[15] E. S. Brightman, *A Philosophy of Religion,* New York, Prentice-Hall, 1940, pp. 327, 328.

[16] Peter A Bertocci, *Introduction to the Philosophy of Religion,* New York, Prentice-Hall, 1951, p. 431.

[17] *Ibid.,* p. 433.

Roman Catholic thinkers and all of the leaders of Islam, as well as many influential Protestant and Jewish thinkers. Characteristic opponents are Nels F. S. Ferre and F. R. Tennant. Ferre is convinced that, if we admit any limitation to the complete perfection of God, the whole idea falls apart.[18] A slightly flat circle is not a circle at all. Tennant rejects the inference of finitude by rejecting the evidence which supposedly leads to it. He holds that the inequities of the created world can be understood without recourse to such a drastic hypothesis. The world does not prove that God is finite, unless we assume some purpose which may not be God's purpose at all. Our world is "adapted by its law-abidingness to the development of rationality and morality." [19]

Archbishop William Temple represents a comprehensive middle ground in that he expresses his reluctance to accept finitism while at the same time recognizing its value. He sees that Rashdall's hypothesis is "immeasurably superior, alike on theoretical and practical grounds, to the doctrine that evil can be dismissed as an illusion." [20] But he thinks that the acceptance of finitism really means throwing up the sponge and admitting that the search for a rational explanation of the universe is a failure. If goodness is the only self-explanatory principle, and if we find in the world something beyond the good, called The Given or by any other name, our search for explanation has failed. Perhaps this is the best we can do, but we can at least conceive something better. If there is something external to God in the "nature of things," which imposes a limitation upon Him, we are far from full ethical monotheism. The God of Plato's *Timaeus* is not very exciting, and the truth is that he is not the Judeo-Christian God at all.[21]

(5) *The fifth proposal is the answer of childlike faith.* This, the working solution at which the unknown author of the Book of Job finally arrived, has always been part of the solution for those deeply religious, whatever their additional views might be. Many of those who have defended one of the first four proposals have admitted some perplexity at the end, and have supplemented their theories

---

[18] Nels F. S. Ferre, *Faith and Reason*, New York, Harper, 1946, pp. 181 ff.

[19] F. R. Tennant, *Philosophical Theology*, vol. 2, p. 201.

[20] *Op. cit.*, p. 264.

[21] This point is carefully developed by Etienne Gilson in *God and Philosophy*, pp. 42 ff.

with the one we are considering now. The positive contribution of the Book of Job comes in the "Speeches of the Lord" which give Job something better than that which is provided by the feeble remarks of his friends. The essential point of these final speeches is that the problem is too great for the finite mind, that Job sees only a small segment of reality, and that his criticisms are accordingly inappropriate. How can Job *know* that either God's power or His goodness is limited? His knowledge of temporal things is admittedly slight; his knowledge of eternal things is still more slight. The conclusion of the book [22] is Job's recognition of his own humble status, with the consequent mood of childlike trust. The trust, if we interpret as intentional the juxtaposition of texts, is not blind credulity, but the consequence of the direct vision of God (Job 42:5, 6).

It seems clear that this fifth proposal, though it has little metaphysical value, must always be part of any satisfactory "solution." The position need not be, it should be noted, merely a deduction from ignorance, which is always logically suspect. The point is that the humble worshiper *already* has abundant reason to believe in God in the full theistic sense. If, then, he runs into some difficulty, even a difficulty as great as the problem of evil, he does not, for that reason, give up his faith. *The reasons for his faith are so great that they can weather a few storms.* Religious insight makes us believe that there *is* a full solution of the problem of evil though we are too ignorant and dull to reach it.

The lesson of Job may be assumed to be a part of any working solution and is consistent with any in which the sense of perplexity remains intact. The fellowship of perplexity is a goodly fellowship, far superior to the fellowship of easy answers. To recognize that no one of the five solutions provides a perfect answer to our total problem is, therefore, not a matter of loss, but of gain. It is desirable to combine the insights that can be fruitfully combined, to omit the suggestions that cannot be defended, and above all to keep a practical attitude toward evil, which encourages our efforts to overcome it. Since it is the practical overcoming of evil in countless moral struggles which gives us our best clue to its theoretical explanation,

---

[22] Disregarding the wholly inconsistent appendix apparently added in the interests of mistaken piety.

we must be especially careful not to adopt any explanatory principle which will in any way undermine this clue.

C. The Idea of Omnipotence

Nearly all of the difficulty which most people feel in connection with the existence of evil arises because of the fact that omnipotence is ascribed to God. Part of the problem, therefore, may be avoided if omnipotence is rightly understood. Clarification at this point can, in fact, be effective in whittling away some of the problems which we admit that we cannot wholly solve. This procedure is a great part of the merit of C. S. Lewis' excellent little book, *The Problem of Pain,* which begins with a reconsideration of omnipotence. Lewis, demonstrating his well-known gift of clarity, states the ancient problem in such a way as to emphasize the notion that God's power is supposedly *almighty.* "If God were good, He would wish to make His creatures perfectly happy, and if God were almighty, He would be able to do what He wished." [23] That He does not do it is known to every one of His children.

We have already made a good beginning when we have realized that the term "omnipotent" is highly equivocal. If it means the ability to do *anything,* then it is practically nonsense. Lewis has pointed out that "the word *impossible* generally implies a suppressed clause, beginning with the word *unless.*" [24] We may profitably add to this that the word "possible" generally implies a suppressed clause beginning with the word "if." Scripture tells us that "with God all things are possible," but this is a truncated statement, and assumes the additional words "if they are not self-contradictory."

The scoffer asks, derisively, whether God is able to make a rope with only one end or a round square. Such questions are supposed to discomfit the simple believer, but they need not do so at all, because the questions asked by the scoffer, in such cases, are strictly meaningless. God's omnipotence, says Lewis, "means power to do all that is intrinsically possible, not to do the intrinsically impossible. You may attribute miracles to Him, but not nonsense. This is no limit to His power. . . . It remains true that all *things* are possible

[23] C. S. Lewis, *The Problem of Pain,* New York, Macmillan, 1948, p. 14.
[24] *Ibid.,* p. 15.

with God: the intrinsic impossibilities are not things but non-entities." [25]

This is a very significant insight which, as Mr. Lewis would be the first to say, is not original in our time. It represents the central tradition of Christian philosophy and was succinctly stated by Thomas Aquinas in the sentence "Nothing which implies contradiction falls under the omnipotence of God." [26] "God cannot" sounds blasphemous, at first thought, yet there is a sense in which the majority of great religious thinkers have expressed the dictum with boldness. It has long been believed that God is limited by the laws of logic. If it is nonsense to expect God to make triangles in which the sum of the interior angles is not 180 degrees, it is equally nonsensical to expect God to make created beings without the dangers inherent in createdness. Even God cannot create an interdependent community of persons without also producing a situation in which evils spread. Professor Bertocci puts its convincingly when he says, "We simply cannot have water which will quench thirst and yet not drown people, fire which will warm homes and not scorch flesh, minds which are sensitive but not capable of becoming insane." [27] Professor Gilson, writing as a Roman Catholic and in conscious harmony with the major tradition of the Middle Ages, notes especially that "these very limitations and mutabilities for which nature is arraigned, are metaphysically inherent in the very status of a created thing as such." [28] This is not to say that createdness necessitates evil; what is affirmed is the notion that it is absurd to expect even God to produce creatures who lack the characteristics of created beings.

If omnipotence means ability to do *anything*, then surely God is not omnipotent, and the problem of evil is not only insoluble but irreducible. But this simple notion of omnipotence is a purely childish notion and one which reflective thought can remove. A. C. Turner, who was killed in France in 1917, has left one of the best suggestions on this subject that modern thought has produced. He was trying to envisage a mature conception of omnipotence and saw it best in the power of love. "Love," he wrote, "is omnipotent be-

[25] *Ibid.*, p. 16.

[26] *Summ. Theol.*, IaQ XXV. Art. 4.

[27] Bertocci, *op. cit.*, p. 414.

[28] Etienne Gilson, *The Spirit of Medieval Philosophy*, New York, Scribner, 1936, p. 113.

cause it can always in any circumstance give a perfect expression of itself. It has no need to manipulate history because it is always sufficient to meet any situation. The activity of love is self-giving; it can afford to give itself away, and no reception which it may meet can be either a limitation or a real defeat. If divine love is the author of all existence, it follows that nothing can exist wherein love cannot find expression." [29]

Here is a really profound idea, which, if understood, may be of assistance to many serious seekers. Much of our trouble has arisen from too close an attention to the kind of experience in which the categories of extension apply. These do not apply to a truly loving Spirit, which alone can give us some hint of what omnipotence is. The essence of the idea of divine omnipotence is the conviction that the partial freedom which we know reflects the perfect freedom, of which we have only hints and which we are entitled to infer. But we must beware of interpreting this perfect freedom in crudely anthropomorphic ways. God's freedom need not be that of choosing between alternative ends and alternative means; it need not involve any indeterminacy at all. His freedom must mean the power to achieve a full expression of His overflowing love. Perhaps the most brilliant sentence produced by the pen of C. S. Lewis is that in which this point is given the following expression: "The freedom of God consists in the fact that no cause other than Himself produces His acts and no external obstacle impedes them—that His own goodness is the root from which they all grow and His own omnipotence the air in which they all flower." [30] To say that God is omnipotent is to say that He has made a world, no part of which can be wholly impervious to enduring purpose.

D. The Price of Freedom

Our task of reducing the difficulty is already partly accomplished by a closer scrutiny of the familiar dilemma. Not only may we gain by a critical look at the popular notion of omnipotence; we may gain even more by a critical look at the assumption that God's purpose ought to be the production of human happiness. He *might* have a nobler purpose.

[29] A. C. Turner, "Faith, Prayer and the World's Order," in *Concerning Prayer,* London, Macmillan, 1916, p. 421.
[30] *The Problem of Pain,* p. 23.

It is easy to make the mistake of thinking of God's love in sentimental ways, but this is by no means necessary. Beginning, as we
always must, with the experience we know at first hand, we soon
realize that love and kindness are not identical. If we really love our
children we must, at times, be apparently cruel. When we are
thoughtful, as well as loving, we realize that we should choose to
have their lives hard rather than contemptible. It is by no means
self-evident that love always entails the easy path. Whatever the
purpose of God may be, it is obviously something better than the
dream of doting parents for their daughters, with parties at night,
sleep in the day, and no pain at all. However bad a hard world is, a
soft world would be worse.

Of all approaches to the problem of evil the most fruitful is that
which starts with an inquiry into the divine purpose and a consideration of the price of its achievement. A valuable preparation for
this inquiry is a clear distinction between two different kinds of evil,
one moral and the other natural. By moral evil we mean that which
arises in or as a result of *sin,* sin being possible wherever there is a
creature sensitive to moral values. Natural evil is that which arises
when self-consciousness is not a factor. Most actions of beasts are
presumably in the latter class.

Moral evil is far more serious than natural evil and yet it is the
more easily understood. Discussions of the problem of evil often
begin by reference to earthquakes, floods and epidemics, but these
are almost trivial in their effects when contrasted with the unmerited
suffering which comes as a result of the actions of wicked men. An
earthquake may destroy life, but it does not torture. Much of the
worst of human suffering is mental anguish, and this is caused far
more by evil men than it is by the forces of nature. Human beings
can, if they choose, move away from known volcanoes or earthquake
territory, but they can hardly escape the animosity of their fellow
men. Moreover, many of the supposed natural evils are chiefly trace-
able to human greed or other moral turpitude. Floods are frequently
the result of an irresponsible policy of lumbering which takes away
from the hills their natural means of holding back the rain water.
Epidemics may be accentuated by the overcrowding which is one
result of a lust for financial gain, irrespective of the human cost.

In attempting to find some explanation of moral evil we must explore more carefully the notion that God is limited. It is instructive to note that all who discuss the matter seriously agree that *there is some limitation*. The only question is *where* the limitation begins. The Catholic writers who oppose finitism all agree that God is limited logically, and those who agree with Professor Brightman merely hold that the limitation is greater.[31] There is some indication, however, that a great deal of the argument is purely verbal. Most of the illustrations given by the upholders of finitism are illustrations, not about the "nature of things," but about the "nature of goodness" or the "nature of personality." The illustrations in John Bennett's valuable paper are all of this kind, while Professor Brightman's observations are similar.

What we suggest is that there is really a tacit agreement among most thinkers in that they combine the third and fourth proposals already outlined. They actually hold that God is limited, but limited in a special way, namely, that He is limited by the conditions of goodness. This may not be the best possible world, but it is, so far as we can see, the only kind of world consistent with the Purpose we dimly glimpse.

If we begin with the notion which we cannot abandon—the belief in the absolute goodness of God—we must suppose that God has a wholly good purpose. Judging by the hints which evolution gives, that purpose is the production of other centers of consciousness capable of spiritual determination which may be defined as "determination by what seems good as contrasted with determination by irresistible compulsion." Perhaps man as we know him represents only a very low form of such spiritual determination, but men at least understand what it is. Now, choice would be an absolute essential in such an enterprise. God's purpose would be defeated if goodness were compelled; moreover, it would not be genuine goodness. The goodness of a machine, which has no alternative, is, of course, not goodness at all. A creature who chose the good voluntarily though poorly would be superior to one who could not do otherwise.

---

31 Why God should be limited by the laws of logic and no more is not as clear as it once seemed. If He is limited by laws of logic, He is, presumably, also limited by the laws of mathematics. But physics is largely applied mathematics. Are physical limitations, therefore, to be excluded *a priori?*

If the possibility of goodness involves choice, it also involves the possibility of evil; and, if the possibility is genuine, it will sometimes be realized. Therefore, the conditions of the occurrence of evil are identical with the conditions of the higher aspects of the moral life. It cannot be said that God directly wills sin or evil desire, because it is not *necessary* that we sin. The sin is *our* fault, not God's, though God made us so that we might sin, because otherwise the best in life could not be. Temple makes a fine distinction at this point which will, no doubt, seem to some readers evasive and to others convincing. "We cannot doubt," he says, "that God foresaw the issues of conferring selfhood upon finite beings, so that sin falls within His purpose, and is even part of it, though it cannot be said that He directly willed or wills it." [32]

Such an interpretation receives impressive support from the devotional writings of that great scholar and saint, Lancelot Andrewes. Perhaps the problem is easier to solve devotionally than philosophically. In his private prayer Andrewes says:

> Two things I recognize, O Lord, in myself:
>   nature, which Thou hast made;
>   sin, which I have added:
> I confess that by sin I have depraved nature;
> but call to remembrance, that I am a
>   wind that passeth away,
>   and returneth not again;
> for of myself I cannot return again from sin.
> Take away from me that which I have made;
> let that which Thou hast made remain in me. [33]

Here we have the abiding Christian paradox of sin. We are to blame for it, but *we* cannot heal it. God did not cause it, but He can forgive and overcome it.

Heresy has come from supposing either

    (a) the power to cause implies the power to overcome, or
    (b) the power to overcome imples responsibility for sin's existence,

i.e., heresy comes from any denial of the paradox.

---

[32] William Temple, *Nature, Man and God*, p. 369.
[33] *The Devotions of Bishop Andrewes*, 1842, vol. 2, Introduction.

The kind of sin which is most serious is man's own; it cannot be attributed to animal inheritance or to the demands of the flesh. Most of the moral evil concerned with animal appetites is comparatively superficial, but that concerned with self-centeredness may be both profound and far-reaching in its effects. The center of our trouble is not the turbulent appetites, but the personality as a whole. "It was not the body that made the spirit sin," writes Gilson, "it was the spirit that brought death to the body." [34] Adam and Eve, according to the legendary story of Genesis, were really both advancing and "falling" in that they made, at the same time, a step which enables us to rise to great heights and to sink far lower than any beast. The same self-consciousness which is the necessary condition of remorse is also the means of vicious self-centeredness.

There is very little evil in the animal creation, in spite of the fact that large animals eat small animals. The necessity of food-getting involves moments of terror, but the modern students of wildlife suggest that the older picture of nature "red in tooth and claw" was sentimentalized.[35] Actually there seems to be a great deal of enjoyment of life in the animal creation. It is with man that the hard problem arises, and this, it would seem, is because man is a creature who is personal as the animals are not. Evil is the price we pay for moral freedom.

It is such considerations as those just mentioned which make it reasonable to maintain that the limitation on God's working, which accounts for the presence of evil, is due, not to the *nature of things,* but to the *nature of goodness.* We can take a step further, however, by showing that the limitation is inherent in the *nature of personality.* A person is a being whose acts are determined, not by external compulsion, but by an appeal to the apprehension of the good. This theory supports the Christian doctrine that God works with men by *grace* and it interprets the Cross as a revelation of the way in which God is always reaching out to win men.

This highly convincing notion has been the chief theme of John

[34] Etienne Gilson, *op. cit.,* p. 114. See also Temple, *Nature, Man and God,* p. 367.

[35] We tend to exaggerate animal pain. If we recognize the limited span of consciousness and memory in animals, our perspective is improved.

Oman and those consciously influenced by his thinking.[36] The book in which Oman has especially developed the notion that personality necessarily involves risk is *Grace and Personality*. In this important volume the point is carefully made that it is impossible to play safe in dealing with persons, since they cannot be manipulated, as things can be, without doing violence to their essential nature. If God, being personal, desired the existence of finite persons in the world, it was necessary that they should be free to fail, since to *force* them into goodness would involve a severance of personal relations. If a man is truly a person he must keep his own house in order with no one to compel him. "In that task," says Oman, "God, no more than man, can help us except through our own purpose, guided by our own insight, dealing with our own world; and, only as grace works in that personal way through ourselves, is it God's dealing with us as His children." [37] Again it is the concept of noncontradiction that is the ruling principle. That God should deal *personally,* and yet compel the avoidance of evil, would be as meaningless as the production of round squares.

It is freely admitted that the "solution" offered is not wholly satisfying, but it does solve part of the problem and give a modicum of mental peace. It absolves God of the authorship of evil; it gives a rational account of why evil is necessary; and it avoids extreme finitism by showing that the limitation is inherent in God's own purpose, rather than in some intractable area outside God's power. It does not show why the exact amount and the distribution of evil are necessary, but it does make us see that the suffering of the innocent is part of the price that must be paid if we are to be really personal beings. We are not personal unless we choose, and men who make bad choices are bound to harm others. In spite of the horrible suffering which choice involves, most of us would prefer such a world to its alternative. Moreover, the very presence of evil tells us something important about the character of God, something which we otherwise might not know. If God, desiring good, nevertheless permits evil, this shows that He is a God of love, using

[36] See, for example, William Wilson's Swarthmore Lecture, *Our Response to God*, London, Allen & Unwin, 1935.

[37] John Oman, *Grace and Personality*, Cambridge University Press, 1919, p. 51.

persuasion rather than compulsion. This, indeed, is the way love works.

E. NATURAL EVIL

Natural evil is far less important, in the modern world, than moral evil, but it is harder to explain. It is relatively easy to see, once the case is made, that to expect personality without its high price is to expect an absurdity, but this will not explain natural evils. It helps to explain suffering in a concentration camp, but it will not explain suffering from the eruption of a volcano. We can agree that God needed to give costly freedom if He desired to make real persons, but why did He need to make earthquakes? There have been developed, in the history of religious thought, three main answers to this particular problem, which may be stated separately but which show their full strength when taken in conjunction:

(1) *The first answer is that personal life cannot develop except in a stable environment.* The crucial question is not whether ours is the *best* possible world, but whether it may be the *only* possible world. The environment which God has provided for the growth of the finite personal beings which we represent, and know, is a material environment and its stability consists in the fact that it is law-abiding. Volcano eruptions occur because the pressures which form in the heated interior of the earth are law-abiding and, when the pressure is sufficiently great, the crust is broken and the lava flows on the earth's surface. If people live near the danger areas, they, in numerous cases, suffer accordingly. The laws, we must remember, can be generally dependable without being absolutely inflexible or mechanical.

The crucial point is that, providing we are to have such a stable setting for our personal development, not all situations can be equally agreeable to all persons. The truth is that the rain may help one set of human purposes and harm another. What we call "accidents" are bound to occur. If knives are sharp enough to do good work, they will also be sharp enough to cut the fingers which guide the work. If automobiles go fast enough to provide needed transportation, they will go fast enough to destroy the lives of those who ride in them and those who unfortunately get in their way.

Though it is not so apparent on the surface, the possibility of natural evil is as necessary to freedom as is the possibility of moral evil. We might try to imagine a world in which God would hold back the volcano every time people were so foolish as to live near it, but free choice would be thereby harmed because choice requires stability. On this point C. S. Lewis is very persuasive:

We can, perhaps, conceive of a world in which God corrected the results of this abuse of free will by his creatures at every moment: so that a wooden beam became soft as grass when it was used as a weapon, and the air refused to obey me if I attempted to set up in it the sound waves that carry lies or insults. But such a world would be one in which wrong actions were impossible, and in which, therefore, freedom of the will would be void.[38]

Thus, we see that the relevant consideration in regard to natural evil is essentially the same as that in regard to moral evil. God's purpose in producing freedom does not, apparently, involve freedom from either inner temptation or outer danger.

(2) *The second relevant consideration concerning natural evil is that much of the resultant suffering is or can be redemptive.* This is particularly true of the suffering occasioned by the natural evil of disease, such as cancer or polio. A life with no element of tragedy is almost sure to be superficial and self-centered, missing the greatest possible richness of human experience. Only those who have suffered much begin to understand what the secrets of life are and they cannot communicate them except to those who have suffered equally. Part of the secret is that there seems to be a close connection between suffering and love. Love, we agree, is the greatest thing in the world, yet the experience of it, in any full measure, does not come to all, but only to the prepared. And an essential element in the fullest preparation seems to be suffering. Suffering can be especially effective in bringing to men and women a sense of *being loved.*

The problem of evil is not wholly answered by the fact that suffering can be redemptive of human character, but this fact greatly lessens the force of that problem. There are many persons alive today who, having gone through deep personal tragedy and having ultimately made their peace with the situation, find in their peace a quality which was not possible before the struggle. When we see

[38] *The Problem of Pain,* p. 21.

this we are still troubled by the fact that some people seem to have far too much sorrow while others seem not to have their share, but we cannot honestly say that it would be a better world if there were no sorrow in it. It looks as though the goal to which our world is pointing, in the development of character, is not mere happiness, but something deeper. This is one of the best indications we have of the ultimate nature of the universe. Ours is a universe of turmoil, and even our solar system, it is widely believed by experts, began with a major disturbance. Starting in the tumult of great tides, the history of our own small planet has itself been tumultuous. There has been the fierceness of cold and heat, the harsh struggle for survival, the rise and fall of species. But it all seems to be pointing somewhere, in the direction of more life, more mind, more spirit in the sense of the self-conscious appreciation of what ought to be. Could it have come without the tumult, the pain, and the endless struggle? That we do not know, but we *can* see that the emergence of character is an end so good that it justifies all the struggle, no matter how many millions of years it has been in the making. A truly good person is so precious, and such a wonderful product in our universe of space and stars, that any amount of pain and turmoil are justified by the ultimate emergence of this product. If sorrow and defeat and tragedy are the necessary price for the tender courage which we sometimes see on some faces, we may be sure that the price is not too high.

In making this significant point we must always take conscious care not to fall into the blasphemy of saying that suffering is a good and, therefore, something to be encouraged or even overlooked. It is an *evil,* but the truth is that ours is a world in which evil may be transcended by being faced and conquered. The paradox is that, frequently, the people who are most resolute in seeking to overcome the world's suffering are the very ones who have been deepened by the struggle with it.[39]

(3) *The third and final consideration is that of the life everlasting.* The ravages of cancer *do* seem unfair, but complete justice can be achieved if life is eternal. Back of every other answer this answer must loom. What we know of this life can only mitigate the problem of evil, but the hope of life everlasting provides the possibility of a

[39] Dr. Schweitzer's "Fellowship of Those Who Bear the Mark of Pain" is a reality.

complete answer. Indeed, the very insistence on the cruel urgency of the problem of evil provides the strongest philosophical argument for a future life. The argument is briefly as follows:

There is good reason to believe that God is and that He is wholly just.
But justice is never perfectly accomplished in this life.
Therefore, if God is not to be defeated, there must be another life in which the perfect justice, denied here, is fully achieved.

This argument has appealed powerfully to many great minds, including that of Dr. Samuel Johnson. "Since the common events of the present life," he said, "happen alike to the good and bad, it follows from the justice of the Supreme Being that there must be another state of existence in which a just retribution shall be made." It is in this mood that we refuse to minimize the problem of evil. The more firmly we grasp it the more it reveals truth about our world and our place in it. There is one thing worse than disturbance over the problem; that is not to feel it.

Part V

SUMMATION

18
God

Do not imagine that these great mysteries are completely and thoroughly known to any of us.

MAIMONIDES

As we approach the conclusion of this study we may appropriately end with the three themes made famous in the philosophy of Immanuel Kant—God, Freedom, Immortality. By these a mature religion will stand, if it stands, and without these it will certainly fall. Furthermore, there is a unique majesty about the really great themes. Consequently, we approach them with wonder and with humility. Whatever the true nature of God is, He is more than we know. The love of God is broader than the measure of man's mind.

A. THE IMPORTANT QUESTION

In previous chapters, particularly those of Part Two, we have seen something of the evidence for the faith that God is and that He is not merely an idea in human minds. The theistic hypothesis is better substantiated and answers more insistent questions raised in experience than is the case with any alternative hypothesis of which we have heard. But we cannot end with this, for the question of God's nature is more important, in some ways, than is the question of God's existence.

The popular question "Is there a God?" is never the right question. Heschel, in his philosophy of Judaism, points out that such a question is really presumptuous. "The ultimate question, bursting forth in our souls," he says, "is too startling, too heavily laden with unutterable wonder to be an academic question, to be equally suspended between yes and no. We can no longer ask: Is there a God? In humility and contrition we realize the presumption of such asking." [1]

---

[1] Abraham Joshua Heschel, *God in Search of Man,* New York, Farrar, Straus, 1955, p. 132.

It is easy enough to believe in "a God" providing we do not much care what kind. If we make the object of our search sufficiently broad and vague, existence is practically assured, but the value of the consequent faith is correspondingly lessened. Though Sigmund Freud is not, in most instances, a reliable interpreter of the religious scene, he does render a service by exposing the situation in which men use the language of practical faith but really mean something else. This Freud considered fundamentally dishonest. "Philosophers," he said, "stretch the meaning of words until they retain scarcely anything of their original sense; by calling 'God' some vague abstraction which they have created for themselves, they pose as deists, as believers before the world; they may even pride themselves on having attained a higher and purer idea of God, although their God is nothing but an insubstantial shadow and no longer the mighty personality of religious doctrine." [2]

It is because nearly all men believe in God in some sense that the question of divine character takes logical precedence over the question of divine existence. All of the major battles of religion are civil wars. Barnabas and Paul were not opposing the irreligious, but the inadequately religious when they cried out at Lystra, "We bring you good news, that you should turn from these vain things to a living God who made the heaven and the earth and the sea and all that is in them." [3]

How easy it is to use the word "God" and mean very little is shown vividly by the history of both deistic and pantheistic belief. The God of the deist is merely the First Cause, required by the demands of intellectual cogency, but such a God is not an active factor in day-by-day experience in the present world. He is not One whom men can love. The conception leaves no room for miracle, for prayer, for providential guidance, and, above all, it leaves no room for the direct religious experience such as Pascal's·conversion or the deep intimacies reported by the author of the *Imitation of Christ*. Though the term is now seldom used, a great deal of what passes for belief today is sheer deism and nothing more and is, therefore, woefully inadequate. If the only God who exists is the God of the deist, it would not be worth while to write a book on the philosophy of

[2] Sigmund Freud, *The Future of an Illusion*, p. 57.
[3] Acts 14:15.

religion. Deism may actually be less religious than primitive atheistic Buddhism, for, though the deist seems to speak of God, whereas the primitive Buddhist did not, he actually fails to have an object of ultimate concern, which the Buddhist undoubtedly had.[4]

Pantheism also involves the use of the word "God," but that is no good reason for taking it seriously. Pantheism is the conception of divine immanence carried to its ultimate conclusion, without the corrective of divine transcendence. The pantheist really identifies God and the world, thus obliterating the distinction between the Creator and the creation. This has taken a deep hold on certain portions of the popular mind, especially that portion which says there is no point in trying to give careful evidence for God, because He can be seen everywhere all the time. This simple faith is even reflected in popular hymns when people sing, "In the rustling grass, I see Him pass; our God is everywhere." The central idea is that God animates the world as I animate my body. With God the soul of the world, nothing is alien to Him, and there is no existence of God apart from the existence of the world. Anything we find in the world is a part of God.

This conception, though more widespread than we usually suppose,[5] suffers terribly from its naïve simplicity, in that it cannot account for the actual complexity and highly paradoxical character of the world as apprehended. Two particular defects are crucial. In the first place, if pantheism is true, God will die when the world dies. A painter may survive the destruction of his painting but, if the painter *is* the picture, the end of the picture is the end of *him*. There is much reason to infer, as Eddington has taught so persuasively, that the material order is due for ultimate stagnation, in which no part will be a scene of life and consequently a world devoid of value.

---

[4] Cf. Tillich, *Systematic Theology*, vol. 1, p. 220. "If God is understood as that which concerns man ultimately, early Buddhism has a concept of God just as certainly as does Vedanta Hinduism. And if God is understood as that which concerns man ultimately, moral or logical concepts of God are seen to be valid insofar as they express an ultimate concern. Otherwise, they are philosophical possibilities but not the God of religion."

[5] Among the most common expressions of essential pantheism in the modern world are the writings of Christian Scientists. Cf. Clyde E. Gunter, "Concerning Disease and Regeneration," *Christian Science Journal*, August, 1952, pp. 405 ff. "Everything in God's universe," says the author, "is under the control of divine Principle."

If there is no basic distinction between God and the world, and if increasing entropy is a fact, the life of God is of limited duration. Such a God is not an object of ultimate concern.

In the second place, pantheism cannot account rationally for sin and evil. If the world and God are identical, then God includes evil in His nature, with the consequence that He is not really worthy of reverence on moral grounds. "If God and man are one, then God, and not man, is responsible for evil." [6] The pantheist cannot evade this crucial difficulty except by some effort to minimize the distinction between good and evil. He may either hold that good and evil are merely human in their reference, purely relative to man's wishes and therefore sheer illusion when applied to the objective world, or he may hold, on the other hand, that what appears to be evil is nothing but some good in disguise. In short, the pantheist is forced, in deference to his central dogma, to deny utterly that there *is* any problem of evil. It ought to be obvious that any philosophy which flies in the face of so much of human experience need not be taken seriously. C. S. Lewis calls it a boy's philosophy and brackets it with the watered-down Christianity which says that "there's a good God in Heaven and everything is all right—leaving out all the terrible doctrines about sin and hell and the devil, and the redemption. It is no good asking for a simple religion. "After all real things aren't simple." [7] The following sentences from Lewis are bound to bring pause to all who are tempted to oversimplification in their conception of God and God's relationship to the world, including those who still speak of the Oversoul, in the way once made fashionable by Ralph Waldo Emerson.

If you don't take the distinction between good and bad very seriously, then it's easy to say that anything you find in this world is a part of God. But, of course, if you think some things really bad, and God really good, then you can't talk like that. You must believe that God is separate from the world and that some of the things we see in it are contrary to His will. Confronted with a cancer or a slum the Pantheist can say, "If you could only see it from the divine point of view, you would realize that this also is God." The Christian replies, "Don't talk damned nonsense." [8]

[6] Peter A. Bertocci, *Introduction to the Philosophy of Religion,* p. 317.
[7] C. S. Lewis, *The Case for Christianity,* p. 35.
[8] *Ibid.,* pp. 33, 34.

B. The Source of Value

It is probable that the best way to gain some understanding of the nature of God is to proceed as on a stairway, not trying to take the top steps first. We invite all to start in such a procedure, each taking as many of the steps as he can.

The common ground on which nearly all devout persons can unite is the conviction that God is the Power in the universe which drives it in the direction of goodness. Unless there is such a power in the world it is really impossible to explain the emergence of such values as are actually known. However imperfect our world is and however tormenting the problem of evil may be, it is a fact that ours is a world of order and that the order is such that it has led to the emergence of· life, of mind and of spirit. The road from the infant planet to the reverent scientist is a long road, but it is all the same road. There is, then, in the world a *thrust* in the direction of increasing meaning, increasing sensibility, increasing appreciation of truth, beauty and goodness. Whatever else God is, He is at least this *thrust*. He is the Eros of which Plato speaks so movingly in the *Symposium* and of which Whitehead, that modern Plato, speaks at the end of *Adventures of Ideas*. Instead of using the word "God" he speaks of the "Unity of Adventure," which, he says, "includes the Eros which is the living urge towards all possibilities, claiming the goodness of their realization." The universe achieves its final justification in the Beauty which the Living Urge produces. "The Adventure of the Universe starts with the dream and reaps tragic Beauty." As we read these highly poetic, yet profound words we begin to get an accurate minimal idea of what there is in the world besides sticks and stones and living cells and finite minds. The dream of youth and the harvest of tragedy are not limited to human experience, but are, Whitehead believed, "at the heart of the nature of things." "God is the adventurous element in the universe. It is the character of God as both adventurous and ultimate that makes possible the best that men can know, the union of Zest with Peace." [9]

Nearly all who believe in God with a sense of wonder, even though they cannot accept the notion of God as personal, would go this far in their characterization of the divine power. Thus, Henry N.

[9] Alfred North Whitehead, *Adventures of Ideas,* p. 381.

Wieman describes God as follows: "God is understood to be the power more than human which saves man from ultimate disaster and transforms him into the best that he can ever become." [10] It is obvious that the man who writes such a statement is trying desperately to be honest and not to go beyond his evidence. He is saying that the God so described is actually known in experience because we *do* find help in our moral endeavor. There is a Power that sustains us on life's darkest as well as life's brightest ways. However inadequate such a characterization of God may be, we can be grateful for the superlative honesty of those who refuse to go beyond their available evidence.

C. God as Personal

It is difficult to see how thinkers, such as those just mentioned, can come so close to ascribing personality to God without taking this important added step. After all, the aspect of our world which most cries out for explanation is precisely that aspect of the ascending series which is most truly personal. There are two major rocks on which religious naturalism [11] must inevitably founder. The first of these is the fact that ours is undoubtedly a world which has persons in it, and the second is the fact that so much of the validated religious experience of mankind is reported in personal terms.

That our world has produced persons is, in many ways, the most astounding fact we know. And we know persons far better than we know anything else, because we ourselves *are* persons. By a person we mean a being with conscious intelligence, equally able to be conscious of self and others, and also able both to entertain purposes and to appreciate values. Though personality as we know it most intimately is associated with bodies, there is no good reason to suppose that such association is necessary. It is certainly possible that there are personal beings without bodies; that is, angels *may* exist. But whereas the existence of angels is problematical, the existence of men is not. The one part of the universe with which we have a fair acquaintance is not only one in which there has been an ad-

[10] Henry Nelson Wieman, "Bernhardt's Analysis of Religion," *Iliff Review*, Winter, 1954, p. 56.

[11] By religious naturalism we mean any system which, even though it rejects the reductionist formula of materialism, fails to adopt a personalistic interpretation of events.

venturous thrust toward life and mind, but one which has flowered in the production of creatures who can sometimes say "no" to their appetites in the light of what is believed to be objectively right and good. The end product we really know is a high type of freedom.

How can the naturalist account for himself? He believes in God, but there is a fundamental absurdity in supposing that the God in whom he believes is inferior to himself in the *order of being*. If God is a mere "power," and not a center of consciousness, then I, the humble creature, am actually superior, in a very important way, to the Creator. Can the "Unity of Adventure" be less rich in content than that which this Unity produces? The strangest feature of Whitehead's philosophy is his failure to see this point.

The tendency, in modern thinking, to suppose that a movement in the direction of impersonality is progress, is a very curious development, and hard to understand, because everything we know points the other way. If any man wants to hold that a creature, such as Socrates, is not superior to a stone, that is his privilege, but he will not be believed.

Our world is one which presents a series of levels of reality, with at least four levels apparent. The level of matter, as represented by a stone, is surpassed by the level of life, as represented in a tree, which unlike the stone, is capable of growth and reproduction. There is much interest today in the possibility that life may now be produced in laboratories by the combination of material factors and without reproduction. Indeed, a few scientists now claim to be close to success in this ancient endeavor. Some suppose that this operation would prove the reductive hypothesis that life is *nothing but* matter. It would, of course, prove nothing of the kind, and would be in no way disturbing. The men involved would simply be fortunate enough to observe a point in which the emergence from one level to another occurs. There would still be different levels, because there would be different laws in operation.[12]

The level of mind, as illustrated in the thinking of a chimpanzee, uses life as life uses matter, but likewise surpasses it. Life is an emancipation from intrinsic passivity, but mind is an emancipation from simple location. A creature which merely lives has no relation-

[12] This is obvious, once it is pointed out, but it was not obvious to me until it was brought to my attention by Professor Lovejoy.

ship with other creatures except by immediate contact, but a creature who thinks is related to others by contemplation. The difference is a difference in kind. Spirit uses and surpasses mind as mind uses and surpasses life. In spirit we observe a final step in the direction of freedom, ôn that spirit is emancipated from the complete domination of the appetites. The biggest step ever taken is the step from "I want" to "I ought."

Now, the point is that if we stop short of thinking of God in the highest terms we know we are guilty of a kind of blasphemy. It is really a terrible thing to suggest that I can be conscious of God, whereas God cannot be conscious of me. Here is where the spiritual genius of Judaism appears most brilliantly. "The God of Hebraic religion," says Herberg, "the God of the Bible, is a *Living God*. In this tremendous phrase—the Living God—which has become so strange to our ears, but which recurs repeatedly in the Bible and continues right through rabbinic tradition, is concentrated the full potency of the Hebraic 'God-idea.' Only it is no longer a mere 'God-idea'; it is the Living God himself." [13] What Herberg and men like him are talking about is not an abstract idea or an intellectual principle, and certainly not the Absolute, but "a dynamic power that is personal." [14] Heschel is even more explicit when he writes: "The living soul is not concerned with a dead cause, but with a living God. Our goal is to ascertain the existence of a Being to whom we may confess our sins, of a God who loves, of a God who is not above concern with our inquiry and search for Him; a father, not an absolute."

The idea of God as fully personal means that God is a center of consciousness and of self-consciousness and, therefore, utterly different from mere brute power or the reign of law, though God is undoubtedly the source both of power and of natural law. God, in the most advanced thought, especially of Christians, is never equated with some abstract quality. The phrase "God is love," though it appears in the New Testament, cannot be considered a definition or an exhaustive statement, and must be understood in connection with other statements, such as "God so loved the world." Love without a lover is a pure abstraction.

[13] Will Herberg, *Judaism and Modern Man,* p. 58.
[14] *Ibid.,* p. 59.

It is Martin Buber, more than any other living philosopher, who has recovered for modern men the wonder and depth of the personal understanding of the mystery at the heart of the world by his emphasis on the ultimate meaning of Thou.[15] The cruel paradox of our time is that, enamored of natural science, we have sought to penetrate the mystery of electrons and have tended to forget the far greater mystery of the persons who study the electrons. To be able to say "Thou" truly and meaningfully is to be a person.[16] God is not an Object merely to be spoken *about*, but One to be spoken *to*, and *listened* to. The mystery of personality is deep enough, at best, but it is absolutely impenetrable if God is merely an impersonal force, a mere *it*.

If naturalism has a hard time accounting for the emergence of personality in the world, it has an even harder time accounting for religious experience. The sophomore may suppose that he can discount all religious experience or explain it psychologically, but the wise man does not think so. To suppose that *all* of those who, in the simplicity of prayer, have felt the sustaining hand of God were deluded is to be guilty of monstrous arrogance. But what is so significant is the great amount of the reported experience, as found in countless journals and implied in countless prayers, that is deeply personal.

"Why is it," Herberg asks, "that we, modern-minded men, are so scandalized when we are seriously asked to think of God as personal?" Part of the answer is no doubt the one which he suggests, that "we have inherited the Greek metaphysical conception of God as Pure Being," but there is an added reason. Being children of a scientific age, we are well aware that new science tends to destroy old science, and we are accordingly skeptical of conclusions which have the antiquity of those of the Bible. Can you trust the judgment of a man who never went faster than a horse could run? Perhaps the

---

[15] William James had previously used similar language in the following sentences: "The more perfect and more eternal aspect of the universe is represented in our religions as having a personal form. The universe is no longer a mere It to us, but a Thou, if we are religious and any relation that may be possible from person to person might be possible here." "The Will to Believe," in which these sentences appear, was first published in 1897. Buber's first draft of *I and Thou* was made in 1916.

[16] *The Writings of Martin Buber*, p. 54.

notion of God as Father is merely another antiquated idea which we ought to outgrow, particularly when we realize that it is rooted in the psychological needs of childhood. But, whatever the explanation, the deep misgiving is usually expressed in a big and ominous-sounding word, *anthropomorphism*. To think of God personally, some say, is really to be anthropomorphic, that is, to think of God in the form of a man.

The criticism is an old one, to which nothing of importance has been added in more than two thousand years, though the attack may be made directly or in an oblique fashion. An unusually clear example of the direct attack on the belief in God as personal is provided by the religious writings of Albert Einstein, writings which indicate that a man may be a great mathematician without being a careful thinker in other fields. Einstein's attack was as follows:

During the youthful period of mankind's spiritual evolution human fantasy created gods in man's own image, who, by the operations of their will were supposed to determine, or at any rate to influence, the phenomenal world. Man sought to alter the disposition of these gods in his own favor by means of magic and prayer. The idea of God in the religions taught at present is a sublimation of that old concept of the gods. Its anthropomorphic character is shown, for instance, by the fact that men appeal to the Divine Being in prayers and plead for fulfillment of their wishes.

Nobody, certainly, will deny that the idea of the existence of an omnipotent, just and omnibeneficent personal God is able to accord man solace, help and guidance; also, by virtue of its simplicity it is accessible to the most undeveloped mind. But, on the other hand, there are decisive weaknesses attached to this idea in itself, which have been painfully felt since the beginning of history. That is, if this being is omnipotent, then every occurrence, including every human action, every human thought, and every human feeling and aspiration is also His work; how is it possible to think of holding men responsible for their deeds and thoughts before such an Almighty Being? In giving out punishments and rewards He would, to a certain extent, be passing judgment on Himself. How can this be combined with the goodness and righteousness ascribed to Him?

The main source of the present day conflicts between the sphere of religion and science lies in this concept of a personal God.[17]

Einstein showed by this statement how little he understood the

17 Albert Einstein, *Ideas and Opinions*, pp. 46, 47.

history of religion. He repeated the ancient claim of Xenophanes
that man has made the gods in his own image, but was he aware of
the prophetic teaching that warns against this very danger, while
keeping the sense of personal immediacy? He presented omnipotence
as though he had not heard of the fact of freedom, which means that
God is not directly responsible for the acts of men which go against
His will. In short, the whole position is remarkably naïve and gets
its apparent strength from its naïveté. Of course, it would be wrong
and inadequate to think of God as limited to the imperfect character
of men, but such an absurdity is a straw man; it is not what is meant
by following the Biblical insight and seeing God as *fully* personal.
There is a middle ground between anthropomorphism and imper-
sonalism.

The direct attack, like that of Einstein, is relatively easy to meet,
but the situation is harder when the attack is oblique and when it
comes from the mind of a man as able as Paul Tillich. There is a
strain in Tillich's thinking in which he attempts, not a denial of
personal characteristics in the divine, but such a radical reinterpreta-
tion of divine personality as to break utterly with what the plain man
of prayer normally means. In the end this might be a more damaging
approach than that of the direct challenge. Tillich speaks of the
personal character of God as a "myth," and says, "Where the myth
is taken literally, God is less than the ultimate, he is less than the
object of ultimate concern, he is not God in the infinite and unconditional sense of the great commandment." [18]

Such a statement calls for careful analysis. What, for example, is
the meaning of "taken literally"? He cannot mean "taken as though
God had a physical form like man's form or appetites and temptations." The inadequacy of that conception would be obvious to
every thinking person and not worth Tillich's attention. He must
mean "taken seriously." But in that case his conclusion does not
follow. If I believe "literally" that God is personal, because I believe
that the highest order of being is personal being, why is God less
than ultimate? Conscious love is not a limitation, but the greatest
emancipation we know or can imagine. To picture God as an impersonal absolute, a mere being with no consciousness or purpose,

[18] "Where do we go from here in theology?" *Religion in Life,* Winter, 1955-
1956, p. 19.

is to involve oneself in one absurdity while trying to escape another. *God is not the object of ultimate concern if He lacks the simple majesty of the freedom which man undoubtedly has.*

The central point is that, if God is not personal, in a literal sense, then God is not the ultimate explanation of that which most requires explanation. What baffles the materialist is the emergence of personal character in a world of chemical reactions. Only one who is supremely personal can be the Ground for the emergence of even the finite personality which we see in our fellows and know intimately in ourselves. If God is only an impersonal force, then the stream *has* risen higher than its source, for we can at least be certain that personality appears in *us.*

The people who have tried to hold to belief in God while rejecting the personal aspect of the Divine have sincerely tried to make an advance over a primitive view, but they have, unfortunately, moved in the wrong direction. Just as life is manifestly superior to matter and as consciousness is superior to mere biological phenomena, the appreciation of personal value is superior to mere awareness of external environment. The line of advance is not *away* from the personal, but toward it and possibly through it. Many of those who resist the notion of God as personal are, no doubt, trying to avoid what seems at first to be a limitation to our size and experience, and this effort is wholesome, but personality is not such a limiting conception. No one in his senses would think of interpreting the personal character of God as limited to the low level of personality illustrated in ourselves. Of course, God is more than we are, but He must be at least *as much* as we are. The alternative to He or Thou is It. Perhaps what we need to do is to coin a big word, from Greek derivatives, which will be as frightening to the "impersonalists" as anthropomorphism has been to the personalists.

To say that God is completely different from us is as absurd as to say that He is completely like us. He may differ from us, C. S. Lewis suggests, not as white differs from black but as a perfect circle differs from a child's first crude attempt to depict a wheel. Human personality makes sense if it is a childish attempt to achieve the complete personality which God, and God alone, demonstrates.

If God is, indeed, truly personal, as so much of experience indicates, we should expect that His most vivid revelation would necessarily be a personal one. The complete way in which He could be shown to us would not be in the majesty of mountains or in the wonder of the stars or even in the intricacy of a cell, but only in a personal life, sharing, as do our little lives, in both affection and temptation, yet perfect where we are imperfect. The good news, according to Christians, is that this has occurred! All other historical persons can be approached or forgotten at will, but there has lived One whom men cannot leave alone. He revealed the truth of God and man, not merely by what he taught, but far more by what he did and, above all, by what he *was*. The major faith of the Western world is centered in a *personal* revelation.

D. Transcendence

The conclusion to which our cumulative argument has led us is that the explanation of the world is to be sought in a Personal Reality, or, to use the Biblical phrase, the Living God. Can we envisage, more precisely, His relation to the world and its process? It seems clear, if our argument is sound, that God is the explanation of the world in such a manner that it is dependent upon Him as He is not dependent upon it. Personality is always more than its own self-expression. The artist undoubtedly puts himself into the painting, but, even on the finite level of personality, the effect does not exhaust the cause; how much less so must it be when we are dealing with infinite personality! In short, the more we take the concept of the personal seriously the more we realize that for God to be truly personal He must be transcendent. Transcendence and immanence are not incompatible, but are complementary concepts. God is seen immanently in the order of the world, but there would not even be this order if He were not more than the order. Only if God is transcendent can the world be the medium of His personal action. It is because God is transcendent that miracle is possible; there is no good reason to suppose that God's freedom is destroyed by the order of nature which He has made. This is why no law of nature, as discovered by physical science, is ultimate; only the Personal Reality is ultimate.

Here is the ground of the chief debate between all naturalism on one side, and full theism, on the other. To be a theist, we remember,

is "to adopt the hypothesis that the process of nature in all its range
is to be accounted for by the intelligent purpose of Mind." [19] In
short, the theist holds that nature is not autonomous or self-explanatory and must look beyond itself for an explanation of itself.
The modern naturalist, on the other hand, rejects all transcendence
as something unnecessary.[20]

The fact of transcendence, which means that the ultimate Object
is a Subject, follows necessarily from the recognition that Mind and
nothing else provides the principle of explanation which the natural
process requires. But if God is a true Subject and not a mere Object,
then our entire relationship to Him is put on a new footing. Religion
is not then a one-way search of man for God, as though we were
searching for a deposit of uranium. If God is the Infinite Subject,
He is reaching for us even as we reach for Him. Too often our
religious philosophy has been posited on the assumption that God
is silent, hidden, and unconcerned about our search. But there have
been strong voices raised in protest. Possibly the most enduring of
the books of the late Rufus M. Jones is one which he wrote early in
his career with the self-explanatory title *The Double Search*. The
familiar assumption that only man is the seeker has been challenged
in contemporary thought by the remarkable resurgence of Biblical
thinking of which the very title of Heschel's great book, *God in
Search of Man,* is illustrative. "All human history as described in the
Bible," he says, "may be summarized in one phrase, God in Search
of Man." [21]

The failure of a number of wise and good men to make the full
deduction regarding Divine Personality is one of the most curious
phases of the philosophy of the recent past. Of these, Professor
Whitehead is characteristic. He says much about God, particularly
in the concluding pages of *Process and Reality,* but he explains that
he is thinking of God in terms of Organism rather than in terms of
Personality. The curious feature is that, though the beautiful things

[19] William Temple, *Nature, Man and God*, p. 257.

[20] This seems to be the position of William H. Bernhardt of Iliff Theological
Seminary. As I understand him, this deeply religious man rejects all supernatural or transcendent conceptions of God and says that he can do so by virtue
of the fact that he sees nature more rich than it is ordinarily seen. Cf. "The
Cognitive Quest for God," *Journal of Religion*, vol. 23, no. 2, p. 99.

[21] *Op. cit.,* p. 136.

he says are appropriate if God is personal, they are not appropriate if God is a mere organism, without conscious purpose and affection such as we know, though imperfectly, in our own lives. "The very reason which gives to the Christian scheme its philosophic superiority is that which precludes Professor Whitehead from adopting it." [22] What is strange is that a man who put us so greatly in his debt and who saw so much did not see more.

Equally mystifying is the stand of Professor Tillich at another level. He goes much further than Professor Whitehead went and speaks of God as "Personal," but refuses to speak of Him as "Person." This is doubly curious in view of the fact that Tillich makes freedom his main point of philosophic departure. Having said that "personal God" is a symbol which is "absolutely fundamental because an existential relation is a person-to-person relation" and that "Man cannot be ultimately concerned about anything that is less than personal," he makes his qualification in the following sentences:

"Personal God" does not mean that God is a person. It means that God is the ground of everything personal and that he carries within himself the ontological power of personality. He is not a person but he is not less than personal. It should not be forgotten that classical theology employed the term *persona* for the trinitarian hypostases, but not for God himself. God became "a person" only in the nineteenth century, in connection with the Kantian separation of nature ruled by physical law from personality ruled by moral law.[23]

Here is a challenge which must be met, but it can be met on several grounds. In the first place, the distinction between "personal" and "a person" is a mere quibble, since the adjective is strictly meaningless without reference to the noun. The only reality that is personal is person. Otherwise, it is a smile without a face. In the second place, it is not true that "God became a person in the nineteenth century." He was clearly a Person for Christ. How else could Christ say "O Father?" Can a direct appeal be made to that which is personal, but not a person? Only a person can reasonably be addressed as "Thou." Furthermore, if we take the trinitarian formula seriously, it is necessary to hold that the language referring to each

---

22 William Temple, *op. cit.,* p. 259.
23 Paul Tillich, *op. cit.,* vol. 1, pp. 244, 245.

part of the Trinity refers to the whole of the Living God, for these three are *one*. The problem which Tillich raises about the Kantian legacy of the separation between the natural and the moral world need not bother us now, providing we have a philosophy according to which Personality, as the ultimate principle, is the explanation of *both* the natural and the moral world.

If it is the indefinite article that bothers Professor Tillich, we can leave off the article, but we are on very shaky ground when we omit the noun. What we are driven to is the conclusion that God is the Personal Reality, in short, the Transcendent Person. It is important to realize that William Temple, who may be justly considered the most distinguished theologian of our century,[24] did not hesitate to use the plain language of common piety and prayer. His central conviction, often repeated in different contexts, was that "God is the explanation of the world because He is Person." [25]

[24] Even *Punch* has written, "If Christian sanity survives in the modern world, none will deserve a greater share of the credit than William Temple." *Punch*, Aug. 11, 1948.

[25] *Op. cit.*, p. 265.

19
Freedom

If man were "just an animal" he would never have found that fact out.

LEWIS MUMFORD

In one sense we are all existentialists. We are deeply concerned about the human predicament, and we are eager to learn what man is. It is one of the special marks of man that, at least since the dawn of serious reflection, he has been a problem to himself. Almost all of the great philosophers, as well as many other men, have been interested in the question of man's precise mode of differentiation from all other animals. It has been said that man is the only animal who laughs, the only one who weeps, the only one who prays, the only one who walks fully erect, the only one who makes fires, the only one who can invent, the only one with a written language, the only one who is proud, the only one who can make progress, the only one who guides his own destiny, the only one who is penitent, and the only one who needs to be. The list could be continued much further, and its very length gives vivid evidence of how keenly thinkers of various periods have been interested in the problem.

The modern study of this basic question is called philosophical anthropology and has involved a number of first-rate minds, such as Heidegger and Scheler. All realize that the answers we give to the problems faced in this particular discipline are crucial, not only for ethics, but also for almost all other areas of experience. Two great answers, one general and the other particular, emerge, by a remarkable consensus, from such inquiries. The general answer is that man is unique in virtue of the very fact that he is puzzled about his uniqueness. So far as we know, no other animal is concerned with questions of this kind. There is one conclusion to which all facts point, the conclusion that man is the animal who reflects, who is eager to understand himself, who is curious about matters which are

unnecessary in the sense that they are not involved in the search for
food and shelter or the struggle for survival. Man, whatever else he
is, is the metaphysical animal, as Schopenhauer called him. This
point is made by many writers, but particularly by existentialists, as
in the following paragraph:

> That being, called "man," who asks philosophical questions, wants first
> of all to know what he is and where he stands. And why is he so anxiously
> and vitally concerned with his own existence? Simply because by his very
> nature he is a questioning being, a philosophical creature. The irrational
> animal, on the other is essentially unphilosophical; it does not question
> the meaning of its existence, nor the meaning of its surrounding world.
> It merely accepts both and uses them to the best of its ability. But man is
> that peculiar kind of being which perpetually questions and wonders and
> doubts.[1]

A. The Fact of Freedom

The particular answer to the question of man's uniqueness involves the revolutionary idea of freedom. Man differs from all others
in that, while he is a part of nature, he is also emancipated from
nature. He has appetites, but he can deny them their satisfaction in
the light of conscious purpose; he survives, but he is capable of
freedom from the mere struggle for survival in that he prizes some
things more highly than he prizes his own continued existence; he
is born into an environment, but he has a remarkable freedom to
alter that environment by conscious thought; he lives in time, but
he is freed from the specious present by the fact that he is always part
of a community of memory and of hope. The human spirit is freed
from animal experience as truly as any living thing is freed from the
limitations of the merely material entity.

Such has been the theme of much of the most brilliant thought of
our day. Gabriel Marcel has presented man as "homo viator"—"never
at the goal, but always on the way." Man's freedom involves danger
as well as wonder; he may, in Goethe's words, "become what he is,"
but he may also fall away from his authentic self. Man's life involves
all of the pains and joys of the transcendence of *fixedness*. Man
stands out from all other modes of existence because, whereas the
minerals, plants and animals simply *are* and cannot actually be
otherwise, man is the creature who "has constantly and dynamically

[1] Kurt Reinhardt, *The Existential Revolt*, Milwaukee, Bruce, 1952, p. 17.

to affirm and actualize his existence in self-knowledge and self-realization." [2] It is man's tragic glory to be suspended between nothingness and the plentitude of being. Because, as Pascal said, man is both a brute and an angel, he is never sure, at any moment, which of them he is.

Nicolas Berdyaev, particularly in his later work, though to a lesser extent in all his books, saw the fact of freedom as the major key to an understanding of reality. In his final phase, the Russian thinker stressed more and more the singleness and unrepeatability of historical events, which distinguish them from the phenomena of nature in which repeatability occurs. "Newness," he affirmed, "does appear in historical time." [3] Freedom he interpreted as the entrance of genuine novelty into the course of events and saw this, when fully recognized, as a damaging blow to all causal determinism. "The causal determinist explanation," he said, "is conspicuously worthless as an elucidation of the emergence of creative genius." [4]

Freedom is so important that it deserves the careful contemplation of anyone who tries to achieve a valid philosophy, and particularly a valid philosophy of religion, because the gift of freedom is a wondrous and a dangerous gift which enters into nearly every distinctively human experience. It bears, for example, upon the reality of sin, because the fact that man *can* sin represents a remarkable ability. No other creature known to us can sin at all. "Only if man *can* do evil is there any meaning in doing good." [5] Because man is free, as no other animal is, he is able to be far more cruel and vindictive than any other animal is, and likewise he can be far more noble. The *range* of human conduct is vastly greater than is the range of animal conduct.

It is much safer, intellectually, to understand human life in terms of freedom than in terms of dignity. Stress on human dignity, in the Renaissance fashion of Pico della Mirandola, has a tendency to make

[2] *Ibid.*, p. 15.

[3] Nicolas Berdyaev, *The Beginning and the End*, New York, Harper, 1952, p. 165.

[4] *Ibid.*, p. 161. It should be noted that Berdyaev went so far as to accept uncritically the dangers of indeterminism and consequently to undermine the strength of the major theistic argument. At the end he was unduly influenced by the philosophy of Jacob Boehme.

[5] E. LaB. Cherbonnier, *Hardness of Heart*, New York, Doubleday, 1955, p. 15.

man proud, and leads to nonsense about natural human goodness. But stress on freedom can provide man, at the same time, with both a sense of wonder and a sense of humility. It is the one sure way to involve conviction about both the greatness and the littleness of man. Reinhold Niebuhr's warning is relevant at this point:

> In the field of speculation about human nature, the crux of the issue is whether the distinctive marks of man as a unique creature shall be so defined that the proofs of his "dignity" are also the proofs of his virtue; or whether his dignity shall be defined in terms of the radical character of human freedom. In the latter case his dignity would have the same ground as his destructiveness or his sin.[6]

The heart of positive freedom is the twin experience of *deliberation* and *decision*. The act of deliberation is a marvelous thing which we consider without wonder only because we engage in it constantly. The person who is trying to deny freedom as a causal factor usually says that different forces are at work and that the stronger motive prevails, but this, as Tillich points out, tells us nothing at all. "To say that the stronger motive always prevails is an empty tautology, since the test by which a motive is proved stronger is simply that it prevails." [7] Unless our universal experience is universally deluding, the decision to which deliberation leads actually involves a new causal factor in the sequence of events. If this is true, it is a very important fact about the world. And it certainly seems to be true. Whether some wood burns this morning depends not merely on the relative dryness of the wood, its location near my fireplace, the existence of a match, etc., but also on *my decision*. In so far as this is the case the mechanistic picture of the universe is shown to be inadequate. That which has no location has altered that which does have location. The mystery of mind and body is still a mystery, but that philosophy is most adequate which faces it realistically. Decision involves consequences. "Each time the child throws its toy out of its baby carriage," says Sir James Jeans, "it disturbs the motion of every star."

The terrific mystery arises from the observation that this amazing experience of effective decision operates, so far as our experience

---

[6] Reinhold Niebuhr, *His Religious, Social and Political Thought*, ed. by Charles W. Kegley and R. W. Bretall, New York, Macmillan, 1956, p. 10.

[7] *Systematic Theology*, vol. 1, p. 184.

goes, only on crass physical bodies. There is no gain in trying to deny matter. Matter is no less material when it is explained, as Eddington explains it, in terms of wave lengths. Electrical impulses are still, so far as we know, radically different from consciousness. Advanced religion does not hold that there are no bodies, but is deeply interested in bodies because it is through bodies that our deepest freedom finds expression. How matter affects consciousness we do not know, and how consciousness affects matter we do not know, but any metaphysic is in great danger if it seeks to neglect the recognition that this double relation is factual.

B. THE DIFFICULTIES OF DETERMINISM

Freedom is not only a fact; it is also a problem. It constitutes a problem of particular significance for those who seek to introduce the methods of natural science into the study of human behavior. The older books on psychology included chapters on freedom, but the current fashion is to avoid the subject, chiefly because it will not fit the scheme that is adopted. The characteristic contemporary textbooks of psychology, as used in colleges, do not even list the word "freedom" in the index. They omit the concept because from the point of view of most of these authors, many of whom have been influenced by behaviorism, even when they avoid the unpopular term, freedom is neither possible nor desirable. Cherbonnier has explained succinctly why this is so. "It is not possible," he says, "because of the assumption that human behavior can be exhaustively explained in causal terms. It is not desirable because it would introduce an element of incalculability in the scientific field of study."[8]

Science would be so much simpler if only there were no men. Then all of the incalculable facts depending on personal decision could be neglected. Psychology would be simple if there were only rats, but who, in that case, would make the analysis? Orthodox social science, in so far as it rests upon the assumption of causal determinism, is always faced, whether its practitioners know it or not, by two tremendous contradictions. In the first place, it is faced with a contradiction concerning truth. Determinism, if taken seriously, would involve the further notion that all intellectual judgment is itself determined, but this would have to apply even to the judgment that

[8] Cherbonnier, *op. cit.*, p. 15.

determinism is true. The point has seldom been made more clearly than in the following sentence from the pen of Paul Tillich. "The determinist does not see that the very affirmation of determinism as true presupposes the freedom of decision between true and false." [9]

The damning fact about mechanistic determinism is that it undermines the possibility of truth and yet claims to be true. It is important, therefore, to see more precisely how this is done. The standard unit of behavior is the conditioned response, for though responses may be simple or complex, they follow the same general laws. When a dog presents the behavior known as salivation, we can account for this behavior by a full consideration of the parts involved. The parts involved can be set in motion by appropriate stimuli, the appropriateness depending upon the physical constitution of the body called the dog and the disposition of the body's parts. These have already been modified by past stimuli and the reactions of the body to them. Here we have a system which can give us reactions according to order.

There is no difference in principle between the dog's salivation and the dog's barking or anything else, except that some actions may be more complex than others. By the same token there is no difference in principle, so the naturalistic creed maintains, between the barking of the dog and the crying, eating or speaking of a man. In the man the body is more complex, and the past stimuli have been more numerous, but again the response is the necessary result. If we really know all the neural and muscular factors and the history of former conditioning, we do not need to appeal to such mythical factors as decision, thought and purpose. It is the movements of bodies that count and that can be studied as other physical objects are studied, by what they do. The movements of the larynx, which we call speech, are as much parts of a complex mechanical order as is the salivation of the dog. Given all the physical constituents, these laryngeal movements could be predicted accurately by any competent observer. And thought, unless it is incipient laryngeal motion, is nothing at all.

But if thought *is* laryngeal motion, it is sheer nonsense to speak of thinking *truly*. A man thinks as his conditioning makes him think and that is the end of the matter. I write as I do now and I think as

[9] Paul Tillich, *op. cit.*, vol. 1, pp. 200, 201.

I think now because of the stimuli and my physical constitution, which produce reactions called thinking or writing. And likewise my opponent thinks and writes as he does for the same reason. It then becomes ridiculous to say that one system is more true than another, for each is what it must be, and it makes no more sense to call a thought true than it does to call a rain cloud true. The rain cloud is produced by a set of physical causes and cannot be other than it is. If all movements of bodies are equally necessary, they cannot be discriminated as true and false. Even my act of discrimination is another necessitated event and no more significant than any other. As Professor Joseph has pithily remarked, "It seems as nonsensical to call a movement true as a flavour purple or a sound avaricious." [10]

All that a determinist can logically maintain is that his books are the necessary outcome of a complex physical system. But, by the same argument, the books of his critics have exactly the same kind of background. There is, then, no way to distinguish between genuine and spurious knowledge. But a system cannot claim to be true and, at the same time, entail a situation in which there is no difference between truth and falsehood. A lie is as much determined as anything else. If I judge that my thought is knowledge and not error, judging, as we say, by comparison with the facts, this new thought or judgment is merely a result of another state of the brain and in no way superior to the former thoughts in this regard.

The climax of this criticism is that determinism provides no intelligible theory of error. It holds that error occurs and is, indeed, extremely common, inasmuch as so many people have not become convinced determinists, but it does not tell us how error is possible, how error can be detected, or even what error is. Certainly there is no valid appeal to logical principles, for the erroneous conclusion is as much necessitated as the correct one. A conclusion cannot help being in accordance with physical fact, for it is nothing but a link in a chain of physical fact. Consciousness may be deluded, but to call an electrical impulse deluded is nonsense.

The second self-contradiction of all social science, in which the *dogma* of causal determinism has been accepted, is that it would destroy the very planning on which so much store is set. It is partly

[10] H. W. B. Joseph, *Some Problems in Ethics,* Oxford University Press, 1931, p. 14.

because the freedom of decision brings in an incalculable element that the planner seeks to avoid it. There is no place on earth in which planning is more highly valued than in Russia, where philosophical determinism is basic doctrine. It is by planning what men do, instead of leaving it to chance decision, that it will finally be possible, we are told, to allow the state to wither away.

But *if* complete determinism is true, the very idea of planning, so dear to the hearts of all dialectical materialists, is, by that fact, itself undermined. The botanist may reasonably be supposed to plan the growth of the tree, since his personal decision is outside the system to which the tree belongs, but the whole logical situation is altered radically once the deterministic system is applied to human thought and actions, including moral actions. The social worker tends to favor a determinist philosophy because, in terms of it, he can plan a project, perhaps one of slum clearance, and his belief in a deterministic system gives him assurance that his experiment will work effectively in changing human life. Since actions follow inevitably from *prior* physical and social conditions, all he needs to do, according to the theory, is to arrange the conditions and wait for the results.

The paradox which the planner must face, however, if he is intellectually alert, *is that in the terms of his philosophy his very effort to plan was itself also determined by prior conditions.* Therefore, he does not actually plan at all, but is merely the helpless and passive performer of deeds which are materially necessitated. It is generally supposed that, by taking careful thought, we can make a better world, but men and women who are truly convinced of the determinist creed cannot be influenced by such foolishness. In so far as they understand their own position they realize that all of their thoughts, purposes and actions are utterly independent of personal *choice.* Therefore, conscious endeavor could not possibly make a difference. Whenever they suppose, in their innocence, that they are planning, the outcome has already been determined by prior events. In short, the planning is only apparent and not real, unless decision is actually a causal factor in the production of events.

C. The Dilemma of Responsibility

It will be generally agreed that the sense of responsibility is one of the noblest features of our lives. So highly is it regarded that the adjective "irresponsible" is almost universally applied as a term of serious condemnation. But how is responsibility possible? It seems to be connected in some way with freedom, yet, as we analyze the problem, we find that the two obvious alternatives, determinism and indeterminism, are equally hostile to the development of responsibility. This is a very sobering observation and one that demands careful consideration.

The way in which deterministic doctrine destroys responsibility is well known. A man is certainly not responsible for that which he cannot help. We do not blame the boulder which rolls down the mountain side and kills a man, and, likewise, we cannot blame a man whose action is forced by events outside himself. If a man kills involuntarily, we hardly speak of the murder as a human act at all. "Man's will is called *animal*," says Kant, "if necessitated pathologically." [11]

Though the complete denial of freedom makes moral experience meaningless, the complete affirmation of freedom, in the sense of indeterminism, has the same result. This striking paradox arises from the fact that complete indeterminism would be inconsistent with the continuity of character. A wholly unpredictable man would by no means be a good man. He would, indeed, be no more an ethical being than is a tossed coin. He would face a decision and, if wholly undetermined, there would be no way of having any idea what his decision might be. Choice, so understood, would be indistinguishable from chance. Furthermore, praise and blame would again have no bearing. The blamed man would be able to say, "I chose that action yesterday, but I do not choose it today." Praise and blame are as meaningless apart from continuity of character as they are meaningless apart from some kind of freedom. The good man is one who is conscious of making a free choice so that he is not an automaton; but the good man is, at the same time, one whose actions are largely predictable because there are enduring elements in his character. The chance that a man of lifelong integrity will steal his friend's purse is almost negligible, but if there is something about his *physical* make-up which makes theft impossible we do not ascribe any *ethical* significance to his apparent honesty.

Here, then, is a serious dilemma. In order to have real responsi-

[11] *Critique of Pure Reason,* Transcendental Dialectic, Bk. II, Sec. IX, par. III.

bility we must reject not only determinism, but also indeterminism. How shall we escape from the horns of our dilemma, finding some way in which the claims of the moral life can be reasonably maintained? Unless we succeed in this effort we must be prepared to hold that a great portion of human experience, and precisely that portion which has seemed the noblest, is sheer delusion.

The beginning of a practical solution is an additional paradox. This new paradox lies in the fact that what seems like freedom from the inside looks like determinism from the outside. It is admitted by all people, either directly or implicitly, that they experience freedom of choice in their own personal lives, whereas it seems possible to explain all other events, including those in the lives of other people, on a basis of strict causal determinism. John is conscious of difficult decisions in his own life, certain that he could go in any one of several different directions if he so chose, but he looks at the action of James and thinks he sees that James was helpless in the presence of external forces and prior conditioning. Herein lies whatever plausibility orthodox behaviorism has, in spite of its fundamental inconsistency. The behaviorist avoids the paradox by the simple expedient of observing all events, mental or physical, from the outside. He looks at other men rather than himself, and he looks at men precisely as he looks at rats. He even goes so far as to state, in a doctrinaire manner, that this is the only way in which observation is possible.

Now, it must be agreed that a good case can be made for the complete causal determination of all acts. The notion that there are no uncaused events, though it is an article of faith in our scientific society, is one which seems unavoidable. The alternative is sheer chance, a concept to which it seems more and more difficult to assign any clear meaning. What we ordinarily call chance is nothing but ignorance of determining conditions, as is obviously the case when we toss a coin or throw a die. There is *some reason* why the die turns up the face it does turn up. In like manner it is difficult to avoid the conclusion that there is *some reason* why a man chooses as he does. Every man is naturally affected by his past training, by the standard of his group, and by the condition of his body. The fact that moral decision can be weakened by the use of drugs is a most sobering consideration. Perhaps there are other factors, quite as determinative as drugs, of which we as yet are ignorant.

If a man's action is lawless it is amoral, and we cannot profitably carry the investigation further. Even when we look back on our own lives we can analyze our former decisions in some detachment and see why we acted as we did. But at the moment of choice we are fully conscious that we do actually choose and that we are responsible as the automaton is not. Even those who write in defense of determinism, interpreting the actions of other men as they interpret the actions of dogs who are conditioned to produce saliva at the ringing of a bell, look upon their own actions as the result of intelligent choice. Even the most orthodox behaviorist apparently is unwilling to believe that his book on the subject is the result of his conditioning, just as that of his opponent or critic is the result of other conditioning. Other men may be the mere victims of circumstance, but not himself! In considering responsibility it is difficult to go beyond the classic words of Dr. Samuel Johnson, when he said in another connection, "All argument is against it; but all belief is for it."

We begin to see light on our problem when we realize that moral experience may be caused, in that it is not fortuitous and lawless, but caused by a different set of factors than those which determine the action of the boulder in the snowslide. The hypothesis which saves both freedom and causality is the hypothesis that the human being is a creature who comes into contact with causes of a different order from those which obtain in physical sequence. The paradox of freedom ceases to be mystifying, provided man's environment includes spiritual as well as physical reality and provided, furthermore, that this spiritual reality can be apprehended. When it is apprehended, the introduction of a new causal order occurs. We, then, have not the indeterminism we are bound to reject, but a determination by *something* other than efficient causation. A man's action, then, is not lawless, but it cannot be predicted because we do not know all his unrealized ideals, which, indeed, he cannot even know himself. The only known theory which avoids absolute contradictions in regard to freedom is the theory that man is affected in his action, not only by conditioning and by physical factors, but also by the true and the good as apprehended. *"Freedom is not absence of determination; it is spiritual determination as distinct from mechanical, or even organic, determination. It is determination by what seems good as contrasted with determination by irresistible compulsion."* [12]

The chief reason why so many discussions of freedom have been so confused and unprofitable is that the billiard-table conception of causation dominates the thought of the examiner, and on this basis there seems to be no solution at all. The truth, as we all know, is that man's acts are determined differently from the movements of billiard balls, and the difference is one of kind rather than of degree. If God really is, if there is a spiritual order as well as a material order, and if man is a creature capable of responding to both orders at once, the mystery of freedom is partly dispelled.

The dilemma of responsibility is avoided by the realization that, in human decision, there is a kind of causation different from that which natural science is now prepared to study. What we face is not a simple dichotomy of determinism and indeterminism, but a triangle in which each point is equally opposed to *two* others. At one corner is *material causation,* at another is *chance,* and at the third is the causation of freedom, which is expressed in the phenomenon of *decision* and which makes *responsibility* possible. When one billiard ball strikes another, the causation is simple, because it is the present shape, size and weight of the objects which determine the outcome. Naturally human action is inexplicable on such a basis, because this is not *its* basis. In truly human action there are a multitude of factors, many of them intrinsically incalculable. Most of them have to do with freedom from limitation to the specious present. Experiences of long ago, perhaps only dimly remembered, and hopes for the long future are major considerations. Everything that a man ever has been and everything he will ever be may be involved in a personal decision.[13] The causation of choice is, therefore, sharply distinguished from all material causation by its inherent magnitude. It is concerned more with the past and the future than with the present; it is concerned more with an objective moral order than with the merely physical order. The causation of freedom is logically unique because it involves another environment than that of nature.

If my actions are the necessary outcome of the agelong play of material forces, so that my consciousness has nothing to do with the

---

[12] William Temple, *Nature, Man and God,* p. 229.
[13] This total background Tillich calls "destiny."

outcome, then there is no place for responsibility at all. The state might destroy me, as it destroys vermin, but it would be ridiculous to talk about *crime*. At the same time, if all of my actions are sheer chance, then I am not responsible either. But if we take personality seriously, rejecting the stupidity of neglecting what we know best in superstitious attention to the kind of causality we know only at second hand, then we can talk intelligently of a responsible society because we can conceive of responsible persons. A responsible person is a self-integrating system of reality in which ideas are the chief instruments of self-determination and in which we are guided quite as much by an imagined and intended future and by a remembered past as by the present.

The question whether man *has* a free will is not the right question. What is significant in this problem is not the will as a psychological abstraction, but the entire person. We need to talk, not about the freedom of the *will*, but about the freedom of *man*. The freedom of man is not something added or debatable, for it constitutes his intrinsic nature. The essential life of humanity is the life of freedom, not as the absence of causality, but as the demonstration of a novel kind of causality which is the best that the created world has to show. It is absurd to reject decision on the ground of its supposed mystery, when it is all that we really know.

There is very little gain in trying, as was done by some scientists a few years ago, to support human freedom by reference to the principle of indeterminacy as applied to atoms. Events have come to a strange pass if we have to defend experience on the highest levels by reference to what occurs at lower levels. What the principle of indeterminacy really means it is too early to know; it *may* mean that there is an element of chance in even the most minute of physical movements. But in any case this is a long way from conscious decision. We are not so hard pressed that we have to get permission from the physicist before we believe in the freedom of human decision, including that of the physicist.

We are helped very much in this whole matter by the recognition of the principle of multiple causation. Nothing that we know occurs as a result of a single cause, but always there are many causal factors combined. Reinhold Niebuhr's way of putting this is very helpful. "In the world of human events and history," he says, "events are related to each other in a system of multiple causation; and the human agent enters the causal chain continually as one of the causes, having a freedom which makes his action unpredictable despite his obvious relation to the necessities of nature." [14]

The philosophical author of *Moby Dick* found in the experience of weaving a mat, with his savage friend Queequeg, a parable of the compatibility of the different constituent factors in events, "chance, free will, and necessity—no wise incompatible—all interweavingly working together." The fact that one of these entered into the completed picture did not, he saw, automatically exclude the others. Melville's major passage on the subject is as follows:

The straight warp of necessity, not to be swerved from its ultimate course—its every alternating vibration, indeed, only tending to that; free will still free to ply her shuttle between given threads; and chance, though restrained in its play within the right lines of necessity, and sideways in its motions directed by free will, though thus prescribed to by both, chance by turns rules either, and has the last featuring blow at events.[15]

D. The Religious Significance of Freedom

The more fully we face the fact of human freedom as a true cause in events, and as the essence of the highest level of experience known, the more we see that it affects seriously our search for religious truth. More than anything else it shatters the dogma of the closed system of the physical world, because, if it can be shown that purely physical events are altered by conscious thought, ours is an open universe. In free causation we have the best single understanding of the meaning of creation. Mind is a cause in a deeper sense than any merely physical cause ever is, because mind provides a principle of explanation. Our best reason for believing that Purpose accounts for the order of the universe is that we actually observe, in the little part of the world that we change, what the ordering effect of free purpose is. It is wiser to base our conclusions on what we know at first hand than on something fundamentally alien to us, as blind force is.

If it could be shown conclusively that human freedom, in the sense of making an actual difference in history, were a delusion, we might as well stop wasting our time on either moral philosophy or

[14] *Reinhold Niebuhr, op. cit.,* p. 14.
[15] Herman Melville, *Moby Dick,* chap. 47.

religious experience. Will Herberg sees this so clearly that his entire philosophy is based upon it. "Man's freedom," he writes, "his capacity for genuine decision—is taken as fundamental, for without it there could be neither religion nor ethics." [16] Without the recognition of freedom we should have a woefully inadequate conception, not only of man, but likewise of God.

The more fully we face the fact of freedom the more we are driven to the recognition of God as intensely *personal*. If purposive freedom is our best explanation of creative change, and if such purposive freedom does not occur except in the lives of persons, then there is good reason to see the basic explanation of the universe in personal terms. Our life is the life of partial freedom, but the life of God is the life of perfect freedom. As we have seen in the preceding chapter, it is only by the hypothesis of Divine Personality that we can account for the appearance of finite persons in the midst of the world order. At the climax of his Gifford Lectures Archbishop Temple stated this argument in a way that has not been surpassed. "If we take as our ultimate principle Personality," he wrote, "not only as purposive mind, but as mind of which the actual purpose is love, then the occurrence of persons within the World-Process is truly explained by the principle to which that process is referred; and there is no other principle known to us whereby human fellowship, which is the culmination of the Process, hitherto, is truly explained at all." [17]

A sobering corollary of the fact of freedom, as we saw in the chapter on the Problem of Evil, is that the reality of human decision constitutes a functional limitation on the divine power. God, it seems, has chosen to produce a creature with the fearful capacity of resisting Him. "The awful responsibility of being alive is just here," says a modern writer, "that our freedom in its measure is real and inviolable. Within a tiny orbit we can withstand even God. We cannot pluck the sun from the sky, or extinguish the stars, or stop the whirling planets, but we can turn our backs upon God and live as though he were not there." [18] A number of philosophers, of whom Professor Charles Hartshorne of the University of Chicago is representative, have concluded, on the basis of such reasoning, that God

[16] *Judaism and Modern Man*, p. 92.

[17] *Op. cit.*, p. 263.

[18] W. E. Sangster, "A Question God Can't Answer," *Christian Advocate*, March 6, 1952, p. 7.

cannot know the future because, if decision is real, the future is not now *anything*. God, the argument runs, can know what *is*, but the fact of freedom leads to the conclusion that the future is not a valid object of knowledge, even for a Superhuman Intelligence.

The emphasis on freedom as the essence of true personality helps us to understand how we ought to treat one another. Because the life of God is perfect freedom, He works by persuasion rather than by coercion, actually respecting our finite freedom.[19] "This doctrine," says Whitehead, "should be looked upon as one of the greatest intellectual discoveries of religion."[20] Its great practical significance is that it leads to the most valid principle of morality that we know, that according to which we, who are free persons, treat others as free persons. The ultimate form of the Categorical Imperative is "So act that you treat all persons as persons and as fellow members in a society of persons."

Because man is unworthy, his freedom may easily be abused. Accordingly, the way of advance is never the empty freedom in which decision is practically identical with chance, but lies instead in the development of choice which comes, not at the beginning of a process, but at the end. There is, moreover, the further paradox that only in bondage is there perfect freedom. "Nobody is anything," said Bosanquet, "except as he joins himself to something."

We are driven to the conclusion that freedom is ultimately meaningful only in the light of the being and nature of God. We are free only because our freedom is derivative. To say that man is made in God's image is to say that, while God is fully free, we are partly or intermittently free. Though man is made in God's image, the difference between human and divine freedom is tremendous. The crucial difference is revealed in the observation that *man makes nothing that is free*. Man makes machines, but they are mere instruments at best. The marvelous computation devices of which modern society is justly proud have no thoughts of their own and make no decisions. They merely give men materials for more intelligent decisions. The omnipotence of God is shown in the fact that He alone has made free beings.

---

[19] Though this idea is usually associated with the Christian doctrine of grace, it was foreshadowed by Plato in both *The Sophist* and the *Timaeus*.
[20] *Adventures of Ideas*, p. 213.

20

Immortality

And finally there is the painful riddle of death, for which no remedy at all has yet been found, nor probably ever will be.

SIGMUND FREUD

What we are concerned to know is the nature of ultimate reality. In the estimate of it we are bound to give full consideration to the moral and spiritual life of men here and now, for these are undoubtedly real. The ultimate reality must somehow include the fact that men know, that they are sensitive to love and duty, that they appreciate beauty, and that they pray. A full consideration of this cumulative evidence leads to the conclusion that the governing principle of reality is the Living God.

A. The Problem

Valuable as this approach is, we cannot stop with it, for it is also a fact that much of man's moral and spiritual life is very baffling. All that we do has upon it, not only the sign of its divine paternity, but also the threat of extinction. The same man who struggles mightily against temptation, holding to a conception of honor or integrity to his own cost, will come to a sudden end. Either he will be killed in an accident or his heart will stop as he lies on a hospital bed. Exactly the same end comes to him that comes to the most self-seeking person. A man stores his mind with knowledge of many kinds so that it becomes a marvelous instrument, able to draw together considerations which have seemed relevant to him for fifty years or more, and to make important conclusions about the natural or the human world, but one day a tumor grows in his brain, and he makes no more careful conclusions.

If it is sobering to think how the life of the individual is thus transitory, it is even more sobering to think of the fact that the

physical scene of our spiritual enterprise, as a people, is slowly becoming uninhabitable. We labor for our children and our children's
children, but someday, in the remote future or, even sooner, as a
result of man's fearful capacity to destroy himself, there will be no
more children. That our earth will one day be wholly unfit for the
continuation of our enterprise is as certain as any of our predictions
can be. No less an astrophysicist than Professor Eddington has compared favorably, in regard to probability, the law of increasing
entropy with that of all other physical laws. Some day, if our present
judgments are at all correct, the works of man will be as though
they had never been. It is wonderful, in preparing a book like this,
to profit from the disciplined minds of the past, but those minds now
seem to be no more, since their physical basis has been destroyed. In
like manner the physical basis of *all* minds, disciplined or undisciplined, will be destroyed. An earth as cold and lifeless as the moon
will revolve around a dying sun. What difference will it then make
whether the Hungarians were courageous in the face of cruel in-
vasion and whether hungry men, in concentration camps, shared
their poor food with still hungrier and sicker prisoners? What difference will it then make whether we now try to be intellectually
honest, to face the negative evidence along with the positive, and
whether we strive to make our world a scene of just peace? Duty and
love will be meaningless when there is no one to love and none to
remember.

The argument for the reality of God as the explanatory basis of
what now is remains valid, but the transitoriness of life and mind
and spirit makes it seem that the very purpose of God Himself will
be frustrated. If the divine purpose is, as evolution seems to indicate,
that of producing free spirits as the end result of a long and tortuous
process, it seems all the more tragic that the purpose will finally be
defeated as physical death stultifies the entire undertaking. The real
hopelessness of such a situation has not been expressed in our time
more eloquently than in the words which Bertrand Russell wrote
more than fifty years ago. If this living philosopher has changed his
major judgment on the matter in question he has not revealed it.
Here is the heart of his well-known statement:

Brief and powerless is Man's life; on him and all his race the slow, sure
doom falls pitiless and dark. Blind to good and evil, reckless of destruction,

omnipotent matter rolls on its relentless way; for Man, condemned to-day to lose his dearest, to-morrow himself to pass through the gate of darkness, it remains only to cherish, ere yet the blow falls, the lofty thoughts that ennoble his little day; disdaining the coward terrors of the slave of Fate, to worship at the shrine that his own hands have built; undismayed by the empire of chance, to preserve a mind free from the wanton tyranny that rules his outward life; proudly defiant of the irresistible forces that tolerate, for a moment, his knowledge and his condemnation, to sustain alone, a weary but unyielding Atlas, the world that his own ideals have fashioned despite the trampling march of unconscious power.[1]

Now, the problem which faces every thoughtful person is this: Do we have any reason to suppose that there is some alternative to the defeat óf the spiritual life which death represents? The only possible alternative would be some genuine form of immortality, by which we mean a continuation of the spiritual life with the appreciation of love and other forms of value, in spite of the death of the body or the physical deterioration of the earth as man's home. Such a continuation either occurs or does not occur. The apparent purpose is either frustrated or it is not frustrated.

If the apparent purpose *is* frustrated, wise men and women will go on doing the best they can and will try to glorify their little day, but there will inevitably be a pensive undertone. Unbelief does not necessarily make men bad, but, if they are wise, it makes them *sad*. Bertrand Russell, because he is a wise man and an honest searcher, however strange some of his conclusions may be, understands perfectly that the situation he faces, with no hope of immortality, is not one to make men laugh and sing.

Because there have been some people who have tried to avoid the sharp disjunction of either real immortality or fundamental defeat, by reference to what is called "cultural immortality," this requires a brief consideration at this point. George Eliot and others like her, of positivistic leanings, have spoken of the Choir Invisible, meaning the long effect on this earth of our present thoughts and efforts, even though each loses his own individual consciousness when his body distintegrates. But this, however valid for a while, is no permanent solution to the central problem. If there is no survival of physical

[1] Bertrand Russell, "A Free Man's Worship," *Mysticism and Logic*, New York, Longmans, 1925. The essay was first published in 1903.

death, the mere continuation of cultural influences on the earth for a few million years does not provide an escape from the central problem which is a metaphysical problem, the problem of the frustration of apparent Purpose. With blunt honesty Professor Montague has written: "However desperate the chance for individual survival may be, the chance for collective survival in the sense of an endless material continuance of its race and its culture is more desperate by far." [2]

B. PERSONAL SURVIVAL

What would be required to avoid the absolute frustration of Purpose which death seems to entail? Would our problem be solved if we could show that, even though the individual personality of my father as a unique center of consciousness is lost forever, his spirit has somehow been conserved, much as a drop of water is conserved in the ocean? The answer is that it would not. It is wholly unprofitable to alter the common meaning of immortality so that we refer to a depersonalized continuation of "spirit." In regard to the latter it is doubtful if depersonalized spirit has any meaning at all. What we prize is not spirit in general, which may be a complete abstraction, but *spirits,* i.e., concrete individuals. Just as God is best understood, not as "Love" or "Good," but as "an independent centre of consciousness," having "a differential activity of his own," [3] so what is precious among men is the particular focus of spiritual life which each represents. It is conceivable that this is destroyed when our bodies disintegrate, but, if so, the notion that history has a meaning is largely undermined and the immortality which most people desire for those whom they love is nonexistent. Even if a depersonalized immortality does have any meaning, it is certainly not desirable and is hardly worth discussing. What we are really concerned about is the kind of belief which refers to something which is exciting and momentous, *if true.*

Immortality may have many meanings, but there is only one that is really worth discussing, *the survival of personal individuality* after the shock of physical death. What so disturbs us, making death a part

[2] W. P. Montague, *The Way of Things,* p. 545.

[3] C. A. Bennett, *The Dilemma of Religious Knowledge,* Yale University Press, 1931, p. 50.

of the problem of evil, is the waste which the destruction of personality would entail if it is final as it appears to be. Personality, as we have described it earlier, is the most precious manifestation of reality known in the world, being infinitely superior to *things* or to *abstractions*. The one phenomenon which gives a hint as to the meaning of the evolutionary process is that of free spirits able to apprehend the good and, in a measure, to be guided by it. The production of such a level of experience would be a meaningful purpose for the world, no matter how much else the purpose might include.

It is insistence on the supreme importance of continued individuality that gives significance to the Christian teaching of the resurrection of the body. What is involved, of course, is not the naïve supposition that the same protoplasm which decays in the coffin will continue in a resurrected form. That is specifically denied in the noble passage in the fifteenth chapter of I Corinthians, in which the resurrection is so eloquently discussed. "There are celestial bodies and there are terrestrial bodies," we are told, the intimation being that what we *shall* have is the former. What is meant is that the individuality, which the organic unity of the body represents, will be maintained. The resurrection faith is that we shall have concrete ways of knowing one another and that we are not to be dissolved into a general pool of spirituality.

It need not be supposed that, in centering the attention on personal survival, it is necessary to adopt any particular scheme of life after death, such as that which became standardized in the medieval world picture. The rigid system of hell, of purgatory and of heaven is thoroughly intelligible, but it involves many difficulties, some of which appear to be insuperable, and in any case there is a manifest lack of evidence. The very idea of enduring torment, in which there is the absence not only of the hope of reformation but even of the *intention* of reformation, is inconsistent with the conception of God as One whose nature is that of the love which never ends. The *Agape* which bears all things, hopes all things, endures all things and which, furthermore, *never ends* is not compatible with vindictiveness, and it is really impossible to absolve from vindictiveness the author of endless torment.

Such considerations have caused the medieval picture of the next world to lose its sharpness, so far as the contemporary mind is concerned. First we lost belief in purgatory, because it has no apparent New Testament basis; second, we lost belief in hell, for reasons just indicated; now all that we have left is belief in heaven, and even that is the subject of endless jokes. But this need not give us great concern, for it is not such a stylized picture that is at stake. If there is survival after death, we seem to be shut off effectively from a knowledge of its details. Accordingly, there is little point in arguing what we do not know. What we *can* argue, and what is worth arguing, is the basic conviction that, in some manner beyond our finite comprehension, the death of the body fails to bring to a tragic end the spiritual process which culminates in the development of conscious individuals. If the individual consciousness, with its capacity to love and to know, does not survive, that is bad news, and if it does or can survive, that is very good news. But what is the evidence?

C. Evidence for Survival

Because we live in an age dominated by natural science, we naturally turn first to the possibility of empirical evidence. We are well aware that we often have to be content with inferential evidence, as in the existence of atoms, but if we could have direct empirical evidence, that would be better. Belief in God, we remember, gains immensely in credibility by the facts of direct religious experience. Is there similar valid evidence for survival? Unfortunately, there is not. Whereas millions of otherwise trustworthy men have reported experience of fellowship with God, we do not have more than a trickle of such evidence regarding life after bodily death. Perhaps the very situation precludes such evidence. What we are talking about is our own future, and that we cannot experience while we are still in the present. The experience of God, on the other hand, runs against no time barriers.

It is conceivable, of course, that we might have some intellectual commerce with other mortals who have survived death much as our rude ancestors supposed. Here is our only chance of empirical evidence. That such evidence is available is the contention of certain groups interested in psychical research. We ought to attend to all such supposed evidence with open minds, sitting down before the fact, here as elsewhere, like little children, and refusing to judge the case in advance.⁴ The truth is, however, that the supposed empirical evidence for survival is not generally convincing. Particularly does it appear unconvincing when contrasted with the empirical evidence for theism. The "spiritualist" evidence is unimpressive, not only in the number and quality of the reports, but far more in the content of the "messages." It is fair to expect some remarkable insights to be made available through communication with those "on the other side," but our expectations in this regard are disappointed. A. E. Taylor expresses what many have recognized when he says that the alleged messages "display a distressingly low level of intelligence." "They are mostly," Taylor continues, "a medley of sentimental gush and twaddling sermonizing. If their authors are, as it is often alleged that they are, the great moral and intellectual heroes of our past, it would seem that the brightest prospect the unseen world has to offer is that of a gradual declension of mankind into an undying society of trivial sentimental bores." ⁵

The phenomena of necromancy are likewise suspect because of the lack of moral effects, such as we have a right to expect from experiences so moving. The "fruits of the spirit," often so obvious in communion with God, are not, in necromancy, observable in any unusual way at all. Furthermore, when we consider the amount of conscious and unconscious fraud in such matters, as well as the amount of unrecognized communication between living persons, we are justified in the conviction that very little of the supposed facts is left to explain.⁶

A far more promising approach is that which is frankly inferential. Most philosophers who have tried to deal intelligently with the subject, recognizing the lack of scientific data, have contented them-

---

⁴ So thoroughgoing was the empiricism of William James that he prepared for the possible reception of messages from himself after his decease. He asked his brother, Henry James, to remain in Cambridge a few months to receive communications in case he should succeed in transmitting them.

⁵ A. E. Taylor, *The Faith of a Moralist*, vol. 1, pp. 259, 260.

⁶ Stanford University has for many years had a generous fund set aside specifically for the study of psychical phenomena, including those which are sometimes alleged to prove immortality empirically. Among the supposed communications which have been studied by the scholars assigned to this task some have been attributed to fraud and others to delusion, but no single case has been judged free from both.

selves with showing *what is reasonable to suppose*. They have analyzed the nature of mind, shown its sharp contrast to the body, and then have concluded that the same fate need not befall both. They have found in man's mind, including his logical, aesthetic and moral experience, hints of another order to which he belongs. Our life is meaningful, it has long been argued, only on the supposition that it is the beginning of something uncompleted here which is somewhere to be completed. Josiah Royce was in the main philosophic tradition when he wrote: "Of this our true individual life, our present life is a glimpse, a fragment, a hint, and in its best moments a visible beginning." [7]

The classic use of this method is that of Plato, particularly in the *Phaedo*. In this remarkable dialogue personal immortality is upheld with great confidence and a number of reasons are brought forward. If we eliminate the arguments which now seem to us fanciful or naïve, all that remain refer, in one way or another, to the notion that man *already,* in his life, carries hints of an eternal order about him. Plato's psychophysical dualism, which has been the main tradition through most of the succeeding generations of reflective thought, provides a suitable groundwork for such observations.

The heart of Plato's argument is that we actually do find, in the midst of a world that is wholly mutable, another kind of existence, with definite marks of stability. The further we get from the body, with its appetites and the falsifications of sensory experience, the closer we get to the truth. Our real life seems not to be a physical life at all. Therefore, the philosopher welcomes release. "The seen is the changing, the unseen is the unchanging." [8] But it is the body which is akin to the seen.

This way of dealing with the fact of death gains as we dwell on the strangeness of human life in its earthly setting. Human life promises more than it attains, and, if death ends all, is a mere fragment. Now, when we find a fragment of a vase, it seems a fair guess that the rest of the vase is in existence, even though we do not see it. Man's life, however, seems to be not only fragmentary, but truncated. The truncated part seems, thus, to give us some idea of

[7] Josiah Royce, *The Conception of Immortality*, Boston, Houghton Mifflin, 1900, p. 76.
[8] *Phaedo*, 79.

the nature of the part which is unseen, but without which the part that is seen has little meaning.

Man's mind is always something of a stranger to bodily existence, as though it is a pilgrim from another realm. The soul is "simply fastened and glued to the body" until philosophy sets the soul free. Being free, the soul recognizes that its true destiny lies elsewhere and prepares for that destiny. The emancipated soul "will calm passion, and follow reason, and dwell in the contemplation of her, beholding the true and divine (which is not matter of opinion), and thence deriving nourishment. Thus she seeks to live while she lives, and after death she hopes to go to her own kindred and to that which is like her, and to be freed from human ills." [9] Death seems to be reasonable as the portion of the body, but it looks like an intruder in the spiritual life, which has a different lineage.

An approach fundamentally similar to the Platonic one is the Kantian inference from moral experience. Again we pass from something in man's mind to the kind of world which must be if what is in man's mind is a clue to reality. The moral argument for immortality points out that we are impelled to seek moral ends and that the destruction of human personalities would make these moral ends unattainable. Since the moral obligation cannot be fully realized in this life, that obligation is a delusion unless there is a wider plane of existence on which further realization of the obligation is possible.[10] It would, Kant argues, be a curious world indeed if man were obliged to do what he cannot do. But only on the hypothesis of immortality is there a possibility of the fulfillment of the obligation. Obedience to the moral law, says Kant, requires endless progress, but endless progress is possible only "on the supposition of an *endless* duration of the existence and personality of the same rational being." Immortality, Kant supposed, can be shown to be a *necessary postulate* if moral experience is to be taken seriously.

This argument has been given an impressive treatment by A. E. Taylor in Chapter VII of his book, *The Faith of a Moralist*,[11] but

[9] *Ibid.*, 84 (Jowett).

[10] This is essentially the same as the argument from the existence of evil, stated at the end of Chap. XVII.

[11] Taylor's succinct statement is "that since the moral law can rightfully command us to live as aspirants to eternity, eternity must really be our destination" (p. 281).

he is careful to point out that it is not a demonstration valid for everyone, but valid only for those who believe in the absolute objectivity of moral obligation. Rufus Jones states the case in one sentence when he says, "If we are to have values of the intrinsic and eternal type, we must take by faith as real the kind of world in which they *can* be." [12]

All such arguments are met in the modern mind with a strong objection to the effect that the higher things of the mind, including moral experience, are wholly dependent upon the body. This was known long ago and received its classic expression from Lucretius. There are, in fact, no new arguments against immortality, although we have been able to present the classic objection in enormous detail. However, no modern objection is really any more weighty than that which Plato used in the *Phaedo,* putting it in the mouth of Simmias. Simmias was in full agreement about all that was said concerning the wonder and glory of the spiritual life, but he could not see that this wonder and glory was itself an evidence of continuance. To make his point clear he used the illustration of the lyre and the wonderful harmony which it produced. The harmony, he said, is something superior to the lyre; it is invisible, incorporeal, perfect and divine, whereas the lyre and the strings are material, composite and earthy, just as the body is. But when someone breaks the lyre, the harmony is gone, however wonderful it has been. In fact the harmony is gone sooner than the crass materials which made up the lyre. "The thought, Socrates," said Simmias, "must have occurred to your own mind that such is our conception of the soul; and that when the body is in a manner strung and held together by elements of hot and cold, wet and dry, then the soul is the harmony or due proportionate admixture of them. But if so, whenever the strings of the body are unduly loosened or overstrained through disease or other injury, then the soul, though most divine, like other harmonies of music or of works of art, of course, perishes at once; although the material remains of the body may last for a considerable time, until they are either decayed or burnt." [13]

This is the modern objection exactly. The modern man is often willing to admit that there is a real difference between body and

[12] Rufus M. Jones, *Spirit in Man,* Stanford University Press, 1941, p. 46.
[13] *Phaedo,* 86 (Jowett).

mind, but he sees so much evidence that the mind is dependent upon the body that he cannot see how the glory of the mind is itself an evidence of its going on. The things that matter most seem to be at the mercy of the things that matter least. Our treasure is very great, but how can it be kept if the earthen vessel which contains it is broken? Just as a change in the materials of the lyre affects the harmony produced, a change in glandular balance or some disease of the central nervous system may alter radically the functioning of the individual mind. We now know enough about brain surgery to be sure that the noblest of mental and moral characteristics may come to an end, not merely at death, but as a result of purely physical changes before death.

The answer of Socrates, according to Plato, was the rejection of the analogy of the lyre. The soul, he said, is not like a harmony, for a harmony is purely passive, unable to initiate anything. Man's soul, by contrast, is wonderfully *active* and often dominant. Though the condition of the body affects the mind, this is not the whole of the story, since, by means of thought, we deliberately curb or change the body, as well as external objects. As William James maintained in his Ingersoll Lecture, the body seems more like an instrument than anything else—a tool which the mind uses to attain its ends. The amazing ability of some men and women to rise above physical weakness provides part of the evidence for the truth of this thesis. The extent to which the tired body can be driven in pursuance of some cherished aim makes it clear that, if we are to use any analogy at all (which is probably inevitable), it would be far better to represent the mind as a charioteer than as a harmony. The mind frequently denies the body its natural satisfactions, especially when a moral obligation is recognized. Hunger and imprisonment are often chosen when dishonor is the alternative. The refusal of Socrates to flee is the classic illustration of such experience. The notion that the soul *leads* and thus cannot be understood as passively dependent upon the condition of the body is, no doubt, the heart of Plato's argument. We discover, he says, the soul "leading the elements of which she is believed to be composed; almost always opposing and coercing them in all sorts of ways throughout life, sometimes more violently with the pains of medicine and gymnastic; then again more gently;

now threatening, now admonishing the desires, passions, fears, as if talking to a thing which is not herself." [14]

The question of the absolute dependence of the mind upon the brain is still an open question. The data, as James insisted, are still amenable to more than one hypothesis. Though this recognition is an important factor in our study, we must note that it is only a negative factor. It gives no positive argument for immortality, but only *leaves the way open* for such positive argument if any is forthcoming. Indeed, the whole philosophical approach to the question is inconclusive, giving little help unless something is added. Why, we may reasonably ask, does the presence of a fragment give evidence that there is more to come? Because, it may be replied, the world would otherwise be unreasonable. But how do we know it is not unreasonable? The world, indeed, is far more intelligible if what is most precious is not wantonly destroyed, but what is the ground of belief in intelligibility? Certainly the mere existence of a material structure gives no such ground; a material structure might be fundamentally unintelligible. As we have seen in Chapter VII, the whole notion of an order, which science explores, implies a genuine matching of mind with Mind. Thus, the basal assumption of science that the universe is intelligible is really the assumption of theism.

Apart from theism or some similar belief, the Platonic and Kantian evidences for immortality have little persuasiveness. The reality of God is the only assurance we have of ultimate rationality. To one who believes in God as the cosmic support of moral obligation the Kantian argument has cogency, but it has such cogency for no others. Unless God is the author both of our moral nature and of our total environment, there is no reason to posit a fundamental harmony between them. On the other hand, if there is good reason to believe in God, as we have seen that there is, the arguments of Plato and Kant become valuable in a secondary way.

We are driven to the conclusion that immortality is best approached, not from the point of view of science, and not from the point of view of philosophy alone, but from the point of view of religion. Professor A. E. Taylor supports this conclusion strongly when he says, "Apart from an adequate doctrine of God it is, as I believe, impossible to find any secure foundation for a doctrine of

[14] *Ibid.*, 94 (Jowett).

human immortality." [15] Thus, we are pointed forward to our final approach to the subject of immortality. The scientific evidence for immortality is practically worthless, the philosophical argument is inconclusive, but the religious argument is fruitful.

D. The Corollary of Faith

One of the apparent paradoxes concerning immortality is the fact that the subject of life after death is often of far less concern to the deeply devout man than it is to the unbeliever. A nontheistic thinker, like McTaggart, may face anxiously the old question, "If a man die, shall he live again?" but to the majority of those who believe in God, experiencing reality in worship, the subject is largely incidental. It is surprising to us to note how small a part any argument about immortality played in the thought of Jesus, if we may judge by the Gospel narrative. He dealt briefly with the question of the resurrection when the Sadducees insisted, but he based his faith on the logically prior faith in God. "He is not the God of the dead, but of the living" was the sufficient answer. President Eisenhower was in the very center of the Judeo-Christian tradition when he minimized, in his news conference of August 1, 1956, the problem of his own death. In response to a question about his possible death, in view of the hard demands upon him, the President said, "I don't think it is too important to the individual how his end comes, and certainly he can't dictate the time." Here is the authentic voice of living faith. The unbeliever is naturally deeply concerned, for he has no conviction of cosmic support. He must hold desperately to this life, since he thinks he will never have another, but the person who believes in God so firmly that he is convinced God's purpose *cannot* be frustrated can face death in a mood which, at best, is positively gay, and in any case is lacking in anxiety. It is wholesome to see the growing recognition of the fact that Christian funerals should be joyous in tone. When they are somber and tearful the faith is being denied.

One of the most moving passages in the Platonic dialogues is that in which we read of joy in the face of death. It is one of the evidences that for Plato, as for the modern Christian, the belief in immortality

---

[15] A. E. Taylor, *op. cit.*, vol. 1, p. 256.

was really a corollary of faith in God. The passage is that in which
the dying Socrates compares himself to the prophetic birds that are
sacred to Apollo.

For they, when they perceive that they must die, having sung all their
life long, *do then sing more than ever,* rejoicing in the thought that they
are about to go away to the god whose ministers they are. For because they
are sacred to Apollo they have the gift of prophecy, and anticipate the
good things of another world; wherefore they sing and rejoice on that day
more than ever they did before.[16]

Belief in personal survival is secondary to belief in God, both
temporally and logically. It came late in the development of Hebrew
faith, and it came late because it is strictly derivative. Because it is
derivative, it can never be precise. The faith does not tell us exactly
what happens after death, either to ourselves or to those whom we
love, but it is not such knowledge that we require. It is enough to
know that, in our sorrow and loneliness, God cares and that God
still reigns. We do not need to know the details of heaven, which may
be as much beyond our grasp as poetry is beyond the grasp of an
animal, but it is enough to know that we cannot drift "beyond His
love and care."

Since this is the logic of the situation, it is right that, in conclusion, we should stress the center of our faith and that alone. If
we have adequate reason to believe that the Ultimate Reality is such
as to account for moral and spiritual life in its *occurrence,* we can
reasonably trust that Reality for its *endurance.* The only good
argument against personal survival is that the continuation of consciousness after the brain has decayed is incomprehensible. But the
relevant point to make is that the very appearance of man, with all
of his pain and glory, is itself incomprehensible. Bertrand Russell's
blunt honesty was extremely helpful when he wrote, against a background of complete atheism, that "a strange mystery it is that nature,
omnipotent but blind, has brought forth at last a child, subject still
to her power but gifted with sight, with knowledge of good and evil,
with the capacity of judging all the works of his unthinking
mother." [17]

16 *Phaedo,* 85 A.
17 Bertrand Russell, "A Free Man's Worship," *Mysticism and Logic,* New York,
N. W. Norton, 1929, p. 48.

Yes, it is a strange mystery, but it is infinitely more strange to the atheist than it is to the believer in the Living God. We cannot validly use the argument from incomprehensibility in a world in which all natural things are incomprehensible. That men should survive bodily death is not more strange than a thousand other things that are. Specifically, it is not more strange that consciousness should *survive* than that it should *arrive*. That it did arrive we truly know, and, starting from this knowledge, we are driven to accept the only picture of Ultimate Reality which makes the strangeness less strange. Personal survival is a valid conclusion, because it makes more sense than does its alternative, the alternative of a world of meaning which becomes meaningless at the end.

Appendix

A. The Fundamental Theistic Argument of Plato's Laws, Book X [1]

CLEINIAS. But is there any difficulty in proving the existence of the Gods?

ATHENIAN. How would you prove it?

CLE. How? In the first place, the earth and the sun, and the stars and the universe, and the fair order of the seasons, and the division of them into years and months, furnish proofs of their existence; and also there is the fact that all Hellenes and barbarians believe in them.

ATH. I fear, my sweet friend, though I will not say that I much regard, the contempt with which the profane will be likely to assail us. For you do not understand the nature of their complaint, and you fancy that they rush into impiety only from a love of sensual pleasure.

CLE. Why, Stranger, what other reason is there?

ATH. One which you who live in a different atmosphere would never guess.

CLE. What is it?

ATH. A very grievous sort of ignorance which is imagined to be the greatest wisdom.

CLE. What do you mean?

ATH. At Athens there are tales preserved in writing which the virtue of your state, as I am informed, refuses to admit. They speak of the Gods in prose as well as verse, and the oldest of them tell of the origin of the heavens and of the world, and not far from the beginning of their story they proceed to narrate the birth of the Gods, and how after they were born they behaved to one another. Whether these stories have in other ways a good or a bad influence, I should not like to be severe upon them, because they are ancient; but, looking at them with reference to the duties of children to their parents, I cannot praise them, or think that they are useful, or at all true. Of the words of the ancients I have nothing more to say; and I should wish to say of them only what is pleasing to the

---

[1] *Dialogues of Plato*, tr. by B. Jowett, 3rd ed., Oxford University Press, 1892, Vol. V, pp. 269-83.

Gods. But as to our younger generation and their wisdom, I cannot let them off when they do mischief. For do but mark the effect of their words: when you and I argue for the existence of the Gods, and produce the sun, moon, stars, and earth, claiming for them a divine being, if we would listen to the aforesaid philosophers we should say that they are earth and stones only, which can have no care at all of human affairs, and that all religion is a cooking up of words and a make-believe.

.   .   .   .

ATH. Come, then, and if ever we are to call upon the Gods, let us call upon them now in all seriousness to come to the demonstration of their own existence. And so holding fast to the rope we will venture upon the depths of the argument. When questions of this sort are asked of me, my safest answer would appear to be as follows:—Some one says to me, 'O Stranger, are all things at rest and nothing in motion, or is the exact opposite of this true, or are some things in motion and others at rest?'—To this I shall reply that some things are in motion and others at rest. 'And do not things which move move in a place, and are not the things which are at rest at rest in a place?' Certainly. 'And some move or rest in one place and some in more places than one?' You mean to say, we shall rejoin, that those things which rest at the centre move in one place, just as the circumference goes round of globes which are said to be at rest? 'Yes,' And we observe that, in the revolution, the motion which carries round the larger and the lesser circle at the same time is proportionally distributed to greater and smaller, and is greater and smaller in a certain proportion. Here is a wonder which might be thought an impossibility, that the same motion should impart swiftness and slowness in due proportion to larger and lesser circles. 'Very true.' And when you speak of bodies moving in many places, you seem to me to mean those which move from one place to another, and sometimes have one centre of motion and sometimes more than one be- cause they turn upon their axis; and whenever they meet anything, if it be stationary, they are divided by it; but if they get in the midst between bodies which are approaching and moving towards the same spot from opposite directions, they unite with them. 'I admit the truth of what you are saying.' Also when they unite they grow, and when they are divided they waste away,—that is, supposing the constitution of each to remain, or if that fails, then there is a second reason of their dissolution. 'And when are all things created and how?' Clearly, they are created when the first principle receives increase and attains to the second dimension, reach- ing the third becomes perceptible to sense. Everything which is thus changing and moving is in process of generation; only when at rest has it real existence, but when passing into another state it is destroyed utterly. Have we not mentioned all motions that there are, and comprehended them under their kinds and numbered them with the exception, my friends, of two?

CLE. Which are they?

ATH. Just the two, with which our present enquiry is concerned.

CLE. Speak plainer.

ATH. I suppose that our enquiry has reference to the soul?

CLE. Very true.

ATH. Let us assume that there is a motion able to move other things, but not to move itself;—that is one kind; and there is another kind which can move itself as well as other things, working in composition and decomposition, by increase and diminution and generation and destruction,—that is also one of the many kinds of motion.

CLE. Granted.

ATH. And we will assume that which moves other, and is changed by other, to be the ninth, and that which changes itself and others, and is co-incident with every action and every passion, and is the true principle of change and motion in all that is—that we shall be inclined to call the tenth.

CLE. Certainly.

ATH. And which of these ten motions ought we to prefer as being the mightiest and most efficient?

CLE. I must say that the motion which is able to move itself is ten thousand times superior to all the others.

ATH. Very good; but may I make one or two corrections in what I have been saying?

CLE. What are they?

ATH. When I spoke of the tenth sort of motion, that was not quite correct.

CLE. What was the error?

ATH. According to the true order, the tenth was really the first in generation and power; then follows the second, which was strangely enough termed the ninth by us.

CLE. What do you mean?

ATH. I mean this: when one thing changes another, and that another, of such will there be any primary changing element? How can a thing which is moved by another ever be the beginning of change? Impossible. But when the self-moved changes other, and that again other, and thus thousands upon tens of thousands of bodies are set in motion, must not the beginning of all this motion be the change of the self-moving principle?

CLE. Very true, and I quite agree.

ATH. Or, to put the question in another way, making answer to our-selves:—If, as most of these philosophers have the audacity to affirm, all things were at rest in one mass, which of the above-mentioned principles of motion would first spring up among them?

CLE. Clearly the self-moving; for there could be no change in them arising out of any external cause; the change must first take place in themselves.

ATH. Then we must say that self-motion being the origin of all motions, and the first which arises among things at rest as well as among things in motion, is the eldest and mightiest principle of change, and that which is changed by another and yet moves other is second.

CLE. Quite true.

ATH. At this stage of the argument let us put a question.

CLE. What question?

ATH. If we were to see this power existing in any earthly, watery, or fiery substance, simple or compound—how should we describe it?

CLE. You mean to ask whether we should call such a self-moving power life?

ATH. I do.

CLE. Certainly we should.

ATH. And when we see soul in anything, must we not do the same—must we not admit that this is life?

CLE. We must.

.   .   .   .

ATH. And what is the definition of that which is named 'soul'? Can we conceive of any other than that which has been already given—the motion which can move itself?

CLE. You mean to say that the essence which is defined as the self-moved is the same with that which has the name soul?

ATH. Yes; and if this is true, do we still maintain that there is anything wanting in the proof that the soul is the first origin and moving power of all that is, or has become, or will be, and their contraries, when she has been clearly shown to be the source of change and motion in all things?

CLE. Certainly not; the soul as being the source of motion, has been most satisfactorily shown to be the oldest of all things.

ATH. And is not that motion which is produced in another, by reason of another, but never has any self-moving power at all, being in truth the change of an inanimate body, to be reckoned second, or by any lower number which you may prefer?

CLE. Exactly.

ATH. Then we are right, and speak the most perfect and absolute truth, when we say that the soul is prior to the body, and that the body is second and comes afterwards, and is born to obey the soul, which is the ruler?

CLE. Nothing can be more true.

ATH. Do you remember our old admission, that if the soul was prior to the body the things of the soul were also prior to those of the body?

CLE. Certainly.

ATH. Then characters and manners, and wishes and reasonings, and true opinions, and reflections, and recollections are prior to length and breadth and depth and strength of bodies, if the soul is prior to the body.

CLE. To be sure.

ATH. In the next place, must we not of necessity admit that the soul is the cause of good and evil, base and honourable, just and unjust, and of all other opposites, if we suppose her to be the cause of all things?

CLE. We must.

ATH. And as the soul orders and inhabits all things that move, however moving, must we not say that she orders also the heavens?

CLE. Of course.

ATH. One soul or more? More than one—I will answer for you; at any rate, we must not suppose that there are less than two—one the author of good, and the other of evil.

CLE. Very true.

ATH. Yes, very true; the soul then directs all things in heaven, and earth, and sea, by her movements, and these are described by the terms— will, consideration, attention, deliberation, opinion true and false, joy and sorrow, confidence, fear, hatred, love, and other primary motions akin to these; which again receive the secondary motions of corporeal substances, and guide all things to growth and decay, to composition and decomposition, and to the qualities which accompany them, such as heat and cold, heaviness and lightness, hardness and softness, blackness and whiteness, bitterness and sweetness, and all those other qualities which the soul uses, herself a goddess, when truly receiving the divine mind she disciplines all things rightly to their happiness; but when she is the companion of folly, she does the very contrary of all this. Shall we assume so much, or do we still entertain doubts?

CLE. There is no room at all for doubt.

ATH. Shall we say then that it is the soul which controls heaven and earth, and the whole world?—that it is a principle of wisdom and virtue, or a principle which has neither wisdom nor virtue? Suppose that we make answer as follows:—

CLE. How would you answer?

ATH. If, my friend, we say that the whole path and movement of heaven, and of all that is therein, is by nature akin to the movement and revolution and calculation of mind, and proceeds by kindred laws, then, as is plain, we must say that the best soul takes care of the world and guides it along the good path.

B. KANT'S MORAL PROOF OF GOD'S BEING FROM THE CRITIQUE OF JUDGMENT[1]

The moral law as the formal rational condition of the use of our freedom obliges us by itself alone, without depending on any purpose as material condition; but it nevertheless determines for us, and indeed *a priori*, a final purpose towards which it obliges us to strive; and this purpose is the *highest good in the world* possible through freedom.

The subjective condition under which man (and, according to all our concepts, every rational finite being) can set a final purpose before himself under the above law is happiness. Consequently, the highest physical good possible in the world, to be furthered as a final purpose as far as in us lies, is *happiness*, under the objective condition of the harmony of man with the law of *morality* as worthiness to be happy.

But it is impossible for us in accordance with all our rational faculties to represent these two requirements of the final purpose proposed to us by the moral law, as *connected* by merely natural causes, and yet as conformable to the Idea of that final purpose. Hence the concept of the *practical necessity* of such a purpose through the application of our powers does not harmonise with the theoretical concept of the *physical possibility* of working it out, if we connect with our freedom no other causality (as a means) than that of nature.

Consequently, we must assume a moral World-Cause (an Author of the world), in order to set before ourselves a final purpose consistently with the moral law; and in so far as the latter is necessary, so far (i.e. in the same degree and on the same ground) the former also must be necessarily assumed; i.e. we must admit that there is a God.

(Note added in 2d ed.) This moral argument does not supply any *objectively valid* proof of the Being of God; it does not prove to the skeptic that there is a God, but proves that if he wishes to think in a way consonant with morality, he must admit the *assumption* of this proposition under the maxims of his practical Reason.—We should therefore not say: it is necessary *for morals* (Sittlichkeit), to assume the happiness of all rational beings of the world in proportion to their morality (Moralitat); but rather, this is necessitated *by* morality. Accordingly, this is a *subjective* argument sufficient for moral beings.

[1] *Critique of Judgment,* tr. by J. H. Bernard, New York, Macmillan, 1914.

This proof, to which we can easily give the form of logical precision, does not say: it is as necessary to assume the Being of God as to recognise the validity of the moral law; and consequently he who cannot convince himself of the first, can judge himself free from the obligations of the second. No! there must in such case only be given up the *aiming at* the final purpose in the world, to be brought about by the pursuit of the second (viz. a happiness of rational beings in harmony with the pursuit of moral laws, regarded as the highest good). Every rational being would yet have to cognise himself as straitly bound by the precepts of morality, for its laws are formal and command unconditionally without respect to purposes (as the matter of volition). But the one requisite of the final purpose, as practical Reason prescribes it to beings of the world, is an irresistible purpose imposed on them by their nature (as finite beings), which Reason wishes to know as subject only to the moral law as inviolable *condition*, or even as universally set up in accordance with it. Thus Reason takes for final purpose the furthering of happiness in harmony with morality. To further this so far as is in our power (i.e. in respect to happiness) is commanded us by the moral law; be the issue of this endeavor what it may. The fulfilling of duty consists in the form of the earnest will, not in the intermediate causes of success.

Suppose then that partly through the weakness of all the speculative arguments so highly extolled, and partly through many irregularities in nature and the world of sense which come before him, a man is persuaded of the proposition, There is no God; he would nevertheless be contemptible in his own eyes if on that account he were to imagine the laws of duty as empty, invalid and inobligatory, and wished to resolve to transgress them boldly. Such an one, even if he could be convinced in the sequel of that which he had doubted at the first, would always be contemptible while having such as regards its (external) effect as punctiliously as could be desired, for (he would be acting) from fear or from the aim at recompense, without the sentiment of reverence for duty. If, conversely, as a believer (in God) he performs his duty according to his conscience, uprightly and disinterestedly, and nevertheless believes that he is free from all moral obligation so soon as he is convinced that there is no God, this could accord but badly with an inner moral disposition.

We may then suppose the case of a righteous man (e.g. *Spinoza*) who holds himself firmly persuaded that there is no God, and also (because in respect of the Object of morality a similar consequence results) no future life; how is he to judge of his own inner purposive destination, by means of the moral law, which reveres in practice? He desires no advantage to himself from following it, either in this or another world;

he wishes, rather, disinterestedly to establish the good to which that holy law directs all his powers. But his effort is bounded; and from nature, although he may expect here and there a contingent accordance, he can never expect a regular harmony agreeing according to constant rules (such as his maxims are and must be, internally), with the purpose that he yet feels himself obliged and impelled to accomplish. Deceit, violence, and envy will always surround him, although he himself be honest, peaceable, and kindly; and the righteous men with whom he meets will, notwithstanding all their worthiness of happiness, be yet subjected by nature which regards not this, to all the evils of want, disease, and untimely death, just like the beasts of the earth. So it will be until one wide grave engulfs them together (honest or not, it makes no difference), and throws them back—who were able to believe themselves the final purpose of creation—into the abyss of the purposeless chaos of matter from which they were drawn.— The purpose, then, which this well-intentioned person had and ought to have before him in his pursuit of moral laws, he must certainly give up as impossible. Or else, if he wishes to remain dependent upon the call of his moral internal destination, and not to weaken the respect with which the moral law immediately inspires him, by assuming the nothingness of the single, ideal, final purpose adequate to its high demand (which cannot be brought about without a violation of moral sentiment), he must, as he well can—since there is at least no contradiction from a practical point of view in forming a concept of the possibility of a morally prescribed final purpose—assume the being of a *moral* author of the world, that is, a God.

C. Pascal's Experience of God[3]

The year of grace 1654,

Monday, 23 November, day of Saint Clement, pope and martyr, and of others in the martyrology.

Eve of Saint Chrysogonus, martyr, and others,

From about half past ten in the evening until about half past twelve,

.... FIRE ....

God of Abraham, God of Isaac, God of Jacob, not of the philosophers and scholars.

Certitude, certitude, feeling, joy, peace.

God of Jesus Christ.

Deum meum et Deum vestrum.

---

[3] Morris Bishop, *Pascal, The Life of Genius,* New York, Reynal E. Hitchcock, 1936, pp. 172, 173.

Thy God will be my God.

Forgetfulness of the world and of everything, except GOD.

He is to be found by the ways taught in the Gospel.

Greatness of the human soul.

O righteous Father, the world hath not known thee, but I have known thee.

Joy, joy, joy, tears of joy.

I have been separated from him.

Dereliquerunt me fontem aquae vivae.

My God, wilt thou forsake me:

Let me not be separated from him eternally.

This is the eternal life, that they know thee as the only true God, and the one whom thou hast sent, Jesus Christ.

Jesus Christ,

Jesus Christ.

I have been separated from him; I have fled him, renounced him, crucified him,

Let me never be separated from him.

He is preserved only by the ways taught in the Gospel.

Renunciation, total and sweet.

D. BIBLIOGRAPHICAL NOTE

It is assumed that many of those who read this book, whether or not they are enrolled in colleges, are serious students who may develop strong interests in several of the subjects discussed and may achieve real competence in a few. The numerous footnotes scattered throughout the volume are intended as aids to such an endeavor. Wherever possible, the reference has been to specific passages in other books, which, in turn, through footnotes of their own, point to still other books. Thus the person interested in a particular problem may, by diligent following of such leads, come to use many books, from many traditions, though he cannot predict his course in advance. The procedure of advancing step by step is much more profitable than is dependence upon a single list of volumes, with no indication of relevant passages.

Reference may profitably be made here to a few general works in the philosophy of religion. Of the recent volumes, two deserve especial attention. Samuel M. Thompson, of Monmouth College, has written *A Modern Philosophy of Religion* (Henry Regnery, 1955), which is philosophical in method and unapologetically theistic in conviction. Professor Thompson seeks to take seriously "the implications of the twentieth century revolution in physical science." Another is that of John Hutchison of Columbia University, *Faith, Reason and Existence* (Oxford University Press, 1956). Dr. Hutchison is sympathetic to Biblical theology, having been much influenced by both Reinhold Niebuhr and Paul Tillich.

A valuable book in the field, which is not quite so recent, is that of Professor Peter Bertocci of Boston University, who keeps alive today the personalistic tradition of Edgar Brightman and of Borden P. Bowne. The book, *Introduction to the Philosophy of Religion* (Prentice-Hall, 1951), is much more comprehensive than Professor Brightman's well-known volume, *A Philosophy of Religion* (Prentice-Hall, 1940), which is limited, in large measure, to the problem of divine finitude. As numerous footnotes indicate, it is my conviction that the very best philosophy of religion of this century is *Nature, Man and God* by William Temple. Many of Temple's leading ideas appear in a slightly simpler form in *Mens Creatrix* (Macmillan, 1935). An older book which helps to clarify the exact nature of the philosophy of religion as a separate intellectual discipline is A. Seth Pringle-Pattison, *Philosophy of Religion* (1930). The Introduction is especially helpful. For sheer logical competence, no modern writer has surpassed J. Cook Wilson, in his "Rational Grounds for Belief in God," *Statement and Inference* (vol. 2, pp. 835 ff.). A valuable contemporary work which includes Eastern as well as Western religions insights is Sarvapolli Radhakrishnan's *Recovery of Faith* (Harper, 1955).

Of general philosophical books dealing with the subjects handled in Part I, a current book of outstanding value is that by J. Harry Cotton of Wabash College, *Christian Knowledge of God* (Macmillan, 1951). Professor Cotton deals in this book with the logic of religion, stressing such themes as "The Limits of Reason," "Our Knowledge of Persons," and "Revelation and Reason." Similar topics are included in William J. Wolf, *Man's Knowledge of God* (Doubleday, 1955), and Nels Ferre, *Faith and Reason* (Harper, 1946). Similar in scope is H. Reinhold Niebuhr, *The Meaning of Revelation* (Macmillan, 1955).

Those interested in pursuing further the moral argument for theism are advised to look carefully, not only at the large volumes already mentioned but also at C. S. Lewis, *The Case for Christianity* (Macmillan, 1947). The argument is presented succinctly and brilliantly in Part I, "Right and Wrong as a Clue to the Meaning of the Universe." Other helpful approaches to the moral argument, not already mentioned in the footnotes, are A. C. Garnett, *Religion and the Moral Life* (Ronald, 1955), and Hastings Rashdall, *Philosophy and Religion* (Scribner, 1910). The Rashdall volume, which has become something of a philosophical classic, states the moral argument compactly. For a persuasive restatement of the teleological argument, see Gerald Heard, *Is God Evident?* (Harper, 1948) .

A valuable older essay on the nature of religious experience is provided by A. Clutton-Brock, "Spiritual Experience," *The Spirit* (Macmillan, 1921) . The argument from religious experience is given new freshness in the public lecture given at Oxford in June, 1945, by C. C. J. Webb, *Religious Experience* (Oxford University Press) . Professor Webb takes account of recent criticisms and of changes in philosophical climate. Arnold J. Toynbee's Gifford Lectures, *Historian's Approach to Religion* (Oxford University Press, 1956) , are largely disappointing, but cannot be wholly neglected. Reinhold Niebuhr, *Faith and History* (Scribner, 1949) , makes an important contribution in this field of inquiry.

Those who are seeking to understand the challenge of logical positivism may be helped by A. J. Ayer, *Philosophical Essays* (Macmillan, 1954) , and by G. Ryle, *The Concept of Mind* (Hutchinson University Library, 1952) . Further light on the challenge of Freud is given in R. S. Lee, *Freud and Christianity* (James Clarke, London, 1948) . Students desiring to go more deeply into existentialism are directed to F. H. Heinemann, *Existentialism and the Modern Predicament* (Harper, 1953) , and to the current writings of Gabriel Marcel, especially *Dreadful Freedom, A Critique of Existentialism* (University of Chicago Press, 1948) . Karl Jaspers, *Reason and Anti-Reason in our Time* (S. C. M. Press, London, 1952) , is a valuable translation. Another important translation is Ernst Cassirer, *Determinism and Indeterminism in Modern Physics,* translated by O. Theodor Benfey (Yale University Press, 1956) . The relation of faith to science has been the subject of many recent books. One especially suitable for mention is Karl Heim, *Christian Faith and Natural Science* (Harper, 1953) .

When we consider the problem of God's nature we can still find nothing more pertinent than C. C. J. Webb, *God and Personality* (Macmillan, 1918) . Two very different positions, stemming from Harvard philosophers, are provided by W. E. Hocking, *The Meaning of God in Human Experience* (Yale University Press, 1923) , and Alfred North Whitehead, *Religion in the Making* (Macmillan, 1926) A contemporary consideration of science in its relation to both ethics and religion is James A. Pike, *Doing the Truth,* (Doubleday, 1955) . A valuable contribution to the problem of evil, not already mentioned in the footnotes, is Nels Ferre, *Evil and the Christian Faith* (Harper, 1947) . A little known book by Albert Schweitzer is *Christianity and the Religions of the World* (George H. Doran, 1923) . Though much has been written on immortality and related subjects, one book stands out remarkably in this area, John Baillie, *And the Life Everlasting* (Oxford University Press, 1934).

No bibliography is ever complete and, even when it approaches completeness, it tends to lose its usefulness for the general reader or student, because it is so overwhelming. We need not, however, be overconcerned with completeness. A more modest and a more satisfactory approach is to find a few expressions of intellectual integrity, which we can truly honor, and then, with their help, try to follow the argument wherever it leads.

Index of Names

Index of Subjects